ME A SADDLE-PAL
MY LIFE AS A HOLLYWOOD STUNTMAN

MICKEY GILBERT
WITH REBECCA ROCKWELL

outskirtspress
DENVER, COLORADO

The opinions expressed in this manuscript are solely the opinions of the author and do not represent the opinions or thoughts of the publisher. The author has represented and warranted full ownership and/or legal right to publish all the materials in this book.

Me and My Saddle-Pal
My Life as a Hollywood Stuntman
All Rights Reserved.
Copyright © 2014 Mickey Gilbert With Rebecca Rockwell
v2.0

Cover Image and Author Photo by Yvonne Gilbert
Interior Images used with permission.

This book may not be reproduced, transmitted, or stored in whole or in part by any means, including graphic, electronic, or mechanical without the express written consent of the publisher except in the case of brief quotations embodied in critical articles and reviews.

Outskirts Press, Inc.
http://www.outskirtspress.com

ISBN: 978-1-4787-4033-9

Outskirts Press and the "OP" logo are trademarks belonging to Outskirts Press, Inc.

PRINTED IN THE UNITED STATES OF AMERICA

Contents

Author's Dedication i
Roping the King 1
The Early Years 3
Graduating High School and Meeting Yvonne 13
Alvarez Kelly and *When the Legends Die* 22
Beau Geste 27
Africa: Texas-Style! 34
Cowboy in Africa 52
The Wild Bunch 55
Butch Cassidy and the Sundance Kid 60
Stunts Unlimited, *The Undefeated*,
    The Ballad of Cable Hogue and *Little Big Man* 70
Sometimes a Great Notion 82
Pocket Money 87
Junior Bonner 93
Chino 98
The Sting, Blazing Saddles and *Earthquake* 109
The Great Waldo Pepper 113
The Wind and the Lion 116
Rooster Cogburn 126
Breakheart Pass 134
The Return of a Man Called Horse 142

Silver Streak	151
Our Winning Season	155
The Prisoner of Zenda	162
The Electric Horseman	167
The Frisco Kid	177
The Blues Brothers	181
The Workings of the Lord	186
The Fall Guy	189
Above the Law	205
Raising a Family of Stuntmen	210
Renegades	214
Old Gringo	221
We're No Angels (A Wild Ride for Troy)	238
Problem Child	242
Young Guns II	246
City Slickers	251
The Last of the Mohicans	256
Striking Distance	275
City Slickers II: The Legend of Curly's Gold	283
The Amazing Panda Adventure	287
Waterworld	299
The Nutty Professor	309
Being Around Big Stars	314
Metro	317
The Horse Whisperer	324
The Academy Awards	330
Looking Back…and Forward	333

Contents

Author's Dedication i
Roping the King..1
The Early Years...3
Graduating High School and Meeting Yvonne 13
Alvarez Kelly and *When the Legends Die* 22
Beau Geste 27
Africa: Texas-Style!..34
Cowboy in Africa...52
The Wild Bunch..55
Butch Cassidy and the Sundance Kid 60
Stunts Unlimited, *The Undefeated,*
    The Ballad of Cable Hogue and *Little Big Man* 70
Sometimes a Great Notion..82
Pocket Money 87
Junior Bonner..93
Chino 98
The Sting, Blazing Saddles and *Earthquake*........................109
The Great Waldo Pepper 113
The Wind and the Lion 116
Rooster Cogburn 126
Breakheart Pass..134
The Return of a Man Called Horse.......................................142

Silver Streak 151
Our Winning Season 155
The Prisoner of Zenda 162
The Electric Horseman 167
The Frisco Kid 177
The Blues Brothers 181
The Workings of the Lord 186
The Fall Guy 189
Above the Law 205
Raising a Family of Stuntmen 210
Renegades 214
Old Gringo 221
We're No Angels (A Wild Ride for Troy) 238
Problem Child 242
Young Guns II 246
City Slickers 251
The Last of the Mohicans 256
Striking Distance 275
City Slickers II: The Legend of Curly's Gold 283
The Amazing Panda Adventure 287
Waterworld 299
The Nutty Professor 309
Being Around Big Stars 314
Metro 317
The Horse Whisperer 324
The Academy Awards 330
Looking Back…and Forward 333

Author's Dedication

I dedicate this book to my wife Yvonne, my three sons Tim, Troy and Lance, and let's not forget my adopted son—not by law, but by love—and that's you, Chuck. I also dedicate it to my closest friend, my Saddle-Pal, the Lord above. If it wasn't for the Lord watching over me and answering me throughout my life, I wouldn't have all these stories to tell. To be able to talk to the Lord every day and take Him with you, wherever you go, is a wonderful joy and blessing.

As you read the following pages, you will see how He brought me through life and death experiences and even a miracle. Yes, I've lived a full and dangerous life, but if I got the chance to have another go at it, I'd do it all over again.

I also want to thank my good friend Don McCuaig, who has been my cinematographer for twenty-eight years. Don, without your camera experiences and cinematography ideas, we wouldn't have captured the footage we got. Love ya, man.

There are other people that made this book possible: our Christian and golfing friends, Jeff and Laurie Knudson, along with my co-author, Rebecca Rockwell. This came about out of Jeff and Laurie's curiosity about movies and the experiences I had while making them. Well, they kept after me to write all my experiences down in a book, and they also found my co-author Rebecca, who already has three books out on the shelf today. I'm so happy that I took their advice, and you know why?

Because it's nice for my grandchildren to read about; and, I won't lie to you—I had a great time writing about myself.

      God bless you all.
      -Mickey Gilbert, 2014

Roping the King

I'm sitting on my horse, ready to go, and my father-in-law Joe Yrigoyen, himself a seasoned stuntman and a veteran of the movie business, rides up next to me. I look over at him and motion out about a hundred yards ahead of us. "There he is," I said tensely. "He's a *big* one. It's a good thing we rode in downwind from him, or he'd be having us for lunch right about now."

It's an African Lion I'm talking about, a large male, sleek and magnificent. He's laying in the tall grass, his amber eyes fixed on us, his nostrils flaring delicately as he tries in vain to pick up our scent, wondering what we are.

"You ready?" I ask with a grin.

He nods. We build our loops and take off, swinging our ropes and hollering at the top of our lungs. The lion tenses up even further, standing, rising to his full height. He's massive, likely close to seven hundred pounds or more, and his size—and ferocity—is not lost on me as I gallop closer.

The lion stands still, trying to catch our scent, not intimidated in the slightest. We're fifty yards from him, now, getting closer, and he starts shifting his body to the right and the left, lifting his head up, then lowering it as he tries to scent us. Finally he's had enough, and he takes off, leaping away from us. As he runs he looks back every now and then, still trying to figure out what the hell we are, and what we want with him.

ME AND MY SADDLE-PAL

I ride up on him, fast, swinging my rope. Joe's about thirty feet off to my right. I close in and throw my rope. It settles neatly around the lion's neck, and I dally my rope around my saddle-horn, turning my horse sharply to the left. The lion jerks around, more interested in fighting the rope than he is in me. I keep him going in a wide circle so Joe can ride in behind him and get his loop around him, too.

Joe throws his rope. Damn, he missed him. The lion turns towards Joe, but I jerk him hard again. I holler to Joe, "I'm gonna choke down on him a little more, so take your time!" I've learned from experience that when animals are being choked, their first instinct is to pull back, which chokes them even more. Keeping a tight rope on the lion assures me that he's not going to charge. Joe throws again and ropes him clean, this time.

Together, we get him to the point where he's between our horses with nowhere to go. He's furious—fighting the ropes, growling deep in his chest, trying like mad to get free. He rears up, looming over us—wow, he's got to be around seven feet tall—but we keep going, moving him forward so the natives could get him into a cage. They get him in, we get our ropes off, and it's done.

It's all for a movie, this amazing thing we just did—but we *really did* it. It wasn't some trick of the camera, or a fake lion. The lion was real, the danger was real, and so is my reaction to it all. The adrenaline is rushing through me; my heart's pounding, and I don't think I've ever been this exhilarated before. I'm coiling my rope as Joe rides up beside me and I start laughing as I lean over in my saddle and give him a high-five. "Do you realize that we just roped the King of the Jungle?" I'm shaking my head. It's the most gratifying thing in the world to me: I just did something no one's ever done in a movie before. It wouldn't be the last time, either.

Excitement. That emotion is something I feel often in my line of work, and feeling it now takes me back, suddenly, to when I was a kid and I found out I was going to be moving from our small home in Pasadena to the ranch my dad bought when I was six. That's kind of how it all started.

The Early Years

My father was something of an entrepreneur, and he had the idea to purchase a chicken ranch during World War II, when meat commanded a high price due to rationing. It was a good way to make a good living, but by no means easy. To this day, I remember that my brother Freddy and I, at five and six, were shooting hoops at the garage behind our house in Pasadena when my father drove up, all excited. "Well, boys," he said as he got out of the car, "we did it!"

"What'd we do, Pops?" I asked eagerly.

He smiled. "We got the ranch!"

Excitement flooded through me, and I remember jumping up and down, hollering with joy, Freddy joining in. When I calmed down I asked my dad if there was a tree outside my bedroom window at the ranch.

He looked puzzled. "I'm not sure, Mickey. Why do you ask?"

"Because if there's a tree, I'm going to tie a rope in it and pull the rope in through the window, and in the mornings I'll use the rope to swing down and land right on my pony," I told him, as if the answer was obvious. Is it any wonder I ended up in stunts?

Ranch life meant one thing, first and foremost: hard work. Besides our chickens, we had hogs and cows, and raised vegetables, as well. I learned the value of hard work on that ranch, and we all did our share—me, Freddy, and Mom and Dad, too. I'd milk the cow in the mornings, squirting milk at the barn cats who hung around begging, and Freddy milked in the evenings. We kept hogs in the barn, and I'll never forget the time one of them got loose. My mom tried to catch it; she ran after it as it headed for the fence. As I watched, she launched herself at it, tackling it and throwing both arms around its neck. Our eyes were huge—our mother just *tackled* a pig. It kept running, scared out of its wits, as Mom hung on, her body flapping alongside it like a flag. I was yelling at her to let it go, but she hung on. Mom was a determined type of person who finished what she started.

We were a close-knit family, and a team. Because of the multitude of chores we had to do to keep the place going, Freddy and I never had time to go to church, but even so, God was prevalent in my life from a young age, and has been ever since. My mom would always have us say our prayers at night, I would drag a bale of hay out of the barn, lay on it on my back and talk to God as I looked up at the stars above me. I would talk to Him about how far up Heaven was, and ask Him if I was really *here*, or was I dreaming it all? I found that all the talking I did to God, laying out there on my hay bale, made it all so much more personal to me that way, more one-on-one.

Life on the ranch wasn't *all* work and no play, of course. It was on the ranch that I first demonstrated the talent to come up with rather *unusual* ways to amuse myself and my brother, a talent that would carry over into my work in films.

There was, for instance, the way I devised to get the two of us a ride into Van Nuys to catch a movie. Our ranch was on a rather lonely road that few cars traveled down; hitch-hiking the traditional way could take so long that Freddy and I would have gray hair before a car even appeared, let alone stopped. We needed a way of guaranteeing that whatever car passed by first would stop and pick us up.

How did I solve this minor issue, one might ask? By threading a piece of fishing line *very* carefully through an egg with a needle and letting it dangle out off the limb of one of the trees that hung over the road—right at windshield level. Then Freddy and I would move well away from that tree and wait for a car. When a car would show

THE EARLY YEARS

up, Freddy and I would put our thumbs out to hitch a ride. And guess what? *Splat* went the egg—all over the windshield. They never noticed the thing hanging there before they hit it, and once they did, of course they stopped. Time and again, my little trick worked like a charm, the driver getting out, scratching his head as he looked at the goo plastered across the glass, then looking over at the two of us, sitting innocently on the roadside, always far enough away, of course, so that they wouldn't think we had anything to do with it.

"Where'd that egg come from? Did you boys throw it?" the driver would demand.

Freddy and I would shrug and smile. "Oh, no, sir!" we'd always reply stoutly, then make our way over to the car. "But as long as you're stopped…" We always got our rides to town.

Somehow, I learned how to hypnotize chickens. Yeah—no kidding. Next to the building where we housed our laying hens was a cleaned-off dirt area. I would take a hose and lightly sprinkle down the dirt there, then let it dry on top. The reason for all this prep-work was that when I'd take a stick and place one end of it into the dirt and drag it, a line would be left from the dampness underneath the dried-off surface. Then I'd go catch a hen and bring her back to that dirt area, gently pushing her down into a squatting position. I'd push her beak down to the ground, placing my stick to her beak while continuing to hold her head down. Then, I'd slowly draw my stick away while she stayed in position, staring down that damp line I'd drawn. I could let her go, get up and back off, but she'd still stay there, right where I'd put her, still as a statue. I'd go get more chickens and do the same thing until pretty soon I'd have ten chickens, about four feet apart, all hypnotized in the same manner. I never did figure out what made it work, but it did—every time. Where the hell did I learn how to do this? I have no idea. All I knew is that if my dad ever caught me, I'd get a hell of a whipping.

My dad had some interesting hobbies, too—he held the world's record for motor boat racing, and had also been a superstar in track and field back in the late twenties. I remember while we were living in Pasadena, our garage was a third full of trophies he'd won—trophies

ME AND MY SADDLE-PAL

I wish I had now. He started working with me, training me in all the same events he'd competed in, throughout the time I was in third grade, all the way until I'd reached the sixth. We set up an area at the ranch for high and broad jumping, pole vaulting, discus throwing and hurdles, and when we'd get done with our ranch work he'd take me out there for training. Wouldn't you know, with all that one-on-one training I got, I ended up winning all there was to win in all of my grammar-school track meets—except the pole vault, because seeing as how I was the only student who knew how to pole vault, it wasn't an event they offered.

I sometimes got into fights at school, but it led me into a new hobby: rodeos. A kid I'd gotten into a fight with turned out to be one of my best friends. His brother was learning to rope calves, which got me interested. Along with roping I also got interested in riding bulls. A few of us rigged up a bucking barrel, which consisted of two cables tied into each end of the barrel, and connected to four telephone poles out aways from the barrel. There would be one person per cable, jerking down and pushing up, to simulate the movement of a bull, while one of us would ride it. Our version of a mechanical bull worked well, and I got in a lot of practice, but pretty soon I'd decided I needed to try my hand at the real thing. Our local tack store had steers penned behind it, and in the evenings Freddy and I would sneak over and rope one of them to practice on. Miraculously, we never got caught doing it.

∽∞∾

After the war was over, meat prices came back down, so Dad got out of the chicken business. He sub-divided the ranch and built houses, but kept part of the property because Freddy and I wanted to make some money boarding horses. The main chicken shed was around three hundred feet long and about twenty feet wide, so we converted it into a stable by sectioning off stalls and building corrals behind them.

During that time, I also had a paper-route delivering *The Valley*

THE EARLY YEARS

Times—and my route was the biggest in the valley. Prior to this my dad had bought us a horse, a mare named Susie Q. Freddy had sort of taken her over, so my uncle took pity on me and bought me a mustang gelding that our farrier had to lay down to shoe; I named him Monty the Mustang.

Most of the streets in the valley in those days were dirt, only the main roads were paved. Woodman Avenue, the street that the ranch was on, was paved, so I'd deliver the papers on my bike on that street. When I'd finish, I'd straddle my double-sack paper bag over Monty's back and do the rest of the route, the north part, that way, since all the streets were dirt. Freddy would do the south part on Susie Q.

Monty had a single-foot style to him when he loped, going just a little quicker than a fast trot. After awhile I wouldn't have to rein him in to make a turn; he knew the route so well that he just went where he was supposed to go. The last part of my route was three-quarters of a mile across the Panorama Dairy's alfalfa fields. I delivered there regularly and eventually made a horse path right through the fields. Sitting comfortably in my saddle with Monty going lazily along, I sometimes fell asleep as I rode. If that happened, Monty would walk up to Old Man Youst's house at the end of that path I'd made, turn around, and head back into the alfalfa field—horse cruise-control! Halfway back, I'd wake up, not remembering if I'd thrown the paper or not. When I'd get home, Mom would come out of the house.

"You fell asleep again," she'd tell me. "Old Man Youst called and said he saw you with your chin bobbing on your chest, sound asleep on that horse." I'd jump in the car with her and we'd drive around to deliver the paper to him.

On the weekends, I'd ride Monty to the weekly horse show and enter us in the breakaway calf-roping, an event where your time starts when you leave the chute, chasing the calf, and rope him. You stop your horse and the rope tightens and breaks away from the calf; at that point, time is called.

Freddy and I had built a rodeo arena at the ranch by that point, complete with a calf chute and a bucking chute to practice in. We'd put some of the horses we were boarding into the bucking chute with my rigging cinched on and a bucking strap round their flanks and ride them out, one by one. Luckily, no one ever caught us doing it.

⚜

There was this kid that was boarding a two-year-old filly with us who didn't know too much about horses. One day he came to the ranch to check his horse, taking a cotton lead-rope and tying it around her neck. He led her outside and tied her to a four-by-four post that was partially supporting the roof. There was a clump of grass growing at the base of the pole, so naturally, the filly tried to get to it. As she did so, the lead-rope slipped down to the bottom of the post. When she raised her head, the rope, still tied around the post at the bottom, tightened around her neck and started choking her. She jerked back, violently, ripping the post out from under the barn's overhang. *Adios, amigos*—the filly took off, dragging the post along with her, which, of course, scared her so much that she kept going. She ran through the gate that separated the house from the barn, tearing up the driveway, which was all dirt. Out of control, she turned and headed down Woodman Avenue.

By this time, my dad had built four homes within the ranch, so we had a fairly new house next door to us. The filly turned left and raced up the neighbor's driveway, still dragging the post along with her, and ran between the cars parked there. It was summertime, so the neighbors had their door open with only the screen door closed.

This happened around dinner time, six or so, and the neighbor lady had just set a pot roast down on the nicely-set dining room table inside.

Can't you folks guess what happened? The filly came crashing through the screen door, dragging that post. The neighbors scattered in all directions as the horse burst into the dining room, crashing into the table and sending food, dishes and silverware flying. She kicked at

THE EARLY YEARS

the post behind her, and in doing so kicked a hole in the dining room wall, giving them a new door into their bathroom.

I'd been coming out of the hay barn at the time, and, seeing and hearing what was happening, grabbed a lead-rope and halter. I raced over to the neighbors, but of course the damage was already done by the time I entered the house. The neighbor kids were hiding behind chairs and couches, their parents backed into the kitchen, scared to death. Wouldn't you be, if a horse crashed through *your* front door?

I got to the filly and talked soothingly to her, trying to calm her down, and eventually I got the halter and lead-rope on. I untied the rope around her neck and led her out of the house, walking her home. As you might expect, this little fiasco made the papers, with the headline, 'Horse Crashes Into House Next Door.'

Another strange day in the life of the Gilbert boys occurred after Freddy and I joined up with a group of kids called the D.A.P.—Deputy Auxiliary Police. We had a drill sergeant named Pat Murphy, who would teach us how to do drills while we rode in parades. By this time the valley was growing; General Motors had put in a huge plant about a mile west of us, and the Panorama Dairy, where I'd done my famous "sleep-riding," was no more. A big contractor bought up all the dairy property and plowed the land up, getting ready to sub-divide it all. Some man went to the Van Nuys Airport and hired a pilot and plane to fly him out over the G.M. plant so he could take pictures from above. That didn't turn out to be the case, however. When the plane was over the plant, the man opened the door and baled out, trying to make a splash by landing on top of the G.M. plant. Instead, he missed and landed in the plowed-up alfalfa fields around it. The fields were deep from working the land; no vehicles could get out onto them. Our drill sergeant called me and Freddy up and had us get onto our horses to go out and look for the guy, who we knew probably had not survived the fall.

ME AND MY SADDLE-PAL

We spotted him after we'd been out for a good hour or so; I'll never forget it. He'd landed flat on his back, and because the field had been deeply plowed, he'd made a depression in the earth when he'd hit and when we found him he looked like he was laying in a shallow grave—which, I suppose, he was. We looked down at the body, and I have to admit I didn't really feel sorry for the man; it had been such a *stupid* thing to do, and look what had come of it. Freddy and I called Sergeant Murphy and told him we'd found the body, giving him our location. He showed up with the police, and we pointed out to where the body was.

The trouble then became how to get him out of there—as I mentioned, no vehicles could get through those soft, deep furrows. I knew an old cowboy by the name of Walt who lived in the area who had a mule. At the time there was a television series called *Francis the Talking Mule* that was popular, so, you guessed it, this mule was known as Francis. I rode down to Walt's place, and fortunately he was home. I told him what had happened, and asked him to help us out. Freddy and I, several policemen, Walt and Francis plowed our way through the field. They rolled the victim into a body bag and loaded him up onto Francis, and we took him out that way.

෴

Most people living in the neighborhood—along with the Van Nuys Police Department—knew about the Gilberts. There were always animals getting loose, and people would call in and report us. One morning one of our neighbors called and told my mom that one of our roping calves was grazing on her front lawn—not the way she'd intended to have it mowed. I grabbed my rope, and Mom and I jumped into our '41 Buick to go retrieve it. Two hundred yards down Woodman Avenue, we saw the calf. I jumped out to rope it, but it took off down the street. I leapt onto the front fender, and we took off in pursuit.

As the calf swerved to the left side of the road, it turned into a driveway and ran through an open backyard gate. I jumped off the fender

THE EARLY YEARS

and went after it. As I reached the gate I heard a loud *splash*—the calf had fallen into the homeowners' swimming pool! I heard one of the neighbors hollering out her bedroom window, "Alice! Alice, there's a *cow* in your swimming pool!"

"It's okay, ma'am," I called quickly, "I'll get him." I roped the calf and got him out of the pool, then made a nose-loop so I could control the calf and get it the hell out of there.

Once I was in high school, I kept on coming up with rather unique solutions to problems—like the time I got around a sticky situation in my high school Future Farmers of America class.

We were each supposed to plant out a garden plot as our class project, but instead of completing my own, I spent my time coming up with creative ways to "help" my fellow students out with theirs—flooding them with the hose, digging them up a bit…harmless schoolyard pranks. It finally caught up with me, though, when I found myself confronted at the end of the school-year by my FFA teacher, a man we all referred to as "Chrome-Dome," for his shining bald head.

"Gilbert," he told me in exasperation, "I'm done with your fooling around. You haven't completed your garden plot, and if you don't get it done, you're going to fail this class."

"Aww, come on, Chrome-Dome," I cajoled, trying to wheedle my way out of it. He just shook his head.

"You've got two hours," he said firmly, then moved off to oversee some other students.

I stood there for a second, thinking. I'd been screwing around, and now I had to come up with a way out of it. I suddenly caught sight of a pile of dead chickens in one corner of the yard. They'd had lice, and their carcasses were due to be burned. I felt a smile come up over my face as I looked at them. I had an idea.

Two hours later I ran up to Chrome-Dome. "Hey, Chrome-Dome, I did it! I got my garden done, and it's growing, and everything! Come see it!"

He rolled his eyes at me, but he tagged along as I led him over to my plot. When he saw it, he stopped short and simply stared.

ME AND MY SADDLE-PAL

In my garden-rows I had neatly "planted" chickens, leaving their heads sticking straight out of the ground, their beaks propped up with sticks so they looked like they were standing at attention, their vacant eyes staring straight ahead. I looked over at Chrome-Dome with a wide smile on my face. *Let's see what you make of* that!

After a minute he let out a sigh. "Well, Gilbert," he said, "I don't really see how I can fail you, after *this*!"

That was my life up to that point, and it was never boring! When I think back to those days, I thank the Lord for giving us such a beautiful, different life, and a life I'd live all over again, if I could.

Graduating High School and Meeting Yvonne

I graduated from Van Nuys High School in 1954. One of my classmates, interestingly enough, was a young man by the name of Robert Redford (yes, *that* Robert Redford). He would be an actor/director I would work with many times over the course of my career, but we didn't know each other back then. We traveled in different circles—I was in FFA and hung out with the other agricultural types; he was in the upper echelons; the kids on the football team, the ones in student government, that sort of thing—none of which was *my* thing. We wouldn't actually meet and get to know each other until we did *Butch Cassidy and the Sundance Kid* together, but it shows how small a world we live in.

After I graduated, I went to Pierce College in Woodland Hills to continue my studies in agriculture. They had a rodeo team that wasn't real high-ranking among other collegiate teams at the time; they hadn't been around long. By the time I got there they were starting to do better, and I joined. I competed in bareback bronc-riding, calf-roping, bulldogging and the optional event of either team roping or wild cow milking. My prior experience with gymnastics in high school, along with all of my previous rodeo experience, served me well and I won the National Championship in bareback bronc-riding and calf-roping. From there I went Pro, and did very well my first year, never taking less than second place in any bronc-riding event I entered.

ME AND MY SADDLE-PAL

Here I am in action at the Thousand Oaks Rodeo, 1965. —M.G.

The biggest rodeo in the world was held at the Coliseum in Los Angeles, and because of the prestige and the large cash prizes, competition was always fierce. Cowboys came from all over the country to compete in it. I had a fantastic bucking horse and a great ride in general, and took second place in the bronc-riding event in 1955, something I was quite proud of. When I got home, my dad asked how I'd done, and I showed him the check. It was around fifteen hundred dollars, and my dad was impressed; that was a hell of a lot of money in those days.

It was my dad's idea to use that prize money as a down payment on a ranch some friends of ours were selling. "Think about it, Mickey. You'll have your own place," he urged. I thought about

GRADUATING HIGH SCHOOL AND MEETING YVONNE

it and decided to go for it—there was nothing else I needed the money for at the time. My father made the deal, and I became the proud owner of my own ranch. My monthly payments were $116.99 a month, and I used my rodeo winnings to make them. I didn't move onto it for a few years, but it was nice to know I had it there, waiting for me.

Competing in the Colosseum Rodeo. –M.G

Around this time, I developed an interest in getting into the movie business. As most people know, that's not an easy task. I was naturally inclined toward stunts, but if you're an unknown, it's difficult to find anyone willing to give you a chance. So, to get my foot in the door, I started working as an extra. About the same time, a woman named

ME AND MY SADDLE-PAL

Mary Williams rented the house my dad had built behind our main house. She had a horse and brought it along to board with us.

Mary worked at NBC studios, and she had a girlfriend there by the name of Yvonne Yrigoyen, who was cute, available, and whom she wanted me to meet. Mary was relentless. "You've got to come to the studio and meet Yvonne, Mickey," she kept on insisting.

"Oh, Mary, I'm always busy, I'm always off at rodeos…" My protests made little difference, and she persisted. I ended up meeting Yvonne, all right...but I'll tell you about that in a minute.

While at NBC Studios, Mary also introduced me to Frank Cleaver, who'd worked as a writer on several western T.V. shows, primarily *Bonanza*. He was planning a western series with Grant Sullivan called *Pony Express*. He mentioned he was interested in buying a couple of horses, and Mary suggested he board them at my family's ranch.

During the conversation, Cleaver brought up *Pony Express* again, and he told me, "you know, you could double for Grant Sullivan, easy. You're maybe an inch taller or so, but still, you'd be perfect."

Needless to say, I was excited about this prospect. The series was about the Pony Express riders back in the early 19th century, and Cleaver got me on as an extra—but I also doubled as the actual Pony Express rider every time they showed one going onscreen, and I got Screen Actor's Guild pay for that.

I did about twelve or thirteen episodes of *Pony Express,* doing the mounts. These were the way pony express riders changed to a fresh horse—you'd ride in on one horse, jump off with your mailbag in hand, which was made to fit over the saddle, then do a running mount, vaulting yourself up into the saddle of a fresh horse that's already going at full-speed after having been released by someone holding it at the ready. I was good at these mounts because I'd go over to the barns that were supplying the horses to the production, and I'd work with the wranglers there to figure out which horses were best for what I needed to do with them. As a result I made the mounts look really easy when I did them on camera. One day the production manager came to me and told me they were reluctant to pay me the screen actor's guild salary I

GRADUATING HIGH SCHOOL AND MEETING YVONNE

was collecting for doing the mounts, because they thought they weren't difficult enough to warrant that type of pay.

"You're going to have to work as an extra when you do these, from now on," he told me.

"Well, then, I'm not gonna do them," I replied.

"Then we're going to get someone else," he told me.

The first day my replacement came in, the crew of *Pony Express* got a little more than they bargained for. He got off the first horse and went to try to vault up into the saddle of the second, which was one of the horses I'd trained for the pony express mounts. But the new guy didn't make it all the way when he tried to vault up there, and to top that off his pants split clear up the backside. He wasn't wearing any underwear, so the camera caught a nice view of his bare butt sticking through his pants as he went past. I couldn't help but feel a little vindicated at that--maybe now they'd realize these things weren't as easy as I made them look.

The production manager came to me and asked me to get back out there because the new guy couldn't cut it. "Fine," I told him, "but you've got to put me back on my Screen Actor's Guild contract before I do. You've seen that these mounts aren't easy, so I need to be fairly compensated." He agreed, so I didn't have to worry about that little headache any longer.

Back to Yvonne. While I was still working on *Pony Express,* Mary kept up her pleas to have me come by NBC and meet Yvonne.

"Okay, okay," I finally said. I wasn't interested at the time; in truth neither was Yvonne, either, but we each gave in to get Mary off our backs.

My first impression of Yvonne was this: she was a really cute, attractive redhead, but my attention was drawn, first and foremost, to the beehive hairdo she was wearing. It must've stood about six or seven inches off her head. I swear I thought she could've hidden something inside it—that's how big it was. So I'm looking at her, thinking, *I need this like I need a hole in my head,* and she's looking at me, clearly thinking *why am I even meeting this cowboy?*

ME AND MY SADDLE-PAL

Mary said, "Mickey, this is Yvonne. Yvonne, this is Mickey."

My elegant, charming greeting? "Hi."

Hers? "Hi."

That was it. I was out of there. "Nice to meet you. Gotta go." I left.

Around this time I was moving out to the ranch I'd bought. I fell in love with the place and worked hard to make it home. After a few months had gone by and I'd gotten the ranch set up like I'd wanted it, I decided to throw a barbecue for the cast and crew of *Pony Express*. I told Mary to trailer her horse over and we'd all go on a big horseback ride.

Mary went to Yvonne and invited her along. "We're going to go up to Mickey's place and go for a ride, it'll be so much fun!"

She didn't want to go. "I ride my dad's horses all the time, Mary," Yvonne pointed out. "I don't need to go up to his place to do it." But as you've probably surmised by now, Mary was persistent, and she kept after her until she finally gave in, and she and a few other people came along with her and Mary to the barbecue.

I saddled up a bunch of my horses, and we set off on our ride, going out of the ranch. We had come to some railroad tracks and were all stopped in a row, waiting for an old freight train to pass, near a trestle. Near Yvonne's horse was a telephone pole that had a support cable coming down off it and going into the ground. Yvonne had swung her right leg over the saddle, relaxing as she waited for the train to go by, and though my horses were pretty bomb-proof, her horse backed up a bit when she did it and ended up backing right into that cable. As a result it spooked, moving forward toward the train and then turning to its left, bolting and heading over the trestle.

I acted quickly and took off after her, going as fast as I could go. At the other end of the trestle I could see another telephone pole with a similar cable coming down off of it, right in the path of the horse. Yvonne was unable to reach the reins to pull the horse up since they were sitting right up behind its ears, so she was powerless to do anything to steer the horse away from the danger.

I inched closer, and as I saw that cable my heart sank. If the horse tried to go under the cable, the cable would hit Yvonne and severely

GRADUATING HIGH SCHOOL AND MEETING YVONNE

injure her. If he tried to go over, he'd trip and throw her. Scenarios—all of them *bad*—were racing through my head as I tried to catch up with them.

Before I could reach them, the horse ran head-on into the cable and turned a perfect somersault over it, throwing Yvonne off to the right. She landed on her back in the rocks alongside the train tracks, and the horse got to its feet and took off running again. All of this happened so fast it left my head spinning.

I got off my horse and rushed over to her, expecting the worst. Amazingly, nothing was broken. "I'm okay, I'm okay," she kept saying. "I have to get back on the horse. My dad always taught us to get back on the horse if you fall off. We're going to finish this ride!"

"Hold on a minute," I said. "I want to make sure you're not hurt. I want you to move your arms and legs, move your neck, take a deep breath and make sure you're ribs aren't broken…"

She did all of that, and she was okay. A friend of mine went and caught the horse, and Yvonne was ready to get right back on. "Come on, let's go!" she said.

"No, we're going to go back to the ranch now," I said.

She protested, but I was firm. I knew that once the adrenaline wore off she'd start shaking—and I was right. Before we were back across the trestle she was shaking like a leaf. I got her back to the ranch and got her comfortable, then called her father to let him know what had happened.

The next evening I called over to the Yrigoyen place to see how Yvonne was doing, and Joe, her father, answered the phone. I told him I was just calling to check up on Yvonne.

"She's okay," he told me. "She's sore, but she's okay."

"She's lucky," I said. "If that cable had hit her, it would've cut her in half."

"Well, God was with us," he replied.

"He sure was! Give her my best, and tell her I'm glad she's okay." I hung up.

Well, Yvonne was sitting right next to her dad the whole time, and

ME AND MY SADDLE-PAL

when he'd hung up she'd asked him, "didn't Mickey want to talk to *me?*"

"No, he just wanted to make sure you were okay," Joe replied.

"Well, that just pisses me off," she'd told Joe, fuming. "He should've asked to speak with *me,* not you! If he ever asks me for a date, or anything, he won't get one! He's off my list after that! I'd say no so fast, his head'll spin!"

So, that was that—for now.

Some time later a friend of mine from college, Ernie Righetti, asked me to go on a double date with him and his girlfriend, who boarded her horse at my ranch. I told him I would see what I could do. I was so busy with my rodeo career and the ranch in those days that I never had much time for dating, so I searched my brain for someone I could ask out on this double date. Who did I think of? You guessed it—Yvonne Yrigoyen. I gave her a call to test the waters.

Now, I probably should've called her at home, but I called her up at NBC instead. "Yvonne, this is Mickey Gilbert, and I wanted to know if you'd want to go out on a date."

I'm sure you're thinking: *if he ever asks me for a date, I'll say no so fast it'll make his head spin!* Fortunately for me, that's not what she said. She said, "Oh, yeah, sure, that'd be great!"

I told her when and where, and some time later she told me that after she'd hung up the phone she'd told herself she couldn't believe what had come out of her mouth. She'd vowed to turn me down cold, after all. That double date with Ernie and his girlfriend was our first date—the first of many.

My sense of humor came into play here and there and made for some rather interesting evenings, like the time we went to a Dupar's restaurant at midnight at my suggestion to get some coffee and a bite to eat. Yvonne got up to go to the restroom, and while she was gone I gathered up a bunch of silverware, some ashtrays, and some salt-and-pepper shakers and slipped them all into her purse. When she came back I told her I was going to head to the restroom, too. Instead I went to the manager, took him aside and told him I'd seen the little redhead

GRADUATING HIGH SCHOOL AND MEETING YVONNE

gal over at that table stealing flatware, etcetera. He went over to grill her, and I saw her shake her head. Then I saw her open up her purse for him. Her face drained of color and I could tell she was telling him she had no idea how those things got in there. I could tell she was really getting upset, so I went over and confessed to masterminding the whole thing. Some joke, huh? But that was me.

As time went on, Yvonne stopped being interested in the type of guys she'd dated before me—the football players and jocks—and from then on she was with the cowboy, yours truly. We ended up getting married about a year or so later, and that was our beginning.

Alvarez Kelly and *When the Legends Die*

I've always felt strongly that God is playing a role in my life, and the way I got my first big job in the motion picture industry confirmed that for me.

Before I met Yvonne, I used to practice my roping at a ranch in Tarzana, California owned by an old-time cowboy named Harry Hill. This is where I met Yvonne's dad and my future father-in-law, Joe Yrigoyen. Joe and his youngest daughter Juanne would ride their horses over to Harry's arena and watch me practice. Joe was a big-time stuntman and also a rancher; he had around seven hundred head of cattle that he pastured on Bob Hope's property in the Malibu Canyon hills, so he knew how to rope, too—just not on a professional level. He had a lot of respect for my abilities as a rodeo cowboy, so we got to know each other pretty well. At that point I was still working the rodeo circuit and trying desperately to get into the stunt business, which was not working very well.

It was just one of life's great coincidences that I had met Yvonne through a mutual friend, Mary Williams, and that Yvonne happened to be Joe's daughter. Well, as time went on, Yvonne and I fell in love, got married and had our first son, Timmy. During our first few years of marriage, Joe was working on some of the big western movies, and he would call me and ask if I'd like to go along on these shows and start my stunt career. He knew my abilities as a horseman and a gymnast, and knew I'd be good at stunt work because of them. But as much as I wanted to be in the industry, I turned Joe down—because I was married to his daughter. I didn't want people to think I had married Yvonne just so I could have an easy avenue into the picture business.

So, I kept going to rodeos, making enough to keep us going. As time went on, Joe had another big Western coming and called me once again with the invitation to join him. I talked it over with Yvonne and this time, decided to go.

Joe had a son, Joe Jr., who was working as a stuntman, too, and doing very well. Little Joe, as I'll refer to him, became very good friends and shared many good times together. Months before we were to leave for location, Big Joe decided to have Little Joe and I start training to do different types of horse falls and drags underneath horses. We practiced these stunts on my ranch, and Big Joe let us use his two falling horses, Gypsy and Rebel, to practice on. Everything went great, and before you knew it, we were on our way to Baton Rouge, Louisiana to do a movie called *Alvarez Kelly* starring William Holden, on which Big Joe was the stunt coordinator and second unit director.

Besides me and Little Joe, Big Joe brought on some of the big-time stunt coordinators to work as stuntmen on the film. He had me performing many types of stunts in *Alvarez Kelly*, and I figured he was showing off some of my skills in front of them so when they were coordinating other shows, they might remember me and hire me on. I was doing explosions off of my mini trampoline so it looked like bombs were throwing me into the air; forty to sixty-foot high falls and being shot out of trees besides all the horse work I was doing. Little Joe and I did a head-on horse fall where we were both charging at one another and our horses, Gypsy and Rebel, collided into one another and fell to the ground. That was one of the stunts he and I had practiced extensively at my ranch.

My toughest stunt on the film was a stirrup drag that Big Joe wanted me to do, using Gypsy, his falling horse that I'd already been practicing with at the ranch. It wasn't a problem when I'd done it at the ranch,

ME AND MY SADDLE-PAL

but now I was in amongst three hundred head of cattle, being shot off my horse and dragging alongside of Gypsy's rear leg.

The stunt was planned like so: Joe hollers *"action!"* and they stampede the cattle as I'm riding in the middle of them. Underneath my wardrobe is a blood packet (called a "squib" in the industry), which I can detonate at any time. Joe gets a shot of a soldier up in a tree shooting at me, and I press the button, blow the squib, and fall off my horse at the same time. I'm wearing a stunt vest under my wardrobe that has a nylon strap hooked into it. The strap runs down my leg to a release unit. Hooked into this release unit is another strap that is tied into the stirrup. Also hooked into the release unit is a small cable that, as I'm dragging, I can pull at any time to release myself from the horse. Sounds a little complicated an dangerous, right? Well, you know what? It is.

We go to do the stunt, and here's what happened: I blew the squib, fell of Gypsy, and was being dragged alongside of her hind legs. I'd been dragged about forty feet or so and was doing fine, when, out of nowhere, a steer cut in front of the horse. Gypsy swerved to the right momentarily, then straightened out again. The sudden swerve caused my body to be thrown into her right hind leg, and my upper left thigh slammed into Gypsy's leg just below her hock, snapping her bone. It all happened in the blink of an eye.

She kept running on three legs, still dragging me on my back. I looked up and saw her wobbling as she ran, so I pulled my release cable. Once my weight was released from her, Gypsy stumbled and fell to the ground. I got to my feet and raced to her head to hold her down, talking to her to keep her calm.

Big Joe came rushing over, and after seeing the extent of Gypsy's injuries, decided to put her down. It was a terrible ending to such a wild camera shot, but I've got to tell you, it could've been worse. My saddle-pal, God Almighty, was with me all the way that day. My leg could easily have broken, too, when I'd slammed into Gypsy; instead all I came away with was a bad bruise.

My father-in-law and I shared a lot of tears over Gypsy's unfortunate end, but as with any trauma that happens in life, you eventually have to move on. I always look back on this incident as an example of the way the Lord above, my Saddle-Pal, is working in my life and looking out for me, too.

One of the other stars of *Alvarez Kelly* was Richard Widmark, a veteran actor who'd gotten his start in film noir in the 1940s. Joe had me doubling Widmark, who was playing Confederate Colonel Tom Rossiter, I was dressed in the same costume he was, of course. While on set he'd often pass by me and give me a quick glance, never saying anything. Widmark was a quiet man. All the time I was working on the film, I kept hoping they'd bring Widmark in so I could get to know him a bit, and perhaps give him some advice about staying safe during riding scenes. Unfortunately, it never happened, and we never even formally met one another; he simply knew me as his stunt double by sight.

Some years later a job came up on a film being shot in Durango, Colorado called *When the Legends Die*, and I had the opportunity to double Widmark once again in that film. He saw me on set one day from afar and recognized me. He came up to me. "Weren't you on *Alvarez Kelly?*" he asked me.

"Yeah, I actually doubled you in it," I told him.

"Oh, okay, I remember you," he told me—and that was it; he walked off.

A few minutes later I happened to be standing next to a crewmember holding a walkie-talkie, and it crackled to life. Richard Widmark's voice came through. "Hey, what's the name of my stunt double?" he asked, obviously unaware I was standing next to the guy. The assistant threw a glance my way, and then told Widmark my name. Widmark repeated it, then thanked the assistant and signed off.

We were all staying at the same motel in Durango, and one evening I walked in to see Widmark sitting at the bar having a drink. He saw me come by, and to my surprise, called me over. "Hey, Mickey! Come here, let me buy you a drink!"

I was surprised he remembered my name, and at how friendly he

ME AND MY SADDLE-PAL

was being; he'd always been so quiet on set. "What'll you have?" he asked me.

"Well, I'm not really much of a drinker, but I'll have a beer," I told him, and took a seat. We started talking together; I told him about my days on the rodeo circuit, and how I lived on a ranch and loved that lifestyle. Widmark owned a ranch, too, in Thousand Oaks, California; one of my stuntman buddies named Jimmy Burk happened to manage it for him. We had something in common, and it made for a nice evening of conversation and getting to know each other.

We went back to work on the film the next day, and I did some more doubling for him. When filming wrapped on the movie, we said our good-byes and parted ways, and the next time I heard from him was on a western released by Universal Pictures called *Death of a Gunfighter*, in which he played a character called Marshal Frank Patch. I heard of it after the fact, but apparently at a production meeting for the show that Widmark attended, there was some discussion about stunts and Widmark practically brought the entire meeting to a halt by asking where I was, and if they'd secured me for the movie yet. He told them he specifically wanted me to double him and wouldn't hear of attempting any of those scenes unless they brought me on. You can't imagine how good hearing *that* made me feel—and though there hadn't been any plans to bring someone in for stunts initially, they ended up calling me in to double for him and do some stunt coordinating.

I didn't see much of him after that since he stopped making a lot of the type of films I worked on, but hearing about that meeting made a lasting impression. There are milestones in any career, and being asked for specifically—almost demanded, from the sounds of it—by a big-time, highly respected actor like Richard Widmark was definitely one of mine.

Beau Geste

After I finished *Alvarez Kelly*, which started a whole new career for me thanks to Yvonne's dad Joe, I received a call from Hal Needham, whom I'd just worked with on *Alvarez Kelly*. Hal was working as the stunt coordinator on a movie called *Beau Geste*, based on an adventure novel from 1924 that had been adapted to the screen several times before. I guess I'd impressed Hal on *Alvarez Kelly*, because he wanted to know if I'd be interested in working with him again on this new project.

"Need you ask?" I said. "I'd love to!"

About two weeks later, Yvonne drove me down to Universal Studios to catch a bus with about twenty other stuntmen that I would eventually get to know. As we pulled through the main gates, I saw the buses being loaded up with stuntmen. "Holy shit!" I exclaimed, spotting a guy wearing bright orange cowboy boots with his pants tucked into them, carrying a bag. Those boots were something else!

"What's the matter?" Yvonne asked me.

"See that guy in the orange boots over there?" I asked her.

"Wow," she said, spotting him, "who do you suppose that is?"

"I have no idea, but I'm sure I'll find out soon enough," I said.

I got onto the bus and we were soon on our way to Yuma, Arizona, to a place called Buttercup Valley. This was nothing but sand dunes after sand dunes. Universal had built a huge fort there where we were going to be filming battle scenes. On the bus were several stuntmen

ME AND MY SADDLE-PAL

I'd worked with on *Alvarez Kelly* so it wasn't like my first day on the job. I spotted the fellow with the orange boots as we got off the bus in Yuma, so I walked over and introduced myself to him. His name was Freddy Waugh. "Those boots of yours are really something, Freddy," I commented.

"Yeah, you like 'em?" he asked.

"Well…they wouldn't stand out so much, maybe, if you didn't have your pants tucked into them," I said.

"Yeah, you're right," Freddy replied, glancing down at his fancy footwear. "I guess wearing them that way does make 'em light up a little, doesn't it?"

"Like a Christmas tree," I said, and we both laughed. He pulled his pant-legs out and slid them down over the boots' tops. I checked the results out. "Much better, Freddy, much better."

A stuntman I knew walked by and glanced at Freddy's feet, taking in his wardrobe adjustment. "I see you told him," he said to me, as he kept walking.

Later that day, we were all going to be bused out to the fort set to meet with Needham to talk about the actions scenes, and what each of us would be doing on the show. Hal picked me to be one of the horsemen riding the falling horses, and he told me he would also have me as one of the Legionnaires, doing high falls off the fort walls.

One day I was working with my falling horse when I noticed Hal watching Freddy and two other stuntmen as they were working out on some small trampolines called mini-leapers. These were to be used for ground explosions that would catapult men into the air when they went off. I rode over to watch, and as I was looking on I noticed that each guy would run and leap off both feet on the trampoline, then do a trick in the air, as if an explosion had gone off. Hal saw me watching them and called, "Hey, Mickey, do you know how to work a mini-leaper?"

"Yeah," I said. Hal didn't know that my gymnastic workouts included training on trampolines.

"Come on over and take a run at it," he said, so I dismounted and walked over. Freddy introduced me to Chuck and Bill Couch, who were acrobats with trapeze experience, along with several other specialties.

"Go ahead, Mick," Hal said.

I ran at one of the mini-leapers, but instead of leaping onto it from two feet, I just ran, stepped into it, turned a trick in the air and then rolled out of it.

"Wow," Needham said excitedly, "that looked pretty good! Let's see some more."

I did another one off of one leg, turning a lay out "branny" in the air, then rolling out of it. "All right," Hal said, "where did you learn how to do that?"

"I've been a gymnast since the seventh grade," I replied with a grin.

"No, not that," Hal said, "I mean, where did you learn to take off the leaper on one leg?"

"Oh, *that*," I said. "Well, I always thought it would look better and more natural to run into it and go off one leg, instead of jumping into the leaper," I explained. He agreed with me and told the other guys he wanted them to practice off of one leg, too. Later in the day I found the them and made sure they knew that I hadn't been trying to show them up, I just thought it looked more realistic to do I that way, especially since we were supposed to be looking as though a bomb had just gone off. They laughed at me for being apologetic and told me they agreed with me.

One day while we were making the movie, myself and three other stuntmen, all dressed as Arabs, were out working our falling horses in the dunes. We rode up to the top of one of the sand dunes, and out of nowhere, we suddenly saw three Mexicans that had come across the border illegally and were trekking through the dunes. As we all spotted one another, the Mexicans froze. I said to the other stuntmen, "you guys want to have some fun?"

"Sure," they replied, and in unison we all raised our plastic sabers and charged off down the slope, screaming *"ai-yi-yi-yi!"*

You can imagine what those guys were thinking when they saw us come charging down on them. We never got closer to them than about a hundred yards, but that was close enough for them! They threw up their hands, turned and took off like scared rabbits. By this time, we were all laughing so hard that we could barely stay in our saddles. We pulled up and watched them disappear over the next sand dune. I can only imagine what they must have told their friends and family. If you're thinking it wasn't very funny, or very nice, to do what we did, just remember that we were all in our twenties, just a bunch of guys having some fun, and nobody got hurt.

We'd been working on the film by then for about two weeks, doing horse falls, explosions, high falls off the fort walls, and all different types of stunts. Finally we had a day off, so I went with Everett Creach, one of the other stuntmen who was a friend of mine, to the Stardust Motel to grab a bite at the restaurant. While sitting at the bar, I spotted a *huge* steak inside a glass case; a sign on the case said "72-ounce sirloin: eat it in one hour and it's free." If you took over an hour to eat it, the sign said, it cost 13.95. A lot of money—remember, this was 1966.

Now, this piece of meat was about six inches high and around six inches in diameter. I kept staring at it while we were eating, until finally, Everett said, "You're not thinking of doing that, are you?"

I laughed. "No, no." I paused and gave him a wicked grin. "I'm thinking we should *each* get one!"

"You gotta be kidding," Everett groaned.

"Oh, c'mon, let's give it a try," I coaxed. I finally talked him into it, and we waved the manager over to our table. He asked if we were with the movie production, and we told him we were part of the stunt department. Right away, he got the idea to advertise this "stunt" around town, and he'd hold it as a contest, in the bar area. I could see where he was going with this and told him that most of our crew would probably show up, and there would likely be lots of drinking and betting going on, so…

"I gotcha," he said. "if by chance you guys *can't* finish the steak in an hour, you don't want to pay for it, right?"

I nodded. "You hit the nail on the head." This would be good publicity for his restaurant, so I figured he should be able to supply those steaks. He agreed with my proposition and set the date for the contest for one week away, on a Saturday night. He explained that what they did was slice the sirloin in half and cook the first half to your specifications; then while you were eating they put the second half on the barbecue and got it going. Along with the steak came a baked potato, soup or a salad.

"Sounds like *we're* going to have fun on Saturday," I told Everett.

We had a week to get ourselves ready, and when the crew found out about it they were excited. Everett and I met up with the studio cook and would have him make us rice for lunch; we'd stuff ourselves with it to stretch our stomachs, which made everyone laugh at us. As you're reading this you're probably thinking, "those guys are crazy." Well, you're right—we were.

The big night came, and by eight o'clock the bar was packed with crew-members and locals alike. Our table was set up where everyone could see us, and an announcement was made that the two sirloins were on the grill. Everyone let out whoops and laughs. "What you won't do to have a little fun," someone ribbed us.

Two good-looking gals, all dressed up for the occasion, brought out our plates. Before they started the timer, I sliced my potato down the center lengthwise and poured in my cup of soup to moisten it. We picked up our silverware, they started the timer, and in we dug.

You would've thought this was the Kentucky Derby, the way we were getting cheered on. "Don't chew it, just swallow it whole!" someone yelled. One of the actors, a tall, lanky fellow who was sitting at the bar, told me I should cut the meat really thin so I could chew and swallow faster.

We were eating away, and while we were doing it, bets were being made about which one of us would finish first. Just so you get this in perspective—you could make about sixteen quarter-pounder burgers from a seventy-two ounce sirloin. Oh my Lord, what the hell did I get myself into?

I finished my first half, and they plopped the second one down on the plate. I have to say, my soupy potato was tasting pretty good by then, just to have something different going down the hatch, instead of more steak!

"How're you doing there, Everett?" I said jovially around a mouthful.

Everett, cutting and chewing, replied, "don't talk so much, keep eating."

Chuck Hayward, one of the other stuntmen, was sitting at the bar and he laughed and leaned toward me. "How're *you* doing, Mick?"

"I'm in the home stretch," I told him, chuckling.

"Okay, then, I'm betting another twenty on ya. Go for it!"

By now I was feeling like my jaw was starting to think about falling off. There were ten minutes left on the clock, and I had a little over a quarter of a pound left to eat. That's like a thick hamburger. By this time, I could see that Everett wasn't going to make it; he had too much meat on his plate. This horse race is coming down to the wire and I have to say, the crew was going completely nuts, laughing and cheering me on. "Go, Mick, go! Stuff it in!"

Suddenly, my jaw cramped up. I was trying to chew, but couldn't. I put my hands under my jaw, pulling it open and pushing it shut, trying to get the cramp to ease up, but there wasn't enough time. My jaw was so stiff I could hardly talk, and needless to say I didn't finish the steak—but I did better than Everett, and what a good time I had! Everyone talked about that little adventure for weeks.

Freddy Waugh and I became good friends on that movie because we had so much in common, both being gymnasts. Freddy told me he wanted to learn all about horse work—falling, rearing, jumping, etcetera—and I told him that when we got home, he could come up to the ranch and I'd teach him. I also told him that he really should look into buying his own horse and learn how to do some training, ideas that he found exciting. We got back to Universal where Yvonne picked me up. On the way home I said to her, "honey, you'll never guess who I've become good friends with."

She answered me as if she'd already been told, "of course I can guess—the guy in the orange boots!"

BEAU GESTE

I laughed and told her that we were going to be working out together, and that he was going to set up his flying trapeze in one of my pastures. As time went on, Freddy and I worked on more movies together and traded skills, teaching each other everything we could. Freddy married a beautiful girl named Sophia whom Yvonne loved very much. It just goes to show you how working together for just six weeks can lead into a friendship that lasts for a lifetime.

Africa: Texas-Style!

The way I came to work on director Andrew Marton's 1967 film *Africa: Texas-Style!* has always been a clear example to me of how my Saddle-Pal Jesus taught me that if you give all of yourself to others in some way, you'll be rewarded ten-fold.

I was practicing roping in my arena at my ranch one day when I noticed a black limo coming down the drive. As I watched, it pulled into a pasture that was next to the arena. Whomever the occupant was, they didn't reveal themselves right away; instead they sat, concealed behind tinted windows, and apparently watched as I went on with my roping. Finally the doors opened, and a couple walked over to the arena fence. "Can I help you folks?" I asked them.

"We sure hope you can," the man said. He introduced himself as Ralph Helfer and his wife, Toni. They were the owners of a spread called Africa U.S.A., a compound that housed exotic African animals about a mile up the canyon from my place. The Helfers made television shows at the time.

The Helfers told me they'd seen the sign I kept out front that said "Horses Boarded and Trained." "We've got a couple of stallions at our place that need some training," he told me. He said that when they'd bought the two studs, he and Toni had been able to ride them, but as time had gone on they'd become more and more unmanageable, until they were, as he put it, downright mean. He told me he wanted me to come up and take a look at the pair.

"I'll tell you what, Ralph," I said, "I'll ride one of my horses up the river wash tomorrow and if everything works out, I'll halter your studs and take them on leads, and I'll pony them back here."

Ralph shot a look at Toni, then shrugged his shoulders and gave a slight grin. "You know, you can't even go into their corrals without them charging, biting and kicking at you," he warned me.

"Well, that's to be expected of stallions," I told him mildly. I could tell he was thinking, *OK, have it your way—it's your funeral.*

The next morning I saddled up one of my big strong roping horses and rode up the wash to the Helfers' place. Once I'd gotten there I met with Ralph and he took me to the compound where the stallions were. I tied my horse up and walked over to the corral occupied by one of them, a good-looking blue roan.

"So this is one of them, Ralph?" I asked.

"Yeah, he's the worst of the two," Ralph confirmed. The stallion started walking toward me as I leaned my arms on the top rail of the gate. I held out a hand to him, and that's all he needed—he pinned his ears back flat, broke into a charge and came right at me. I pulled my hand back as he snapped at it. Unperturbed, I kept trying to stroke his muzzle, but he wasn't having it and kept trying to bite.

Ralph threw a glance my way. "You see what I mean?" he asked.

I nodded, my eyes still on the horse. "Yeah, he *is* a little nasty," I conceded. I walked back to my horse and grabbed one of the halters I'd brought, coiling up the lead rope that was attached to it as I headed back to the gate.

Ralph eyed the halter. "What are you going to do?" he asked me warily.

"Teach him a lesson," I said simply. As I walked up to the gate the horse came at me again. This time, when he'd gotten to within four feet of me, I swung the halter and lead rope and smacked him right across the nose with them, not hard enough to hurt him, of course, but firmly enough to show him who was boss. He snorted in surprise, turned his tail to me, and I popped him across the back legs this time. He darted away toward a small covered feeding stall with me chasing close behind his rear end all the while. I popped him once more across the hind legs as he turned into the stall, then I started talking to him, nice and easy.

"Easy, boy, whoa, now," I said. As I talked to him I moved slowly towards him. He started turning his rear end on me again, ready to kick, so I popped him again, letting him know I wouldn't tolerate that behavior. At that point, he turned sideways to me, and I kept talking to him, moving slowly up to him as I did. Finally I got to him, and I started petting him. Then I took the halter and lead rope, rubbing his head and neck with it, then walked back to his shoulders, petting him all the while. Finally I moved up to his head and slipped the halter on.

I patted him on his face and led him out of the stall. Ralph and a bunch of his trainers had gathered at the fence; they'd heard the commotion inside the feeding stall but hadn't been able to see what was going on until I led the stallion out. I'll tell you, when they saw that stallion coming along pretty as you please on the end of that lead rope, with the halter secure around his head, their jaws hit the ground—they couldn't believe it.

"I don't believe it," Ralph exclaimed.

"Well, he's gotten away from being disciplined," I explained, "and that's the worst thing you can do to a stallion."

I repeated the same method with the other stallion and was similarly successful, so I left the compound with both horses on lead just like I'd planned and took them back to my ranch. I ended up working with them for about four days, then I called Ralph to come out and take a look at my handiwork. He and Toni arrived and walked with me back to the stallions.

I picked up a halter and lead rope and handed them to Ralph. "Here, I want you to go up to the gate, raise and shake the halter and cluck your tongue at Blue, and he's going to turn and walk right up to you. Don't back off. Just talk to him, real nice and easy, and slip the halter on him." Ralph looked a little reluctant; I could tell he was imagining those sharp hooves and powerful teeth. "Go on," I encouraged him. "He won't hurt you."

AFRICA: TEXAS-STYLE!

So Ralph did as I asked, and it worked perfectly. He led the stallion out after slipping the halter on him. He and Toni were very excited and wanted to try riding them again. We saddled both stallions up and all went out for a ride. During our outing, I told them everything they needed to know about handling the two horses. As we were untacking them back at the ranch I told them that I'd bring the stallions back to their place later that day. It was really great to see them both so excited about being able to ride them again, and I was glad I'd been able to help make that happen. On the way back to his car, Ralph paused.

"By the way, Mick, what do you think I owe you for this, anyway?" he asked me.

"You don't owe me a dime, Ralph," I said. "Someone's already put a lot of time and effort into training those two. I just helped them remember their manners. Just enjoy them and promise me you won't let them get away with bad habits."

Remember when I said this incident made me realize that if I followed God's word and gave myself away to someone, I'd be rewarded? Well, about a month or so later on a Sunday morning, Yvonne was reading the newspaper when something caught her eye. She hollered excitedly to me. "Honey, guess what? Africa U.S.A., Ivan Tors and Ralph Helfer are going to do a movie in Africa about two cowboys roping wild animals." She'd no more gotten those words out than a black limo came cruising up our drive—Ralph and Toni again.

Over coffee, Ralph told me he wanted to know if I'd be interested in going with them to Africa to double Hugh O'Brien during the wild animal roping scenes in the film. "Are you serious?" I asked in disbelief.

"I am," he'd assured me, smiling. After meeting with Ivan Tors and Ralph together, we struck a deal. I would be the stunt coordinator and double for Hugh O'Brien. As the stunt coordinator I had hiring rights, so I hired my father-in-law to double Tom Nardini, who was playing the other wild animal-roping cowboy. In preparation I sold four of my roping horses to the production company—I wasn't about to get horses in Africa to do this job on! I made sure the higher-ups knew that I would only do the show if they agreed to my bringing the horses of my choosing—I was only as good as the tools I had, which, in this case, were my roping horses. They agreed and I stabled them at Africa U.S.A. in preparation, so they could become acclimated to the scent of the animals they'd be working around in Africa. Finally the day came for our departure, so we loaded the horses into an AirFrance cargo plane and away we went to Africa.

After a layover in New York that got extended due to some issue with our permits in Nairobi (more money was being requested than had been originally), we flew on to Paris, then to Lebanon, and finally Nairobi. The journey in total had taken about two and a half weeks.

The rest of the production company wasn't there yet, so Joe and I kept the horses in shape by working them in the big Eucalyptus arena the natives had built for us. Before that we'd had to contend with the side-effects of the Tsetse fly vaccines the horses needed; the vaccines made them sick after administration and we had to spend some time nursing them back to health. Eventually they'd come out of it all right, so we started practicing our roping. The natives there loved to watch us, and the children would run up to the arena fence with long pieces of thistle rope that we'd tie into little lassos for them. Some of the kids would try roping each other like they'd seen us do with cattle, and a lot of them ended up with rope burns around their necks and ankles.

The rest of the production team arrived, and we had a bush pilot, Harold Cope, fly us over different places to scout out herds for roping. We also caught wild animals in pens overnight to use for close-up scenes with the actors and animals.

The director, Andrew Marton, was going to have a scene with us roping Cape buffaloes. The span of the horns on these animals is about four feet across—too wide for me to rope both horns at once, so I decided I'd rope the right horns and heads only so I'd be certain not to miss. We flew out to a location along a river between Uganda and Kenya where there were about two thousand head of buffalo, with zebra and a few elephants mixed in for good measure—it was quite a sight to behold.

We started downwind of the herd so as not to let them get our scent, and I laid out a plan to ride around them and come down unto the herd to rope them. I told the camera crew to stay put and wait for us to come down into the herd to get the shot—I didn't want them pushing the herd at all. "It'll take us about half an hour to get where we need to be," I warned them, "but just hang tight."

As we rode along the cliff that rose above the herd, I rode over into the brush along the edge and glanced down. The director had moved the camera car, and pushed the herd, anyway, to get some stock shots while they waited. I got on my walkie-talkie.

"You guys, you can't do that! If they catch your scent, that entire herd is going to stampede out of there, believe me! Please, just stay where you are until we get down there!"

We rode on, and were about fifty yards from the cliff's edge when we heard this incredible rumbling, like the sound of an earthquake. We could feel the rumbling in our chests. "I think they stampeded the buffalo," Joe told me.

All of the sudden, all of the dried brush along the edge of the cliff exploded as hundreds of buffalo came charging up and over the edge and onto the mesa where we were. "We'd better turn and ride with them or they're gonna run right over us!" I hollered at Joe. They bore down on us and swept past like a wave breaking on sand, and we ran along with them. After about four hundred or so had gone by, the dust got so bad we couldn't see—and that meant our horses couldn't either. I shouted at Joe to mind his horse's head—if our horses lost their footing and went down, we'd go down, too—and if we went down, we'd be trampled.

Finally the entire herd had gone by, and Joe and I pulled our horses up, catching our breath and exclaiming over what had just happened. "We are *very* lucky, Mick," Joe told me, "that we're not dead, and that our horses aren't dead…"

"I know," I told him. I'd wished I'd had a camera with me—that's how incredible the sight had been. And when the dust finally settled, we couldn't see a single buffalo anywhere around us.

I never will forget that moment, nor how right Joe was about us being lucky. It goes to show you how important it is for people who aren't

ME AND MY SADDLE-PAL

familiar with working around animals to listen to the people they've hired to handle it for them. If the director had followed my instructions, the stampede wouldn't have a happened. Fortunately for us and for the production's sake, the director started listening to us after that incident. We ended up roping six different species of animals, and I must say that if Joe and I hadn't had those powerful roping horses, we never would've gotten the job done.

My father-in-law Joe Yrigoyen and I, roping a Wildebeest for Africa: Texas-Style! *–M.G.*

My next piece of excitement on location for *Africa: Texas-Style!* occurred toward the end of the shoot; I fought a rhino on foot. Yeah, you read it right—like a matador. They put this sequence off until the end for a reason. Why, you may ask? Because if I fought the rhino and got seriously hurt, there would be no one to double Hugh O'Brien for the roping scenes. You can't risk using up your resources too early!

The production company sent an experienced wild animal team into Uganda that trapped a pair of rhinos, and brought them back to two small, separate stockades which were placed in the area where I would fight them—one at a time, of course. One of the rhinos was there for a backup in case the other one became sick. Joe was really concerned about this and, being the hunter that he was, he suggested that we bring in two white hunters from the area that really knew their

AFRICA: TEXAS-STYLE!

stuff—they would be my only protection from being gored or crushed by the rhino.

I had an ace in the hole, so to speak, in this crazy situation. During my rodeo career I'd worked with two thousand-pound Brahma bulls, and I'd learned how to get out of their way by dodging around them. My lighter body-weight meant that I could move myself around a heck of a lot quicker than an animal that size could, and I'd use that to my advantage.

The big day came and I started setting everything up. I had them put two camera operators up in different trees to shoot down onto me. We had a cage with a camera operator inside; I'd try to work the rhino around it so we could get some great shots from that angle, and another camera set at the lift gate, shooting out at me as the rhino would walk past.

You may think there's something a bit absurd about a man fighting a rhino; I can tell you what's really absurd about it is the way you get the rhino's attention—you call to them by whimpering like a baby. I'm not kidding.

It was time to go. I put on my cleated football shoes to give me plenty of traction, got the camera operators in their positions, and told Joe and the hunters to position themselves where their instincts told them to be. They rolled the cameras, lifted the slide gate, and there stood the rhino, trying to focus on what was before him. He had to try *hard*—rhinos have extremely poor eyesight.

I was thirty feet out from the pen he was in, a roping coil in my right hand, stepping from side to side and whimpering so that he could see and hear me. *Wham*—suddenly came charging out, past the first camera, his breath coming out of him in loud snorts with every stride. He was about six feet from me, coming strong, when I stepped easily to my left. He started to move with me, but I stepped to my right, staying in close to him as he swung his head at me and pivoted around. He chased me around one of the trees I had a camera in, and I kept going, getting him to follow me around a bush that also hid a camera. I dodged him one more time, then he drew to a stop, staring at me.

I started to weave back and forth again, my eyes locked on the rhino, waiting to see what his next move would be. I was breathing hard and my adrenaline was racing through my body like a flash flood, at that point, and I had to get my wind back while still keeping myself alert enough to be able to get out of his way if he moved again. Out of nowhere I suddenly heard the director screaming at me to "make him charge! *Make him charge!*"

Irritation coursed through me right then, along with the adrenaline—talk about the wrong time to bother me! "Shut the fuck up!" I screamed back. I'd like to see *him* pull this off!

I got my breath back and threw my arms in the air, and he came at me again, but only for about ten seconds. He knew by this time that he wasn't going to get me, and from then on the jig was up—I couldn't get him to charge me. It was just like a bull with a matador, at the point in some bull fights where the matador can walk right up to the bull and put his hand on its head without it charging. I can tell you, I wasn't about to try that with a rhino! Instead, I slapped the rope against his face a couple times. He still wouldn't charge, only lunge a little, then toss his head up and down.

"He's done, guys," I called to the crew. "There's no more fight in him."

"That's great," the director called, "we got enough footage. Go ahead and rope him and snub him to a tree."

I did just that, and after the rhino was safely snubbed, I had Hugh O'Brien get into the scene, with the tree in between him and the rhino—just in case.

I experienced so many things in Africa, many of which didn't pertain to the movie but have stuck with me all these years, like the time I had to deal with army ants. Joe and I were out working one day with our horses and as I looked down I saw a trail of army ants, also known in Africa as Siafu, walking along the ground. A respectful fear of these ants exists in Africa; their bite is severely painful. They're about five times the size of a red ant, and when they travel they tend to form lines about a hundred feet long that are around two inches wide. When they

AFRICA: TEXAS-STYLE!

attack they swarm onto an animal and bite it simultaneously; they've even been known to attack babies or small children. The pain that occurs when they do is excruciating, and they can even kill large animals. I was told they can devour a horse in two days. We reported seeing them, and natives came out with gourds full of gasoline to set them on fire and kill them. How would you like to wake up with a line of those guys crawling all over you? No, thank you!

Here I am, fighting that rhino, during filming for Africa: Texas-Style! –M.G.

Another incident that suck with me was seeing a group of African women squatting in a circle, making necklaces and bracelets of dyed elephant hairs. They had their little babies strapped onto their backs as they worked, their little heads peeking over one shoulder. The flies there were so bad that they'd cover the infants' eyes, causing diseases and blindness. The women all tried to brush the flies away every few minutes, but it never worked for long. When I saw that I got off my horse and tried to help brush the flies off of some of them, but when

ME AND MY SADDLE-PAL

I got close I saw the babies eyes had already turned gray and were protruding out. That particular incident was really when it hit me that I was in the depths of Africa, seeing poverty and poor living conditions.

There was a small Catholic church in the town of Nanyuki that Yvonne and I would attend every Sunday. We had to go to the very first mass of the morning, because if we waited it would get hot and the body odors would become overpowering. We had to take it in stride, though, because we *were* in rural Africa, after all.

Sometimes the best thing about making a movie isn't just the experience of making it—sometimes it's the unlikely friendships you make along the way that really stick in your memory, long after filming is done. In every location there are interesting people to meet and connect with, and sometimes you end up touching someone's life in surprising ways. My time in Kenya was no exception.

While I was working on *Africa: Texas-Style!*, our bush pilot, Harold Cope, became a very good friend of mine. We had a lot of flying time together, scouting out the different herds we'd use for filming; it was the best way to find the herds and get to them, too.

Harold knew quite a few government officials, including Dr. Njoroge Mungai, the Minister of Defense in Kenya. Mungai was a cowboy aficionado; he adored Roy Rogers. He heard about the two American cowboys who were roping African animals for the film and wanted very much to meet us—and what a coincidence that Joe had been Roy Rogers' stunt double during Roy's career. Joe and I were staying in a two-bedroom cottage at the Mount Kenya Safari Club; one night Harold called me there and told me that Mungai had expressed a desire to meet us.

"Bring him up, Harold," I told him, "and we'll take him riding with us."

Mungai jumped at the invitation; the following week Harold landed his plane, Mungai as his passenger, in a cut pasture on the ranch where we were keeping the horses. Joe and I were sitting in our saddles, watching as Harold taxied the plane toward us.

A tall, strapping African man stepped from the plane, dressed in a

AFRICA: TEXAS-STYLE!

cream-colored western suit complete with long fringe hanging off the yoked front and back, a white ten-gallon hat, and two six-guns holstered at his hips. What a sight! I looked at Joe and raised my eyebrows.

"You must be Mickey and Joe," he said in a deep voice that was thick with a Kenyan accent. "Is that right?"

"Yes, sir, that's us!" I said, giving him a smile. I asked him if he'd like to ride with us.

He laughed, raised his arms and said enthusiastically, "Oh yes, yes, yes! I would love to ride with the cowboys!"

It was pretty hot that day, so I suggested to Mungai that he might enjoy his ride more if he put his guns, holsters and jacket in the plane before we set off. He took me up on that suggestion, then mounted up on "Brandy," the horse we'd saddled up for him. We headed over to the arena Joe and I used for roping practice.

Any time we rode up to the arena, bunches of young Swahili kids would climb up on the arena fences and cheer us on, and that day was no exception. I let Mungai chase after some of the steers for a bit, and when we finished we unsaddled the horses and rode bareback into a slow-moving river that came flooding through the Swahili camp. I'd had a generator and a water-pump set up in that area of the river to provide a water massage for the horses, and we sat on their backs in the water as it eased their sore muscles. Afterward I handed Brandy's reins to Mungai and let him hose the horse down. He was having a ball being a cowboy for a day; it was a dream he'd always had, and I was happy to help bring that dream to life.

At the end of the day, he flew back to Nairobi, but Joe and I saw him a few more times after that and he became a good friend. What I didn't realize at the time was that by letting him be part of our world for a bit, we were spreading goodwill among people in the government, and the press as well, because Mungai had nothing but praise for us and gratitude for our kindness.

One weekend Joe and I went into Nairobi to enjoy ourselves on a little break from filming. We had our cowboy hats on, of course, and we attracted attention. Before we knew it we were being waved at and followed by dozens of African fans. I didn't realize at the time that the press was always with our film company while we were roping the different wild animals, and our pictures were appearing in all the papers with regularity, about once a week.

Towards the end of filming, I was on the phone talking to our producer Ivan Tors regarding what we would do with the horses we'd brought over. It was too expensive to fly them home, so I came up with an idea—why not give them to Mungai as a goodwill gift? I knew he would take good care of them and appreciate the gesture, and it would create goodwill between him and Ivan Tors—something that would prove very helpful in the future since Tors was planning to shoot more movies in Kenya. What could be better than to have a guy like Mungai in your corner? Mungai had already been a great asset to our film company, getting us access to places we normally wouldn't have been allowed. I told Ivan I'd present the horses to Mungai on his behalf, and Ivan was thrilled with the idea.

I got in touch with Mungai and told him to come up to say goodbye. Harold flew him out to us, and Joe and I picked him up in our Land Rover, taking him to the barns. When we got there I asked him, "Mungai, which of these horses do you like the best?"

"I like Brandy, the one you rope off of," he told me.

I walked over to Brandy's stall, slipped a halter on him and led him out, handing the lead rope to Mungai. "He's yours," I said with a smile.

Mungai was stunned and asked me to repeat myself as though he hadn't believed what he'd heard. "He's yours, he's a gift from our producer, Ivan Tors."

"Oh, my God, I don't believe it," Mungai exclaimed. I asked him which of the other horses did he like best, and he pointed out the horse Joe rode all the time. Joe walked over to that one, haltered him up and presented him to Mungai as another gift from Ivan. By this time Mungai was so emotional he was actually getting teary-eyed—this six-foot-six man was shedding happy tears over our gifts. "I don't know what to say," he told us. "This is the happiest day of my life."

I couldn't help laughing. "Well, don't get too happy yet, because the others two horses are yours, too!"

AFRICA: TEXAS-STYLE!

His eyes got as round as saucers and he laid a hand over his heart. "I think my heart is going to stop," he told us. When his excitement had leveled out a little I told him he was welcome to keep the horses there until he was ready to move them to his own property. We said our good-byes then, with hugs and tears, and that was the last I saw of Dr. Njoroge Mungai. I'll always remember that big man, so grateful for the gift of those four horses, and the chance to befriend a pair of American cowboys, whose way of life he so admired.

If some of you reading this book don't believe in God (my Saddle-Pal), I hope that perhaps this will help change a few minds.

Joe and I had just finished filming a fight scene in the movie and were walking into our cottage to clean up when the phone rang. It was the production company's first assistant director telling me that our animal trainer Tony Harthorn had just been gored by a huge male Eland, a type of large African antelope with deadly horns that look like corkscrews. He'd been training a young female Eland we called Beauty to work as a pet alongside some African child actors, and it had been going well thus far; he had her good and tame.

We'd built a large fenced-in area where we roped and trained the animals; it opened at one end and funneled down into a narrow passage that emptied into different pens. Sometimes at night animals would wander in through the opened end, and, out of curiosity, walk through the passage into the catch pen. One evening a huge, fifteen hundred-pound bull Eland ended up in the catch pen. Tony planned to put the bull in with Beauty in hopes of breeding them.

The day of Tony's injury, he'd been in the corral with Beauty, working with her, apparently unaware that she'd come into heat. The bull took offense to Tony's proximity to her and charged him. Tony had seen him coming and scrambled to get out of the way, running for the surrounding fence as fast as he could go.

He wasn't fast enough. The bull caught him and thrust upward with his sharp horns, catching Tony in the groin and flinging him off the fence. Then the bull kept up the attack, gouging his horns into Tony's body again and again, only stopping once some of the animal handlers created a distraction. It gave them just long enough to drag Tony out of the bull's reach. Harthorn was unconscious by that time. They loaded him up and rushed him to a Red Cross station on the road going into Nanyuki.

Joe and I hurried to the station and were struck with disbelief and horror at what we saw when we arrived; the station was nothing but cement walls covered by a thatched grass roof that sheltered a concrete table you could lay a person out on. Tony was on that table, his clothes and body both ripped to shreds and soaked with blood, and no one was with him but two other animal trainers. Someone had gone to look for the doctor, but we had no idea how long it would take the find him and bring him back. Seeing all that blood, and the intestines bulging out of Tony's abdomen, I knew one thing for sure—every *second* counted, and every second that it took to bring the doctor back might be a second that Tony didn't have.

We had a couple of towels in our Land Rover, and we got them and tore them into strips, then tied the strips together. We folded one up to make a pad and very gently used it to push Tony's intestines back into his body, then wound the strips around him to hold it in place. As we did that my assistant Ivan showed up and said he was going to drive Tony to Nairobi and take him to a hospital.

"He'll never survive the trip," I told him grimly. "It's a hundred and fifty miles on dirt roads!" I had an idea—call Harold Cope, the bush pilot. I got ahold of him and told him what had happened, and that we needed him and his plane *now*.

"Mickey, it's going to be dark in another hour," Harold told me, "and I'm not allowed to fly after dark."

"Well, then, Tony's going to die," I snapped, "either from all that jarring when he's driven over those dirt roads or from infection setting in."

AFRICA: TEXAS-STYLE!

"All right, all right, I'll do it," Harold gave in, "even if it costs me my license."

"Thank you," I said gratefully.

"But," Harold told me, "I'm going to need you to do something for me if we're going to make this work. Try to round up about twenty cars and have them report to Nanyuki Airfield. Have the cars line up on each side of the runway, facing each other. Then put two cars at the end of the runway facing downwind, so when I land, I'll be landing into the wind towards their lights. When you hear or see my plane, you have everyone in those cars turn their lights on so I can drop in."

My assistant was a British man who'd been raised in Kenya. He told me that on Wednesday nights they showed a movie at the Nanyuki polo field's clubhouse, so there would be many people there who would have cars. While Joe stayed behind with Tony, I drove to the polo field and rushed into the clubhouse, jogging through the maze of seats and standing in front of the screen. "I'm sorry to interrupt your movie, but we have an emergency, and I need some help," I announced loudly. I quickly told them what had happened, and why we needed their cars—and, more importantly, their cars' headlights.

The response I got was amazing. Everyone in that clubhouse jumped up and came to my aid without hesitation, jumping into their cars and driving to the airstrip. With Ivan's help, I did exactly what Harold had told me to do.

They loaded Tony up and drove him to the airstrip. After about an hour (one of the longest hours of my life, and Tony's too!), we heard Harold's plane and saw his lights. I blinked my headlights on and off to cue all of the waiting people from the polo field, and they turned them on in unison, lighting the place up like a Christmas tree. In the sky above us, Harold made one circle and landed.

We drove Tony out to him, and we had to take out three seats in the plane to lay Tony down. After about forty minutes we were airborne, heading for Nairobi, where Harold had radioed the air tower to have an ambulance waiting for our return. Before we'd left, I'd thanked everyone from the clubhouse for their help—I'm sure each person there that night had a story to tell for many years to come.

The next afternoon Ivan helped get ahold of the doctor who'd been working on Tony since we'd gotten him to Nairobi. We were told it didn't look good for the trainer; he was extremely concerned about infection setting in. Tony had a punctured lung, a damaged kidney and many other severe injuries, and the doctor only gave him about a thirty-five percent chance of living. He'd called Tony's parents in the States to let them know what had happened, and inform them of their son's grave condition.

I asked the doctor if he minded me calling him every day to check in. "Not at all," he told me, and so I did. Each time I called, the doctor told me there was no change—Tony was the same, which was bad. He was just barely clinging to life.

"He's gonna make it, Doc," I said to him firmly during one of my calls. "He's got my saddle-pal with him all the way."

"What do you mean by that?" the doctor asked. "Who is your 'saddle-pal?'"

"You'll see," I said.

Another week went by, and I called again. "How's he doin', Doc?" I asked.

"Well, I can hardly believe it," the doctor told me, "but he's actually making some good progress."

Another week passed, and Tony began to get up and walk around the hospital, getting stronger and stronger. Don't get me wrong—he wasn't cured, by any means; he was still having trouble breathing and battling to overcome the other damage done to this body, but he was lean and strong and he had the will to live. By then I knew he was going to make it so I called a little less, letting him concentrate on getting better.

About three more weeks went by, and Joe and I were out on the set one day when I heard a voice calling us—Tony's voice. There he was.

"Oh, my God, look who's here!" I called to everyone on set. We all crowded around Tony and I gave him an easy hug. "You are one, tough, strong son of a bitch," I told him stoutly.

AFRICA: TEXAS-STYLE!

He laughed and thanked me for saving his life. I told him there had been many people involved in that, not just me. "And there was always one person with you the whole time," I told him.

"Who's that?" he asked me.

"He's right up there, Tony," I said, glancing up at the skies above us.

Tony went back to England soon after to heal up the rest of the way, and I never saw him again after that. But I will never forget that day and all those people who helped us in our hour of need, nor will I forget how that tough young man managed to survive such a gruesome attack, against all odds.

Not everyone who works in film is lucky enough to travel to all of the places I've been during my career, but I've been blessed with some pretty amazing opportunities. How many people can say they've roped wild African animals, fought and roped a rhino—and roped the king of the jungle, on top of it all? I truly thanked my Saddle-Pal for taking care of me and Joe during our six months in Africa.

Cowboy in Africa

After Joe and I finished *Africa: Texas-Style!*, the producer decided to do a TV series called *Cowboy in Africa*. It starred Chuck Connors and Tom Nardini. I was hired to coordinate the stunts and double Connors, and Joe would double Nardini. They were planning to shoot the series at Africa U.S.A., the spread above my ranch that was owned by Ralph Helfer, who I'd trained the two stallions for. They were planning to use stock footage of Joe and I roping wild animals in Africa for the series. Joe and I loved that because it meant they'd have to pay us residual monies for using the footage in the new show.

Doubling Connors presented an interesting challenge—he was left-handed, and I'm not. When we met up he asked me if I was going to be able to rope with my left hand. I laughed. "I'm not going to have to, Chuck, because *you're* going to swing a rope right-handed!" I explained that all he needed to do was to be able to swing the rope around his head with his right hand, and then I'd do all the rest. Doing it that way would be a hell of a lot easier than me trying to rope with my non-dominant hand.

Chuck started coming out to my ranch so I could work with him, and to my surprise, he caught on quickly. We realized there was another issue the producers were worried about, though; our height difference. Chuck was six-foot-four, and I'm only six-foot even. The producers had concerns about me doubling him for fight scenes, being so much shorter than he was. I had a solution, though. I explained to them that I'd find a double for each actor Connors was "fighting" that would have the same difference in height to me as the actor did to Connors. For example, if Connors' opponent was three inches shorter than Chuck, then that actors' double would be three inches shorter than me. That way the height difference would be a non-issue. This little trick worked perfectly.

The actor that played the game rancher in the series was James Whitmore, and his double was Gene LeBell, who would become a good friend of mine. Gene and I did quite a few fight scenes together. I used my gymnastics training in some of them; during one I had Gene throw me over a bar and into a huge mirror, and during another I had him throw me through a window. He always ended up body-slamming me one way or another, it seemed. He was considered in our circle as "the toughest man in the world," and he'd earned it. The thing I loved about doing fight scenes with him was that since I was doubling Connors, and Connors was the star of the series, I always ended up winning. Every time we finished a fight, I always kidded Gene by gloating, "ha! I just whipped the toughest man in the world!"

In one of our episodes, Chuck was in a helicopter chasing down a Rhino poacher who was fleeing from him on horseback. Chuck spots the poacher from the air, opens the helicopter door and drops down a rope ladder that's attached to the chopper. He tells the pilot he's going to climb down the ladder, hang onto the last rung, and the pilot should fly him over the top of the poacher so that he drop off and knock the guy off his horse.

We had an inset road that the camera car could travel on to photograph the sequence. I met with the chopper pilot to give him instructions on what I needed; I told him that as I was hanging on the ladder and he started to fly me over the poacher, if he didn't position me correctly, he was to pull off and set me and the chopper down. Pretty simple instructions, right? Well, we got in the air, "action" was called, and the chase was on. I dropped down the ladder and wait as the chopper pilot flies me over the poacher. I wasn't in the right position, so I didn't

ME AND MY SADDLE-PAL

drop off—I stayed there, thinking he would pull over at any second so we can try it again. That isn't what happened. The next thing I knew, I felt a g-force on my hands; he was climbing up pretty fast and turning back to where he'd started from. I knew I needed to attend to my own safety at that point—thank God I was a gymnast. I swung both my legs up and got them over the last rung I'd been dangling from a few seconds before. Then I pulled myself up unto a sitting position on the ladder-rung and waited it out.

Down below, the crew on the insert car was going crazy, waving their arms at the chopper pilot. When we got back to our starting point, he started setting the chopper down. By this point I was standing on the bottom rung so that I could step off and get out of the landing zone. Once he landed, I walked over and opened the door, boiling mad. "What the fuck are you *doing?*" I demanded. The pilot's jaw dropped and he looked like he'd been slapped.

"What are you doing here?" he stammered.

I ignored his question. "Shut the chopper off; we need to have a talk," I said, pointing my finger at him. In the meantime, the stuntman who was playing the part of the poacher came galloping full-speed over to where we were, furious—it was my father-in-law, Joe.

"What the hell is wrong with you?" he hollered at the pilot.

The pilot was pretty shook up at this point. He hadn't realized that I'd never dropped off the chopper, since the ladder was positioned back under the tail and the end of it was about eighteen feet down. He couldn't see me when I was on it. The problem with the whole thing was that he hadn't brought any air-to-ground transmitters with him, so the only way the crew had of communicating with him was by waving their arms. I figured we all needed to calm down a bit before talking the issue out.

Once we'd had a brief meeting about things, we set up for the stunt again. This time around, it worked really well, and was pretty amazing to look at, with me coming down that ladder and knocking Joe off his horse as we both fly through the air and hit the ground. It was no small feat and was quite dangerous, too—so don't think I didn't thank my Saddle-Pal for taking care of me while I did it!

The Wild Bunch

In 1969, Sam Peckinpah directed a western entitled *The Wild Bunch,* about a group of fictional outlaws making a last stand in the final days of the Old West. My father-in-law was working on the film and brought me on. We traveled to Parras, Mexico, one of the filming locations. There were about ten American stuntmen working on it, along with a great deal of Mexican stuntmen.

My brother-in-law Joe Finnegan, who was also working on *The Wild Bunch,* had just invented the air ram about that time, a device that catapults a stunt performer through the air using hydraulics and compressed air. Depending on the air pressure, the air ram can throw a stuntman different distances, and it's activated by the stuntman stepping on a pedal, so he or she doesn't have to depend on someone else triggering the device for them. Joe eventually won a technical Academy Award for the invention, but in 1969 he was just getting it going. He brought it along on *The Wild Bunch* to show it off.

We got to Mexico, and the first thing I noticed that there were a lot of people involved in the production, from crew-members to stuntmen, who were afraid of our director. Sam Peckinpah had a way about him that put people off, and he could be quite demanding. If he wanted something from someone on his crew or otherwise employed on his movie, that person *had* to produce whatever it was Peckinpah had asked for—if they didn't, they were fired on the spot—*no* exceptions.

ME AND MY SADDLE-PAL

I heard him do it, several times. Peckinpah wasn't well-liked, for sure, but he *was* well-respected, even as he was feared.

The more I observed of the situation, the more I started to see that people didn't seem to know how to talk to him. Everyone walked on eggshells around him, being careful with their words and tone when they spoke to him, even his cameramen and his director of photography, Lucien Ballard. I believe he fired a total of thirty-four people on *The Wild Bunch*, so it shouldn't be a surprise that Peckinpah became known for firing members of his crew.

I never had trouble dealing with people. To me, this was a job—not just this particular movie but all the ones I had and would work on. I had learned that to do the job, and to do it well, you had to be able to talk to people, eye-to-eye, no matter if it's a big star, the director or the most menial crew-member. That was how I treated people, and how I wanted to be treated, as well.

In the first part of the movie, there's a scene where the outlaws ride into town during a shindig at the local church. They make their way to the express office, intent on robbing it. As I've mentioned, one of my particular talents is coming up with stunts that no one has ever done before; I really enjoy inventing new ways to do things. This film was no different, and I thought up something to do during that scene. I approached Peckinpah and introduced myself, telling him I was Joe Yrigoyen's son-in-law, since he knew who Joe was. "I'd like to talk to you about one of these stunts, if it's okay," I said, maintaining eye-contact with him as I did so. Peckinpah had small, beady dark eyes.

Right away, I could tell that *he* could tell that I wasn't afraid of him, nor did I hold him on any sort of pedestal because he was this well-known (and well-feared) director. I think, by this time, he was accustomed to just about everybody he came across being afraid of him, even as they treated him like he was better than they were. Maybe it was throwing him for a loop that I wasn't. "I think you'd like this idea, if you heard it," I said.

"Well, what is it?" he asked, rather impatiently.

"Well, when the boys rob the express office, the scene calls for them

THE WILD BUNCH

all getting shot at from a rooftop, right? And the one that has the bag of coins from the robbery gets shot, dropping the bag. Well, I could come riding in on horseback and lean way down and pick the bag up as my horse is still going. The guys in the posse can yell 'shoot the one on the horse!' and shoot me. I'll get shot out of my saddle and drag along by one stirrup, until they yell to shoot the horse, too, so they can recover the money, and the horse can fall while it's dragging me," I explained. The way I envisioned it, it would be a great gag for the scene.

He was quiet for a second, still looking at me, and then he said, "Do you know what you just said?"

"Yeah," I replied, "I laid out something I can do. I'm not the kind of guy who would come to you with a stunt I wasn't able to perform perfectly. I'm not trying to blow smoke up your ass." I said it just like that.

He looked at me again. "You know, I like you," he said, surprising me. "Can you really do it?"

"Absolutely, I can," I said. "I've got a real good trained falling horse here, that I've practiced doing drags on back at my ranch. He'll be great. And my father-in-law can fall the horse for me when we're ready." I told him I would go to the effects guy to rig up a pipe unit for the horse to wear that we could run a long cable through, to act as the method to fall the horse from afar. My father-in-law would be at the other end of that cable, about fifty or seventy-five feet back, ready to pull the horse's head around on cue and make it go down. As the horse's head came around, that would be my signal to pull my release cable that would free me from the stirrup. The horse would fall, I would stand—and get the shit shot out of me. That's exactly what we did, and it worked exactly like I'd planned. A couple of days later Peckinpah came up to me.

"Hey, Kid," he called.

"Yeah?"

"I gotta tell you, that was the best stunt I've ever seen, and it's my favorite stunt, *ever*."

High praise, indeed. "Wow, thank you," I said. "I'm glad you liked it!"

ME AND MY SADDLE-PAL

"I did, I really did. You got my vote."

And thus, I was in with Peckinpah, an honor I did not take for granted.

There I am getting dragged from my stirrup, during the stunt I came up with for The Wild Bunch. *–M.G.*

All in all, I ended up playing thirty-two different people in *The Wild Bunch*, Mexicans who got shot off of rooftops, off of horses, you name it. Every day I went to work I'd have a mustache, or a beard, or different costumes. Peckinpah would call to me every day, "hey, Kid, who are you today?" Every day, I'd answer with a different made-up Hispanic name, complete with accent, and he'd laugh.

So it came as quite a shock when one day, after I'd been working on the film for about eight or nine weeks, Peckinpah came up to me and said, "well, Kid, I gotta let you go."

"Why?" I asked, stunned.

"Because, you are in every damn shot! I see you every time I look at the film—I can tell it's you."

"*You* can tell it's me each time, Sam, but the crowd that comes to see this movie won't be able to!"

THE WILD BUNCH

"Nah, you can only hide so much in these things," he said. "I think you've hit your limit. You've done a great job, though."

"Okay," I said, seeing his point. "Well, thanks, Sam." When he started to head off I called to him. "If you ever do another Western, or a movie like it, would you consider making me your stunt coordinator? I could double someone and coordinate all the stunts."

"Really? You'd want to do that?" he asked.

"Sure, I'd love to. I know I can handle it." I waited to see what he'd say.

"You know what?" he said, after a moment, "I'll call you."

Peckinpah called, all right, true to his word, and invited me to come coordinate stunts on a movie he was making with Steve McQueen called *Junior Bonner*...but that would come a little later.

Butch Cassidy and the Sundance Kid

If you were to ask me to pinpoint a particular moment in my career that really put me over the top in the picture business, it would be my work on the 1969 western classic, *Butch Cassidy and the Sundance Kid*. The film was directed by George Roy Hill, distributed by Twentieth Century Fox and starred Robert Redford and Paul Newman.

I got a call from the production manager, Lloyd Anderson, who asked me a simple question right off the bat: "Mickey, do you do high work?" High work refers to falls and jumps, that sort of thing.

"Sure, I do," I told him. "I've done falls, I've done work on trampolines. I've been in the air a lot." I was pretty good with heights, though they could get a little hairy for me once they got to a hundred and fifty feet up or so, because at that point your body starts to drift a bit in the air and the fall becomes a little harder to control, but I could handle it, just the same.

"Well, I've got a story to tell you," Anderson told me. "We've got a stuntman on this picture who's been scouting locations for stunts, in Mexico and a lot of other places, with our director and producers and myself for about five weeks; our last stop was in Durango, Colorado, on the Animas River."

"I know where that is," I said.

"Well, there's a gorge there, and we have a scene we want to do where Newman and Redford go running and jump off a cliff, into the river below."

"Okay," I said.

"Well, we took the stuntman to the place where we wanted to shoot this stunt, and when we tried to call him about it after we got back we couldn't get ahold of him. We did some checking and found out he took another job, and he's left town."

I knew the stuntman well, whose name I won't reveal here, and so I knew what the problem was—the height. He didn't do a lot of high work. He should've been up front with them about it, and brought in another guy to do the stunt, but for whatever reason he'd chosen not to and simply walked away from the job.

"What are you planning, then?" I asked Anderson.

"Well, you're as good a double for Redford as he would've been," Lloyd replied. "We'd like to bring you on to the picture to double Bob, but before we put you on salary, we'd like to put you on daily pay and have you come out to the location and take a look at it."

"Sure, I'd be glad to," I told him. Inwardly I was thrilled—this would be a *big* deal, if I got this job. Redford was just getting a big start in the business at that time, and I could tell he was going places.

I went out to Durango, and I got to know the director, George Roy Hill. He and the others took me out to the location. There was a large rock Newman and Redford would be against while doing their scene, and then from there it was about ten feet or so to the sheer edge of the cliff. I walked over to the edge and peered down a straight drop right into the river below. Immediately I noticed something concerning.

"Whoa, Mickey, be careful!" they cautioned me, uneasy at how casually I'd gone out to the edge.

"It's okay," I reassured them with an easy smile. "I'm used to this sort of thing. I just want to take a look." I glanced over again, then looked back at them. "Do any of you guys have a problem coming out here and looking off this edge?"

Seemed like everyone did, 'cause nobody volunteered. Hill wanted to look but I could tell he was uneasy.

"Okay, get me a rope," I told one of the crewmembers, "and tie it off

ME AND MY SADDLE-PAL

around that stump back there. Then, George, we'll tie it around you so you can't go beyond it. It'll make you feel safe."

We did that, and when George was about three feet from the cliff's edge, I directed him to look over. "You see that white water down there, George?" I asked.

"Yeah," he replied.

"That means that there are boulders and rocks just below that surface, probably only a foot or so down. The water's moving fast over those rocks and it's frothing as it goes—that's what makes that water white." I caught his eye. "Now, when I do a stunt, I really like doing it and then being able to go to the bank the next day with my paycheck. If I do this stunt here, that won't happen." I gave him a grin. "Catch my drift? There's a river there, but no depth, so you've essentially got no water to land in."

I let him absorb this, then continued. "The only way you could do this jump here is have that riverbed down there dynamited after the spillways to the dam above us were closed up—you'd have to create a hole for me to land in. And besides that, George, I want to show you something." I picked up a rock that was about six inches in diameter and let it fall, the way a body would, over the edge. "Watch where it lands," I told him. The rock reached its maximum velocity and ended up landing just on the other side of the river, barely making contact with water. "You see that?" I asked. "That's where I would land. So all that area over there, about thirty feet wide and twenty feet deep, would have to be dynamited out if we had a chance in hell of doing this with me living through it."

I caught his eye again. "Now, don't get me wrong. I'm not trying to get out of this, George; I *want* to do it. But I'm just letting you know that there's a whole hell of a lot of work that's gonna have to be done, first. Otherwise, we're going to have to do it someplace else. I doubt you'd want to go through all that red tape and expense just to get this one stunt in this particular spot, and even if you do, that dam supplies irrigation to all the farms around here. If it were closed up for a few weeks, like it would have to be, the farmers would raise hell, and I wouldn't blame them."

BUTCH CASSIDY AND THE SUNDANCE KID

I wasn't sure they were going to still hire me because of my bursting their bubble and all, but it turned out that they hired me *because* of it. They could tell I knew my stuff. So I got the job to double Redford.

*That's me doubling Redford,
jumping from his horse to Butch's for* Butch Cassidy. –M.G.

We started off there in Durango with me doing some horseback doubling for Redford, as well as playing a small part in the massive posse that chased Butch and Sundance. Then I did some jumping from Bob's horse to Newman's—you know, the famous "who *are* those guys?" scene. Another scene I did was the equally famous "Raindrops Keep Falling On My Head" sequence, where Paul Newman does the bicycle tricks with Katherine Ross watching from the hayloft.

I have a story about that scene, which was filmed in Moab, Utah. They'd hired a circus acrobat to do the bicycle tricks, including riding the bike while standing on his head. They'd given him six weeks to practice with that bicycle before they needed him to actually do the trick.

We'd done some filming with me doubling in the river prior to this, and I was suffering through a terrible ear infection by the time we got to Moab. George Roy Hill told me to go see what Bill, the circus

ME AND MY SADDLE-PAL

performer, had come up with for the bike trick, so he and I went out to this hard dirt rode with the bike. Bill had constructed a sort of a donut-type getup out of foam affixed to the handlebars that he could fit his head in for the trick. I was doubtful about that—it seemed too bulky, too clunky—but, I supposed, he was the expert.

"Okay, Bill," I said, "I gotta see how you do this."

He made some comment about how he needed to have me run alongside the bicycle while he did the trick, and I shook my head. "Now, wait a minute, I can't be running alongside you in the shot. You're supposed to be on your own." I agreed to run alongside him, just this once, so I could see how he did it.

As I ran, he put his head down into the foam donut and began to lift his body up into a headstand, but he couldn't make it all the way into position—his knees were bent and he started to wobble. "Grab ahold of me!" he said frantically, and I did. To my dismay, once he'd gotten off the bike, he started giving me all these excuses as to why he wasn't pulling the trick off, telling me he'd told the director he needed a guy beside him for safety.

"There isn't supposed to be anyone else in the shot, Bill," I told him, aware now that we had a big problem. "You told them you could do this, and what's more, you've had six weeks with the bike to practice. You should have it aced by now. Have you actually been practicing?"

"Well..." he hedged, and my heart sank.

"Don't say any more," I told him. "I'm going to have to tell George you can't do it. There's no way around it."

I did tell George, and he was furious. He told me to have Bill get on a plane and get off the film—he was fired. We'd have to come up with another way to get this shot.

One day not too long after that, myself and Jim Arnett, who was Newman's double, came about Redford and Newman sitting up in a couple of apple trees, picking apples. Newman had started training with the bike himself at that point, and evidently he was taking a break from it—the bike was leaning against one of the trees.

Arnett and I grabbed a bunch of the rotten apples that were littering the ground around the tree trunks and started tossing them at the two actors, who leapt down and started chasing after us, threatening to get us. I saw the bike there and grabbed it, hopping on and automatically reverting to a trick I'd used to do when I was little.

When I was a kid, around the first grade, my dad had given me a bicycle for Christmas, and I'd to ride it to my Catholic school in Pasadena. Me being me, I'd taught myself to ride it backwards—sitting on the handlebars and pedaling with my knees facing the rear wheel. I did that now with Redford and Newman giving chase, laughing and hollering at them as I pedaled away, backwards, not even thinking about it.

Well, when I did that, Newman stopped short in his tracks, hands on his hips, staring at me like he was seeing me for the first time. He said something to Redford as they watched me zooming around on that bike like that.

He ended up going to George Roy Hill and telling him about it, enthusiastically suggesting that we use me to double him, riding the bike backwards into the bull pen in the show. Hill called me over and asked me about it, and I told him about how I'd learned to do that when I was younger.

"Do you think you could do the headstand?" he asked excitedly, clearly hoping against hope that I could save that trick.

"George, I'm still fighting that ear infection that I got when we were shooting in the river," I reminded him. "I can't put my head down for any length of time, I can't chew—I have to eat through a straw. I'll give it a try, if you want, but I can't promise I'll be able to do it."

I had the effects shop take the donut off the handlebars of the stunt bike and move it to the crossbar so it would be more centered, and I had them put training wheels on the bike to keep it stable. Then I gave it a try, going up into a headstand (my gymnastics background helped me out here quite a bit), though I didn't fully extend my knees, because there was no need to.

I rode around a little bit like that, but my head hurt like hell while I did it. I knew that if I felt better I could practice and get good enough

ME AND MY SADDLE-PAL

to do it without training wheels, but there was no way I wanted this hanging over my head with my ears all screwed up. I went to George and told him that.

"Well," he said, thinking, "let me see you ride it backwards again." I obliged—*that* trick was as easy for me as, well, riding a bike!

"I think we'll skip the headstand-on-the-bike thing," George finally declared, "it's just too difficult."

So that's how I ended up doubling for Paul Newman riding the bike backwards.

I ended up using another little childhood trick of mine that I'd picked up on the chicken ranch of my youth, in *Butch Cassidy*. I taught myself how to hypnotize chickens when I was a kid, and I put that rather specialized skill to use in the scene where Butch and Sundance are riding their horses away from the bank they've robbed in Bolivia. George wanted a bunch of chickens and turkeys in the scene to scatter when Redford and Newman rode their horses through the flock. The problem was, they couldn't get them to stay where they wanted long enough to be scattered in an aesthetically pleasing manner. I piped up "I can make them stay there!"

"What've you got going on *now*, Gilbert?" Redford asked, laughing.

"I know how to hypnotize chickens," I informed him with a grin. "They'll stay were I put 'em, and then when you ride through them they'll come to from their trance and flap around, just like George wants."

I did as promised, recalling that old talent I'd developed for chicken hypnosis. As I'm doing it Newman, Redford and the rest of them are all standing there watching, laughing their asses off and shaking their heads. When they went to do the scene it worked like a charm and the chickens scattered just the way George wanted them to—just another day on *Butch Cassidy*.

One night Redford and Newman and I went out to dinner at a German restaurant outside of Moab. When we pulled up to the restaurant, which was rumored to have excellent food, we could see that the place was pretty crowded and we knew that two movie stars like the two of them coming through the front door was liable to cause a commotion. They asked me to get out and go see if there was a back door we could come in, and table we could have in the back, so we could have some peace while we ate.

I went and got the manager and told him who I had in the car, and why we wanted to come through the back. He told us he had a place in the back for us where we could have some privacy. We did that, eating in a little area sheltered by a partition that was topped by some floral arrangements that sort of hid us from the rest of the patrons.

As we were eating, a woman stood up from a booth on the other side of the partition, talking to her companion. Suddenly she raised her eyes in mid-sentence…and saw us. I couldn't hear what she was saying but I knew she was announcing Redford's and Newman's presence in the restaurant. Everyone would believe her, too, because it was common knowledge that we were filming portions of the movie in Moab.

"Oh, no," I murmured to the two of them, "she's spotted us. That's the end of our peace and quiet."

Sure enough, she came around the partition, shaking like a leaf in nervousness, zeroing in on Newman. "Oh, Mr. Newman," she gushed, "could I please have your autograph?"

Now, you might think that Newman would either be mad he was interrupted at his meal, or grab a napkin and sign away, right? Well, he did neither. He leaned his hands on the table and looked her in the eye. "I'll tell you something, I don't really ever sign autographs, and I'll tell you why—if people see me doing it, they flock over all at once, and I'm put in kind of a spot. So I'd go to dinner with you, I'd go dancing with you, but I don't really sign autographs for that reason." He said it just as nice as could be, and she went back to her table, flustered and flattered—he'd made her day, while getting out of an autograph session at the same time.

We were getting ready to do the big train explosion in the film. The train had been rigged up in the special effects workshop with primer cord and two-foot mortars. The mortars were loaded with prop money, cork, and, in a couple of cases, gasoline—quite dangerous. It made me nervous; I could tell that train was going to be blown to hell and back, and I was damned if I was going to be standing two feet away from it when it did, like Hill was planning on.

The effects guy tried to soothe my fears, telling me it would be fine to stand next to it. I told him he was nuts. Primer cord explodes in no time flat, all along the length of it—and there was *a lot* of primer cord wrapped all over this train.

I got into wardrobe and went down to the set, and I saw the camera guys setting up plywood shields with holes cut into them for the camera lenses to look through, close to the train. Clearly they were figuring on me being right up close to the inferno when it blew. I quickly corrected them, telling them I wasn't going to stand where they thought I was—and telling them why. Eventually word got back to George Roy Hill, and he asked me what the problem was. I told him.

"Are you telling me you know more than the effects guy, Gilbert?" he asked me with one eyebrow raised.

"Well, right now, yeah, I do," I said, refusing to budge, "because I'm telling you I'm not standing there. I'll get burned, and the noise from the explosion will rupture my eardrums. Keep us twenty feet back—we'll still get blown back, like you want, it'll still look good on camera—but Arnett and I will live through it." Minor detail, right?

He gave in and let us move back, and the camera guys, too, thank God—and they set the thing off. You've seen it on camera—it's a white-hot ball of fire. Even being so far away we still got blown back pretty good. It looked great on camera; it was a fantastic shot, and we stayed safe. I shudder to think what would've happened if I hadn't known the danger I was being asked to face. We would've been fried. Literally. Some time later that particular effects guy got his arm blown off in a botched car explosion, and was almost killed.

BUTCH CASSIDY AND THE SUNDANCE KID

In order to stage that famous cliff jump, several still photos were taken of the gorge from a distance, and a matte painting was created on glass to create the illusion we needed—old movie trick.

I picked a spot on the Paramount ranch to recreate the river, and we had backhoes come in and dig the river down to about eighteen feet. This is where I'd land. I brought in generators to power huge fans to blow the water into rapids. All of this coupled with the matte painting created a perfect illusion of that gorge.

They built a platform on the end of a large crane to lift me up to do the jump, but in order to make my proportions correct to the matte painting they had to keep lifting me a little higher up. By the time they got it right I was about a hundred and twenty-five feet up on the crane.

I had a friend of mine that was a professional stunt diver to advise me and jump with me as Newman's double (I wanted someone at my side who wouldn't hesitate at the last minute), and we were ready to go. I called to George that we were ready, he called action, and away we went, into the water—and into movie history. So the famous cliff jump scene in *Butch* was two guys jumping off a crane with a matte painting in the background—but it sure as hell doesn't look that way when you see it, in my opinion. It was an incredible shot, and one that I thought came out really well for the way we were forced to do it. That jump brought me the status I would enjoy over the years as Robert Redford's go-to double, as well, so I always look back on it with gratitude. Once again the Lord was looking out for me, I feel, keeping me safe and granting me an incredible opportunity to contribute to such a classic movie.

Stunts Unlimited, *The Undefeated,*
The Ballad of Cable Hogue and *Little Big Man*

Working with my father-in-law led me into getting some good work, and by the time I'd worked on films like *Africa, Texas-Style!,* B*eau Geste,* and *Alvarez Kelly,* I was making a pretty good name for myself in the industry. A lot of the big stunt coordinators knew me and respected my work. Some of the stuntmen had formed a group called the Stuntmen's Association. The Association had about forty-five members at the time, and membership depended on being voted into the group. My father-in law put my name in for consideration, and fortunately I was voted in unanimously. The group grew larger and larger, until I started noticing that it was separating into different clans, almost like cliques in a high school. I wasn't happy about that at all; in my opinion we needed to be united in our cause, not be split off into groups that would only work to advance the guys in it and no one else.

Hal Needham, the stunt coordinator I'd worked with on *Alvarez Kelly* and *Beau Geste,* agreed with me—he didn't like the clannish environment, either. He decided to pull the top fifteen guys out of the group and form his own; the new group would be called Stunts Unlimited. Besides having all the top stuntmen with him, he was also planning to act like an agency of sorts—he'd get them good jobs and then get a percentage of their earnings in return. He started talking the idea up to some of the guys he was eyeing as prospective members, getting them on board. The Screen Actors Guild got wind of it and told

STUNTS UNLIMITED...

Hal he couldn't do that—it was against the rules.

Hal backed down on the agency part of his idea, but he went ahead with his plan to form a group of stuntmen who worked as a team and looked out for one another. About fifteen guys went with him into Stunts Unlimited. For the time being, I stayed with the Association, along with a friend of mine, Fred Waugh. I tried to rally the group into working more as a team, reminding them that we were making names for ourselves with producers and directors because of our expertise and experience, but it didn't work too well. By the time two years had gone by, I was getting work on shows from my reputation, and I was too busy to worry too much about the Association's issues. Stunts Unlimited was a hot commodity by then, and pretty soon Fred Waugh caved and went over to Needham's group. He kept cajoling me to join him, and after about another year or so, I did, leaving the Stuntmen's Association and becoming a part of Stunts Unlimited. There were about twenty of us in the group at that time, all of us experienced and highly capable at whatever a director needed us to do.

Hal Needham got a job as stunt coordinator on a film called *The Undefeated* starring John Wayne and Rock Hudson, and he called a meeting within Stunts Unlimited about it, telling us he wanted to take as many of us who were free and available with him to Durango, Mexico to work on it. But he had a few rules he laid down first.

"Listen up," he told us. "I know how a lot of you like to party, and get a little loose. That is *not* going to happen on this show. When we go to the airport to fly down there, I want you dressed nicely—none of the cutoffs and crap that you normally wear. I want all of you to be on your best behavior and act like gentlemen at the hotel, no going out and partying at night. You want to go out and have dinner and a few drinks, go ahead, but if I catch anyone getting out of control, I'm sending that person home. Understand?"

We all nodded and told him we did, and that there would be no problems, and off we all went to Durango.

One night after we'd been there a couple of weeks working on the

ME AND MY SADDLE-PAL

film, Fred Waugh and I decided to take a cab and go out to a nice dinner. Just as we were finishing up eating on the outdoor patio, we were approached by a Mexican kid who looked like he was about eighteen or so. He wanted to know if we were working on stunts in the movie. We told him we were.

"I tried to watch you work, but they wouldn't let me near where you're filming," he told us.

"It's pretty much a closed set," I told him, explaining that it was important that onlookers be kept out of the way so they wouldn't get hurt or get in the shot.

"What's your name?" I asked him.

"Daniel Boone," he replied, with a straight face.

I fought back a laugh, and a glance at Waugh showed me he was doing the same. "What?" I said.

"My name is Daniel Boone," he replied.

Fred started laughing. "Kid, if your name is Daniel Boone, then I'm John Wayne," he said.

The kid looked insulted. "Señor, I am telling you the truth," he insisted. "My name is Daniel Boone."

Fred kept chuckling. "If you can prove your name is Daniel Boone, then I'll give you all the money I've got in my wallet."

"Señor, you insult me," he told Fred, and left, heading off the patio.

I turned to Fred. "Waugh, I'll bet you anything he's gonna come back with a bunch of guys and wait for us to leave, and then we're gonna get jumped for your wallet," I predicted.

Uneasily we finished our dinner, and before we could leave, the kid came back with an envelope in his hand. He came up to our table and unceremoniously opened the envelope, unfolding the paper inside and presenting it to us. It was his birth certificate from the hospital in Durango, and the name listed there was Ricardo Daniel Boone Frederico.

I started laughing. "Well, Freddy, it looks like you owe Daniel Boone here some money," I said.

Fred gave the kid a big grin. "Tell you what, Daniel, if you want the money, you've gotta go out and party with us tonight."

STUNTS UNLIMITED...

"Señor, I will go wherever you want," he said.

We left the restaurant and headed out to the nightclubs, going to several in a row. Finally Daniel Boone said he was going to take us to a really nice place. We ended up at the Tropicana, an elegant nightclub in the heart of Durango. All the people there were dressed to the nines, and the place had a stage for dancers (it wasn't a strip club or anything, but the girls were definitely *not* dressed like school marms).

We were sitting at a table near the stage, having a few drinks, and Fred started buying drinks for the people at all the tables around us—spending the money he'd promised to Daniel Boone. Everyone at the other tables thought we were pretty great by that time. The dancers brought a limbo bar out onto the stage, and while the band was playing they took turns going under, then moving the bar down a bit lower before doing it all over again.

I turned to Fred. "Hey, Waugh, you wanna know something? I can do that," I said, jerking my chin at the stage. "I can limbo like that."

He rolled his eyes at me. "No you can't," he scoffed.

"Sure, I can," I said. I was still pretty flexible from my years as a gymnast. I stood up.

"Oh, for God's sake, Gilbert, just sit down and have another drink," Fred ordered.

"No, I'm gonna show you I can do it," I said, and headed for the stage.

The girls got all excited when I came over. "Ooh, we have a contestant!" they squealed. I took off my cowboy hat and plopped it on one of the girls' heads, and they laughed as they watched me lean back and get into position. The bar was about three and a half feet or so off the stage floor at that point, but sure enough, I made it under. When I straightened back up the place was in an uproar, cheering and clapping for the "limboing cowboy."

The girls lowered the bar another six inches or so, and took their turns wriggling under it. I went next—and made it under once again. The place erupted, especially all the people we'd been buying booze for.

Down the bar went again, this time to right above my knee. Waugh

ME AND MY SADDLE-PAL

hollered at me. "There's *no* way you're gonna make it under *that,* Mickey!"

"Oh, yeah?" I asked. "Watch this!" And under I went again. The whole club was cheering me on at that point, with people farther back getting up from their tables and craning their necks to watch.

The girls lowered the bar *again;* now it was only about two feet off the floor. They must've been made of rubber, because they all went under it. I was feeling a bit doubtful now, but I was determined to give it a go.

I managed to flatten myself out, and I started going, with the whole place chanting *"Cow-boy, cow-boy, cow-boy!"* in support. Unfortunately I'd hit my limit, because I got under as far as my waist, then fell flat on my back. I got up to continued cheers, and then I went back to my table, laughing.

By then it was around two-thirty in the morning, so we figured it was time to go. We waved goodbye at all the other patrons, put Daniel Boone into a cab with what was left of the money Fred had promised him and saw him off, then caught one ourselves and went back to the hotel, neither of us feeling any pain at that point, if you catch my drift. We climbed the stairs up to our floor, and as we walked down the long hallway, both of us banged on the doors of the other stuntmen, hollering at them that it was time to get up and go to work. It was all in jest, of course, encouraged by the drinks we'd had at the club. Finally we made it to our respective rooms and went to bed.

The next day was a work day, and the bunch of us filed onto the bus that would take us out to where we were shooting. Finally, once we were all seated, Hal Needham came stalking toward the bus. We could see he was royally pissed. He climbed up onto the bus and stood in the front of it, staring us all down like we were a bunch of misbehaved school children and he was the principal.

"All right," he said sternly, "two of you on this bus came into the hotel last night and woke everyone in it up at around two a.m., and I want to know who it was. I know it was one of my stuntmen, because all of you guys are on that floor. Who was it?"

STUNTS UNLIMITED...

I turned innocently around and looked toward the back of the bus, and Fred, who was sitting next to me, leaned in a little bit. "Gilbert, what are you *doing?*" he hissed.

"I was hoping someone else would take the fall," I told him out of the corner of my mouth, sheepishly.

He shook his head. "Come on. We gotta 'fess up."

"Well?" Needham barked, still waiting for an answer. "Who the hell was it?"

Fred and I raised our hands then, resigned to our fate.

Needham looked taken aback. "Gilbert and Waugh?" he asked in disbelief. "*You* two did it?"

"Yeah, it was us," I confirmed.

"I don't believe it," Hal said. "You guys are the squarest ones in my group. You don't even drink much!"

"Well, we did last night," I said. "It's a long story, Hal. We were with Daniel Boone."

He looked at me like I'd gone off the deep end. "You were with Daniel Boone," he repeated slowly.

"Yeah, it's this Mexican guy we met," I said. "We didn't believe that was his real name, and we bet him it wasn't…" I let my voice trail off. "It's a long story, Hal. But we got a little drunk, and that's why we banged on the doors."

Hal was quiet for a second. "Well," he finally said, "seeing as how it was you two guys, I won't send you home—but I'm still pissed off." He gave us a warning look. "I'll see you all on location." With that, he stalked back off the bus and got into his own car with his driver.

The rest of the shoot for *The Undefeated* was pretty routine, but that crazy story involving a Mexican guy named Daniel Boone and a limbo bar is still one of my favorite memories of my years in the business, and some of the most fun I ever had while out on a shoot.

ME AND MY SADDLE-PAL

Not too long after I'd finished *The Undefeated,* I learned that Sam Peckinpah was directing a movie called *The Ballad of Cable Hogue,* staring Jason Robards, and he wanted me to do some trick riding in it; he remembered me from *The Wild Bunch,* of course. I'd find out later on that Peckinpah had told his assistant to call me right away, but the assistant hadn't done as he was told, since he had another stuntman he was friends with that he wanted to give the job to. Evidently he told Peckinpah that I wasn't available without ever having called me to check, and brought the other guy onto the shoot. It was a disaster, apparently—the guy couldn't do what Peckinpah wanted, so a not-so-happy Sam got rid of the guy and told the assistant to call me again. This time he actually did, and I went out to Tucson to get started.

I met up with Peckinpah, and he told me he wished I'd been available two weeks ago, when they'd first started work. "They brought some other stunt guy out there that didn't work *at all,*" he told me darkly.

I was puzzled. "What do you mean, 'two weeks ago?'"

"My assistant called you and said you weren't available," he said.

I got even more puzzled. "No, he didn't," I said. "I never got any messages from your assistant, or any word that you were trying to get ahold of me. He *did* call me a few days ago, and that's why I'm here, but that was the first time."

I could tell Sam was furious. He called the assistant over. "Did you call Mickey the first time I told you to?" he asked.

"Yeah," the guy said, "But he wasn't available."

"You did *not* call me," I insisted.

An enraged Peckinpah turned back to the assistant. "Get off my show," he said, "you're fired."

I wasn't surprised—that was the way Peckinpah was. You crossed him, you were out. Period. I did the stunt he wanted me to do, doubling for Robards—it was only a couple of days' work—and headed home, my job done. The incident with the unfortunate stuntman before me made me think about how quickly word traveled in the industry. If you couldn't handle your work, or did something sloppy, news traveled fast.

STUNTS UNLIMITED...

The next film I worked on was *Little Big Man,* directed by Arthur Penn and starring Dustin Hoffman, Faye Dunaway, and Richard Mulligan as General George Armstrong Custer. Hal Needham was coordinating the stunts and doing some second unit directing again. As I've mentioned, Needham knew I was dependable and good at what I did, and he liked working with me, so I often got called in to help on shows he was coordinating the stunts for.

I headed to Billings, Montana along with about twenty-five other stuntmen to begin work on the film.

It wouldn't be an easy shoot. There were a lot of Native Americans hired for the project, and unfortunately a great many of them, probably about thirty percent of the total number hired, were not experienced horsemen. They wanted to be part of the film, but lacked the basic skill we needed them to do, There was a lot of drinking among them during shooting hours and they also seemed to have trouble following our directions, both of which made things all the more difficult.

One day we were working on a big battle scene, which involved many Indians on horseback charging down a hill. Roydon Clark, one of the stuntmen I was working with, was doubling for Richard Mulligan during the scene. Roydon would go galloping down the hill with a bunch of Indian warriors giving chase.

Needham wanted to make sure the camera setup was correct, so he told Roydon to put his horse into a lope and come down the hill while he looked through the camera. Roydon was just supposed to stop his horse and get off once he'd reached the camera.

Unfortunately, one of the Indian riders didn't get the memo that we weren't shooting for real, and when Roydon started going, so did he. As Roydon dismounted, swinging his right leg over the saddle, the Indian rider, who'd been doing some drinking, came barreling on through and smacked right into Roydon's extended leg. It spun Roydon around and knocked him right out of the saddle. The Indian, clueless as to what he'd done, just kept going, galloping on past the camera.

The rest of us ran out to check on Roydon. "Whoa! You okay, Roy?" I asked.

"What in the hell was *that?*" he asked, dazed. "What hit me?"

"One of the Indians," I told him. "He thought he was supposed to be chasing you."

Roydon shook his head and got up, brushing the dirt off his costume. Fortunately he wasn't hurt, but it was an example of the challenges we were having to deal with—and there would be more to come.

We were shooting on location at the Bighorn River, and we'd brought in a backhoe and some boulders to create a swell in the river about four feet deep and eight feet long where we would stage some horse falls. Beyond it there were teepees set up for the Indian camp, and many of the Native American extras would actually sleep in them at night. Every person involved in the shoot was warned about that water pit we'd created, and told to be careful around it, particularly when on horseback.

One morning around breakfast time, Needham and myself and several other of the experienced stuntmen were standing on the other side of the river from the Indian camp, directly across from the water pit we'd made in the river. We'd already eaten our share of the breakfast the caterers had prepared and we were going over the day's shots. As we talked, I noticed a couple of the Indian extras laying asleep with their backs against one of the teepees, their horses tied to their ankles so they wouldn't wander.

They must've smelled the bacon and eggs cooking—the scent was wafting tantalizingly across the river—because they woke up and untied their horses, mounting up and riding straight for the water pit. I had a feeling about what was going to happen and I elbowed one of the other stuntmen in the ribs. "Hey, boys, I think you might want to watch this."

The bunch of them turned and looked, and as we did the two

STUNTS UNLIMITED...

Indians put their horses right into the river—and right into the pit. The horses seemed to disappear right from under them as they stepped off the bank into nothing, and the last thing we saw of the two Indians for a few minutes were their eyes, round as saucers, as they were swept off the horses and down the river a bit. The horses got out, and so did the Indians, but it shocked the hell out of them. They hadn't been listening when we'd warned them about that pit we'd had dug. That combined with the rampant drinking among some of them really made me concerned that someone was going to end up getting hurt. We'd been hearing stories about how during the cold weather some of them would drink too much and then go and sleep it off on the highway that ran though the area, because the asphalt would be warm from absorbing the sunshine all day. Several were run over and killed that way. It was really terrible. During the battle-scene shoots, those that had been drinking would break the rubber safety tips off the arrows and fire them that way, which was extremely dangerous, of course. We had horses and stuntmen getting shot with these tipless arrows, and one of our stuntmen, Gary Combs, was blinded in one eye when one of the intoxicated extras shot an arrow right at his face.

We were constantly dealing with the alcohol issue, staying on our toes as much as we could. When we did stunts within the charge scenes, we tried to protect ourselves by having other experienced stuntmen positioned around us so we wouldn't get run over or shot by one of the reckless extras, but even that didn't always work. By the time we were a good ways into the shoot, almost every experienced stuntman there had been shot with a rubber-tipped arrow or run over by a poorly-controlled horse—sometimes both. Things just seemed to get worse and worse. It was definitely one of the most challenging and dangerous shows I've been involved in.

I had to hand it to the film's star, Dustin Hoffman. His character is *extremely* old in the film as he recounts the events of his life to a historian, and to research the part he visited rest homes and talked with elderly men, developing a voice and manner for the character of Jack Crabb. He met an old gentleman whose voice he modeled Jack Crabb's

ME AND MY SADDLE-PAL

after, and the two struck up a friendship. The old man got to see the movie, and to hear his own voice coming out of Dustin Hoffman, which he got a kick out of. Seeing Dustin do that made me really appreciate the lengths actors will go to in order to develop a character.

In the saddle doing horse work on Little Big Man. –M.G.

We finished everything in Billings and headed up to Calgary, Canada, to do some battle scenes in the snow. The ground was frozen and *very* hard, so doing falls was harder on us than usual. Add that to the cold and the whole shoot ended up being less than a good time, but we got it done. One sequence involved one of us crossing a knee-deep part of the river in water so cold it was almost iced-over. None of us wanted to do it. We were about to flip a coin, but before we could Alan Gibbs, one of our guys, volunteered. I told him to just grit his teeth and go for it, which he did.

Good old Fred Waugh was with us, of course. I'd taught him to do all sorts of different saddle falls, like falling forward and to the right if you've gotten shot in the back, spinning to one side or the other if you've gotten shot in the shoulder, or somersaulting over the back of the horse if you've gotten shot dead-on from the front. One day we were getting ready to do a sequence and he came to me and told me he was going to do a header, to be different, and make it look like he landed head-first.

I shook my head. "Freddy," I said, "I wouldn't do that if I were you. We don't have time to bring in sand and cover it with snow to pad your landing, and we can't dig up the ground to make it any softer, either. You'll hurt yourself. This is *not* the place to try something like that."

We got on our horses and started the charge once they'd called action. I fell out of my saddle as I'd planned, and then I heard them calling *cut* frantically. I looked over and saw Waugh out cold on the ground, and I ran over to him, trying to slap him awake. Finally he came to, and I asked him what had happened.

"Oh, I did a header," he admitted sheepishly, wincing as he sat up.

"You dummy," I said in exasperation, "I told you not to do that!"

"Yeah, I know." He winced again.

He'd taken a pretty big whack on the noggin and it kept him out for a day or so, though fortunately he ended up being okay. Yet another example of stuntmen getting too cocky and taking risks they shouldn't take. Between the heavy-drinking extras, the cold weather, and all the injuries that occurred, I have to admit I was glad when shooting on *Little Big Man* was done.

Sometimes a Great Notion

In 1970 Paul Newman directed and starred in a logging industry film called *Sometimes A Great Notion,* based on a 1964 novel of the same name. In it Newman co-starred with Henry Fonda and Lee Remick, and it was produced by Newman's longtime producer and agent, John Foreman. Newman's stunt double James Arnett was the stunt coordinator, and he called me in to do stunts in the picture. Off I went to Lincoln City, Oregon, to get to work.

One scene involved Paul Newman's character working as a choke setter, which is a logger who attaches choker cables to cut trees. The choker cables are attached to a larger cable, which is lifted by a massive crane. This method allows multiple cut trees to be moved all at once, in a large group. Sometimes the logs in the choker cables become entangled in the branches of live trees that lay in their path, and the live trees get ripped out of the ground because of it. In the scene, a massive tree about three feet in diameter and fifty feet tall is ripped from the ground and comes rolling down the hill toward Newman, and I was to double him for it.

I had an idea about how to pull it off. I told them I needed them to lay out another tree horizontally across the hillside, but before they did I needed them to dig out a little trough into the ground to hold the tree snugly in place. We'd need to place stakes against it, as well, to make certain it would stay secure, because I wanted to have the other log roll down the hill and hit it, so that the runaway log would bounce over me on its way down. It went off without a hitch and ended up looking fantastic.

They had built a house on location on one side of the Siletz River about a half a mile up from the ocean that you had to take a ferry across to get to; the river there was calm. The house was the residence of the Stamper family, the film's main characters, and it had a garage for their car and a dock for their boat. There were shots of all the main stars going back and forth across the river on their boat, coming to and from the house, and there was a scene where one of the union organizers comes across the river to try and intimidate Newman's character into going on strike with the rest of the logging companies in the story. Newman's character Hank Stamper grows tired of the man's methods of negotiation and finally decides to show him the door—by way of the sticks of dynamite which he and his brother Joe, played by Richard Jaeckel, start throwing at his boat as the man tries to flee back across the river.

I was doubling the actor playing the union man, and I would be the one in the boat when the dynamite exploded. It wasn't real dynamite, of course; we used pieces of one-inch pipe that were about eight inches long and painted them red. One end had a fuse rigged up that could be lit, and it sparked and fizzled just like a real dynamite fuse, though there were no explosives inside. In order to create the illusion of the explosions that would occur just as each stick was about to hit the water, the effects guy ran wires underwater and weighted them down. They ran all the way across the hundred foot-wide section of river, and there were two-foot wide pieces of cork placed along them at intervals. Each cork marked the place where an explosive charge had been set up just underneath the surface of the water. When the special effects coordinator hit a button, the charge would detonate and blow water up into the air. The corks provided a visual marker for both me and for the actors back on shore, throwing the fake dynamite. I had them set the corks up in a cloverleaf pattern, with each one about fifty feet apart. The plan was for me to go around each one and holler "hit it!"

ME AND MY SADDLE-PAL

to the effects guy when I was ready for him to detonate the charge, so it would look like I was barely dodging these explosions as I raced away from the Stampers' home. For safety's sake, I had them sheet the inside of the boat with plywood to provide me with just a bit more protection from the underwater explosions. I did some dry runs of the stunt, and I could tell it was going to look great.

Then we start doing the real thing. Newman and Jaeckel light their sticks up and start throwing them, aiming for those cork markers. Water's blowing sky-high into the air, soaking me, and all is going great. I turn for the last marker, ready to finish up. By now I'm thinking the whole gig's in the bag. You know the old saying about counting your chickens before they're hatched, right?

Well, I misjudged where that last cork was, and I drove the damn boat right over the top of it, hollering "hit it!" They did, of course—and the charge went off right under the hull of my boat, blowing the bow about four feet into the air and ripping a hole right threw it. I went sailing out, thrown head over heels into the water by the blast.

This sequence was supposed to be a joke on Newman and Jaeckel's part. As each explosion happened, they would laugh and give each other a high-five. Once I was thrown out of the boat, I figured I might as well keep the scene going by swimming toward the other side of the river. I turned around, raised my arm and flipped 'em the finger. They played off that, pointing at me and laughing even more. This all worked out for the best, because the sequence looked better this way than it would have if I'd just gone across the river in the boat.

Newman loved it, Jaeckel loved it, and George Roy Hill loved it, too, and that accident got put into the movie, just as if it was all planned that way. I got lucky that day—I saved the stunt, plus I got off without having a hole blown in myself, instead of just my boat. If you watch *Sometimes A Great Notion,* you will see that little accident fit neatly into the film.

SOMETIMES A GREAT NOTION

Besides doubling for Newman on *Sometimes A Great Notion,* I also doubled Henry Fonda in the film, who played Newman and Jaeckel's father. We were shooting a scene in Newport, Oregon, at the harbor. The scene involved Newman cutting down a tree while Jaeckel was cutting the branches off of another one, a practice called 'bumping." Newman's tree was supposed to fall at an angle, towards Jaeckel, pinning him underneath at the legs, right in the bay as the tide is coming in. Newman's character tries desperately to save him, first cutting pieces of the tree with his chainsaw, then trying to push the massive tree off of his brother. Newman tries everything he can think of to save him, but in the end his efforts fail and Jaeckel dies.

When Fonda was cutting the tree that would fall onto Jaeckel, we rigged up hydraulics to make the tree rock back before it was cut all the way through; in the film it hits Fonda and causes him to lose an arm and eventually die. I doubled Fonda for this scene, and I was really amazed at the good work our effects team did to make this scene realistic.

It was a fun movie to work on, and a lot went on during the filming of it. Newman fractured a bone in his ankle during shooting and we had to stop working for a couple of weeks; Yvonne and I took the opportunity to take a vacation to eastern Oregon until filming was ready to resume.

We had real lumberjacks training us for the film, teaching us how to use their massive chainsaws. There was an art to the way they cut their trees down. I learned how to do it a bit, but Newman was a true champ at it—he could handle a chainsaw. He showed off his new skills when the film was finished by pulling a stunt on George Ray Hill, the director of *Butch Cassidy* and *The Sting*. He walked into Hill's office wielding a chainsaw, fired it up, told Hill to get away from the desk, and promptly cut the desk neatly in half—after which he turned on his heel and walked out as if nothing had happened. The whole thing was a joke to Newman, but an expensive one, since he had to pay about fifteen hundred dollars to buy Hill a new desk. Newman was a fun guy to work with, and he was always trying to loosen George up, who was as serious as the day was long.

ME AND MY SADDLE-PAL

It was so great to have Yvonne and the boys with me while we were making *Notion*. We were staying in Lincoln City, right above Newport, in a house planted right on the sand, and the beach was our front yard. On my days off or on the weekends, Tim, Troy and Lance would gather up our fishing gear and go up river, or we'd drive down to Coos Bay and set out crab pots. There was a restaurant called Moe's Fish House right on the bay that we'd go to; outside the place was a cement jaccuzzi with boiling water that you could dump your crab catch of the day in and cook your own meal. How much better could *that* get?

Just above the house was a small bay where the tide water would come in and out. They boys and I were fishing there one day when Lance hooked something. He was around three years old at that time, and whatever he had on the end of his line was fighting like hell, so I ran to help him. He was jumping up and down, all excited. "I got him, I got him!" As the fish was pulled out of the water, though, it scared Lance half to death. As he'd been slowly reeling in his bait, it had slid over a halibut that had been laying on the bottom. The fish had slapped its tail at the bait, and the tail was what Lance had hooked. Halibuts are a type of flounder, so they're flat with both of their eyes on one side of their head. To say they're odd-looking is an understatement; to a three-year-old kid who's never seen one, they're just plain scary. When Lance saw this thing coming up at him backwards, with its tail flapping up and down, he dropped his pole and high-tailed it out of there. There's nothing like having some laughs and good times, and that's what *Sometimes A Great Notion* was. It was not only a fun film to make, it was also a successful film, and one I'm proud of having worked on.

Pocket Money

Once I was lucky enough to get a job as a stunt double for a high-profile actor, I would often be lucky enough to do so again, as in the case of Redford and Newman, both of whom I've worked with many times. Right after *Sometimes A Great Notion* I did a show called *Pocket Money*, a western based on a novel by Joseph Brown about a cowboy named Jim Kane, a character that would appear in several more of his books. You might guess who played Jim Kane in the film—none other than Paul Newman.

The way the job came about was pretty interesting. The novel's author, Joe Brown, was himself a cowboy, and a former Marine from Arizona who came from a long line of cattlemen. As *Sometimes a Great Notion* was coming to a close and he was in talks with Newman and John Foreman about *Pocket Money*, I got the opportunity to meet him and talk with him a bit when he'd come up to Lincoln City for their meetings. We had a lot in common and he liked to talk to me about my rodeo days. It was Brown, in fact, who suggested that I double for Newman in the film.

"That would be nice," I said, "if they want me to do it. We'll see if I get asked."

One evening Brown was in Lincoln City, and we were all staying at the Shalazam Lodge, a huge, ramshackle place with low-beamed ceilings. We were sitting in the restaurant one evening, and Joe, who'd been drinking fairly impressively that evening (as he did on most evenings), caught my eye. "So, you were a gymnast, huh, Gilbert?" he asked me.

"Oh, yeah," I told him. "I still work out a lot that way."

He jerked his chin at the low beam running above our heads. "You see that beam up there?"

"Yeah."

"I bet you can't do a kip on it," he said.

A kip is an important skill in gymnastics—it's a move that's used both as a mount and as a connecting skill in a bar routine. You swing under the bar and pull your feet to the bar while pushing out with your arms, and you whip out above the bar. Why the hell he knew what it was, I had no idea, but he did.

"Now, what made you think of that?" I asked.

"Well, you're a gymnast, aren't you?" he chuckled. "You think you can do it?"

"Sure, I can do it," I said. "But if I do it, you're gonna have to, too."

I jumped up on the table, the other patrons in the restaurant watching, and, I'm sure, thinking *what the hell is that guy doing?* I was strong, and I kept myself in top shape, of course, to be able to do what I did for a living. I only had to jump up about half a foot to reach the beam, and I didn't have to do a kip to get up there; I just used my body strength and did a muscle up. In a few seconds I was on top of the beam, staring down at Joe. "How's that, Joe?" I asked him with a wide smile.

"Well, I'll be a son of a bitch," he said, still in a good humor from the drinks. "That wasn't even a kip."

"No, it was a muscle up," I said, and jumped down. "So, are you ready for your turn?" I took my seat again. The whole restaurant was staring at us, now, probably thinking we were nuts. Joe jumped up and grabbed the beam, and swung his legs forward with a flourish. When his body came back from that swing, though, the momentum from it snapped his hands free of the bar and he lost his grip on it, flying backwards and smashing into our table. Plates, silverware and glasses flew in all directions. I jumped up and leapt out of the way just in time, laughter making my sides hurt.

POCKET MONEY

"Wow, man, that was pretty good, Joe!" I exclaimed.

He started laughing, too, obviously embarrassed. He kept laughing—what else could he do? The drinks he had in him soothed his pain and bruised ego pretty good, too, I'd imagine. He was a good guy and we enjoyed each others' company, and through him I was able to work on *Pocket Money*.

There was a lot of roping and riding for me to do, doubling Paul again. Jim Arnett, Paul's body double, was doing some coordinating on the film, and he called me in to do the horse stuff. We shot the film in Nogales and Tuscon, Arizona. Lee Marvin was cast in the film and I became friends with him. For some reason I never did figure out, Marvin didn't get along with Paul Newman and was always saying sarcastic things to him in between takes. One morning I woke up and went out on the balcony of my hotel room just as Marvin was standing out on his. I'd gone to a gun show in Tuscon the day before where I bought a .44 Magnum like the one Eastwood used in Dirty Harry, and I showed it to Lee, who was impressed. He told me to go get some ammo for it and bring it out so he could shoot it.

"It's pretty early," I cautioned him, "and that's a loud gun. You're probably going to wake the whole hotel up."

"Nah, let me try it." He cocked back the hammer and fired, and you would've thought a cannon had gone off, the damned thing was so loud. It was a powerful gun and it looked like a hand grenade had gone off where he shot it. Despite my protests, he shot it again, and people started coming out of their rooms, pissed about the noise and alarmed about the shots. Once they saw it was Lee Marvin who'd fired the gun, they backed off, and no one reported us.

Once we started working, Newman came up to me and talked to me in confidence; he was upset about the bad blood between him and Marvin and was puzzled as to its origin. He'd noticed I seemed to get on well with Marvin, and he asked me to talk to him—Marvin's sarcastic remarks were getting threatening, in Newman's way of thinking, and it was flustering the hell out of him. I agreed to see what I could do.

ME AND MY SADDLE-PAL

I went to Marvin. "What's the deal with you and Newman?" I asked.

"Eh, I just don't like him," Marvin replied sourly.

"It's messing up the picture, Lee," I said. "You need to back off a bit, take it easy on him, so we can get this movie made." Marvin laughed it off and went back to drinking—which he was doing far too much of while making the film.

One night I was having dinner with Stuart Rosenberg, the director, and Newman came charging in, saying that Marvin was making threats against him again. Rosenberg demanded to know what was going on, and Newman explained the situation. I told Rosenberg I'd talked to Lee, but Marvin had just laughed it off. "He's drinking too much, that's his problem," I said.

One Saturday night, I suggested that we all go see the bullfights in Mexico the next day—Newman, Rosenberg, Arnett, me—and Marvin. We got a driver and went down into Mexico, and we got there early. We went into a bar to wait, and for some strange reason I asked for twenty-five shots of tequila—five apiece. As I've said, I've never been a drinker, but when I'm in Mexico I've been known to enjoy a shot of tequila here and there. We did our toasts and drank our shots, and by the end, we were feeling pretty damn good—no pain there. When we got to the bull ring, Marvin started heckling the bullfighters, paying no heed to my attempts to get him to shut up.

When we left the ring, the matadors were all waiting by their cars, arms crossed as they leaned against their cars, staring us down. "Just keep walking," I muttered to the rest, hoping we wouldn't get killed but pretty sure we were going to. We walked on by, got into our car, and drove off.

We went to the Cavern, a fabulous restaurant at the border of Nogales Mexico and Nogales Arizona, for dinner. As we were ordering our meals, John Foreman, the producer, walked in with about six members of the crew. While we're sitting there, a small boy walks in with a big cardboard box. He came up to Stuart, the film's director, tapped him on the shoulder, and handed him the box.

POCKET MONEY

"What's this?"

"For you, Señor," the kid said. "From the Matadors." *Oh, no.* They'd tracked us down and sent the kid in. Inside the box were the horns and the tail of a bull.

"That's not a gift, Stuart," I said, "that's an insult." I don't think I have to spell out what that gesture means, and it was payment for Lee Marvin's heckling. We got rid of the box, and then I went over to John Foreman's table.

"You like tequila, John?" I asked.

"Sure. I can drink tequila like you wouldn't believe, Gilbert."

I ordered a couple of shots—not a good idea, I know—and before I'd even swallowed my shot, Foreman's glass was already empty on the table. "What the hell—how'd you drink that so fast?" I demanded of Foreman.

"I told you I could drink like you wouldn't believe," he said.

I ordered two more, and he did the same thing—his glass was empty and on the table before I'd even lowered mine from my lips. Turned out he was dumping his shots into a half-empty water glass on the table, but I hadn't quite figured it out yet. I ordered one more round, eyeballing the long tray of food on the table.

"If I don't see you drink this, Foreman, I'm gonna dump that tray of food all over your table," I told him.

"Whatever. I'm drinking it," he said.

Same thing happened, and I did as promised, spilling their food all over the place. Everyone else in the restaurant was looking at us like we were nuts, but all of us in the production were cracking up.

"I'm not going to drink with you anymore, John," I told him, and went back to my table. They picked what they could off the table and kept right on eating it, tray or no tray.

Throughout shooting, Marvin kept up his antagonistic attitude toward Newman. I tried to talk to him again, telling him he was a good enough actor to *act* the part of an alcoholic cowboy, without actually doing all the drinking for real, and I was worried about it affecting his career later on. I reminded him of another film we'd done together

ME AND MY SADDLE-PAL

called *Monty Walsh,* and how he'd disappeared from the set on a drinking binge. I told him I remembered that incident, and so if *I* remembered things like that, surely producers and directors would remember it, too—and maybe not cast him in such good films. I tried to be helpful, because I genuinely liked Lee, but it didn't work. *Pocket Money* was not a success, and it wasn't a good film for Paul, for obvious reasons.

Junior Bonner

Just like he'd promised at the end of *The Wild Bunch,* Sam Peckinpah called me up and told me a bit about the premise for *Junior Bonner;* it was a rodeo picture, shot in Prescott, Arizona. Both of these things were right up my alley; my background as a rodeo champ and my experiences at the big rodeo in Prescott made me tailor-made for this job.

I drove out to Prescott and headed to the production office, where I introduced myself as the stunt coordinator and stunt double for Steve McQueen. I asked after Sam and told them I needed to meet with him, and they told me he was out at his motel and they weren't sure when he'd be back.

"I'll just go out there and see him," I said. They looked at one another, unsure what to say, because they weren't aware of the rapport I'd developed with him. *They* were all scared to death of him, like everyone else seemed to be. They never wanted to give anyone any direction regarding Peckinpah if Peckinpah hadn't given *them* direction first.

I headed out to the motel and saw two SUVs filled with producers, waiting for Peckinpah to come out of his motel room. He had some girl in there and they didn't want to interrupt.

I parked my truck and got out, walking past the SUVs toward the director's room. One of the producers stuck their head out of the car window and frantically hailed me. "Hey, cowboy, where are you going?"

"I gotta see Sam," I said, wondering what the deal was.

"Well, I wouldn't bother him right now. We've been waiting for him for a bit—I don't think now's a good time."

I'd already knocked on the door by then. "Who is it?" Peckinpah hollered from inside.

"It's Mickey Gilbert," I called back. "It's the Kid!"

"Hey! You out here, now?"

"Yeah!"

"Hang on a second." He came to the door and opened it—and he was stark-ass naked. I was too stunned to say anything. He pounded me on the back and looked out at the producers waiting in the cars. "I'll be right with you guys," he said breezily, then yanked me into the room—which pissed the producers off to no end.

Inside, Sam wrapped a towel around himself and we talked a minute, then I stood up. "I'll let you guys be, I didn't mean to barge in on you," I said quickly. "I just wanted to let you know I was hear. We can catch up and go over things at the next production meeting."

"Don't worry about it," he said, waving off my apology.

Eventually we got to work on the film, and I was coordinating a huge bar fight at the Palace Bar. I needed about twenty stunt people, both men and women, for the sequence. When the production team found out how many I wanted to bring in, they said 'no way,' so I talked to Sam. I told him I'd go out and find some local people that I could work with and train for use in the sequence. He gave me the go-ahead, so that's exactly what I did, training them at the YMCA and arranging to pay them five dollars a day.

The second day I was working with my new recruits, someone from the production came and got me; Peckinpah wanted to see me right away at the Palace Bar.

I headed over there and when I walked in I saw Sam sitting at the bar, with all the producers and production managers lined up, sitting on either side of him. What the hell was *this* about?

"You wanted to see me, Sam?"

"Yeah. Who told you you could hire eighty people for this sequence at the bar?" he asked me grimly.

So *that's* what it was. "I'll tell you something, Sam," I said. "How much is this movie costing, per day, to shoot? Fifty-thousand?"

"I don't know, something like that. What about it?" he asked suspiciously.

"They won't let me bring in enough trained stuntmen for this sequence; they're only giving me seven people. If I don't train these folks I've pulled off the street, they're not going to have a clue what to do when it comes time to shoot. So if you don't let me train them up at the Y, I'm going to have to bring them down here and shut the production down while I train them on location. If you do that, you're going to kiss off about twenty or thirty-thousand dollars while I'm trying to train them here." I was completely frank with him.

I knew it wasn't Sam who was upset—it was the producers. Ever since that day I'd breezed into his hotel room while he kept them waiting, they'd had it in for me. Sam stood up, turned to face the row of producers, and said, "you see? I *told* you this guy knows his shit! Go back to your work."

I chuckled under my breath. "Okay, I'm out of here," I said, and went back to the Y to continue my training.

Over the course of training, I'd find people who just had a certain look about them that was just what we needed for the movie. I'd grab them and drag them into the bar for Sam to inspect, and he was always enthusiastic, sharing my opinion on whatever it was about each person that had caught my eye. He'd always give me the go-ahead to hire them.

One of the guys I saw was a big six-foot-six Native American guy that I'd see driving a tractor in town. He as a *huge* man, about two-hundred eighty pounds. I went up to him. "Hey, you want to make some money doing some fights?" I asked.

"Yeah, who do I have to kill?" he asked enthusiastically.

I laughed. "No, you're not going to kill anyone; it's for a movie. I'll train you to do what you need to do. You'll be part of a big bar fight, and you'll be tossing guys into tables and knocking them back, that sort of thing."

He lit up. "Yeah, I'd *love* to do that!"

"Okay, come with me!" I had him lumber behind me into the bar. "Hey, Sam!" He was just about ready to shoot. He called cut and looked over at us in the doorway. When he saw the newest recruit I'd brought in, he almost jumped up and down.

"He's *perfect!* Bring him on in and sign him up!"

Lucian Ballard, the director of photography that always worked with Peckinpah, came up to me one day and gave me a poke with the cane he always carried. "You know what, Kid?" he said dryly, "you're gonna get yourself fired one day, butting in on Peckinpah like that all the time. One of these days he'll be in a mood and you'll be gone."

"Oh, no, I never but in on him," I corrected Lucien. "I watch him very carefully and I always talk to him when I can see he's got a second or so of free time." I smiled.

He didn't. Instead, he shook his head. "You be careful, Gilbert. You know how he is."

"Yeah, I know how he is, but I also know how to talk to him," I said. "I'm fine, Lucien."

And I was. For whatever reason, whether it was because I stood up to him or treated him at the same level as anyone else I dealt with, or perhaps both, I had Sam Peckinpah's respect—an accomplishment which didn't come lightly, and one I always remember as noteworthy in my career.

Prior to shooting that fight scene at the Palace Bar, when I was training all the guys at the YMCA, they were having fun pretending to throw punches and tackling one another during training. The day came to shoot the actual scene, which would be filmed in cuts so we wouldn't have to do everything all at once. I had a few trained stuntmen in there, but the rest were extras, and when they got positioned in front of the camera I could see the telltale signs of nervousness coming out.

We shot one section of the sequence, and nobody did anything as they were supposed to—they were moving too fast. I called cut, then went to Peckinpah and spoke to him and his director of photography, Lucien Ballard.

JUNIOR BONNER

"I know what we need to do to get this right," I told them. "I'm going to rehearse them, and then, when I'm ready, I'm going to look over at you and give you a nod and a wink, and you'll roll the cameras without calling action. I'll tell everyone we're going to rehearse one more time, to take it slow and do it right. We'll get it."

I told the guys we were going to rehearse, and I winked at Sam and Lucien, who started the cameras rolling without letting them know. "Let's go through it, now, nice and easy," I told the guys—and what do you know, they did it perfectly. Later on Peckinpah came up to me.

"What made you think to do that?" he asked me.

"Well, because I've noticed during my career that when people get really nervous, they start moving too fast and getting jerky in their movements, too. They want to get it over with, instead of taking their time and doing it right."

Being observant and doing what I can to get around nerves, as well as respecting people's feelings and treating them like human beings has always helped me be successful in the movie business, and I hope I've inspired that in others I've worked with, too, if even just a little bit.

Chino

In 1973 I got called in by director John Sturges to work with him on a Dino De Laurentiis-produced film called *Chino,* starring Charles Bronson, Bronson's wife Jill Ireland, and Vincent Van Patten. Sturges was interested in having me coordinate some horse stunts in the film, as well as double Bronson for the roping and horse-breaking scenes. The director also wanted me to find a head wrangler for the film who could care for all the livestock that was going to be used, so I contacted a buddy of mine, Rudy Ugland, who was one of the best horse trainers in the business and who had lots of experience with westerns. Sturges entered my salary into his contract so that there would be no way I could be taken advantage of.

John and I flew to Rome to meet with De Laurentiis and discuss the film. When we got there, we had to walk up a red-carpeted stairway, flanked by two armed Italian tough-guy bodyguards, to get to his office.

De Laurentiis had a way of promoting finances for a film, but also skimming finances off of them at the same time. We walked into his office and he shook hands with each of us while giving us his best Charlie Bronson stare-down, at the same time. I always had a knack for looking into horses' eyes and being able to tell if they were gentle and easygoing, or as wild as feral cats, not to be trusted for a second. As I moved through my film career I was able to apply the same knack to people

I met in the business, and I did the same with De Laurentiis. After he and Sturges had a conversation about the movie, he looked over at me, sizing me up, and asked, in his heavy Italian accent, if I thought I could handle the job okay. That remark did not endear him to me any, but I just said, "Yes, Mr. Dino, I wouldn't be here if Mr. Sturges didn't have confidence in me and think I was a good fit for the picture."

He stared me down, slowly cracked a smile and said, "I like that name, Mr. Dino. That's very clever of you, Mikilito." He chuckled, and so did I, and we said our good-byes.

Sturges and I separated then while still in Rome. John wanted me to fly down to Spain with a construction foreman to supervise the building of the housing for all of our cast horses, as well as a roping arena for me to train them in. The foreman's name was Mariano, and we became very good friends after working together for awhile. After about two weeks of working with him, I started scouting the country around Almeria to find the two hundred head of horses I needed; these would work in the film as our wild herd, since the film's plot centered around a horse-breeder who also broke and trained wild horses. This herd would be used for me to rope when I was doubling Bronson.

I met up with Antonio "Tony" Tarruella, a Spanish native who was employed as the first assistant director on the production. Tony spoke seven languages and knew lots of people around Southern Spain. I also met Augustino Medina, a gypsy wrangler who helped me scout for horses. He was a very wealthy man who made his money from motion picture companies that shot films in Spain. When they finished a production, Medina would buy all their lighting equipment, the wardrobe, and anything else that the production company didn't want to pay to have shipped back to the states. Then in turn, Medina would rent these items back to other production companies coming to Spain to shoot movies. Pretty smart guy.

So, Tony, Medina and I took off on a road-trip that lasted three weeks, making deals with different ranchers to use their horses. Some places we'd rent ten horses, at others we'd rent forty. We kept going until we'd secured the full two hundred head we needed. Each rancher we made a deal with had the responsibility of shipping his horses to Almeria on a given date.

On our first day of travel, Medina wanted to take us to lunch in Segovia, at a special restaurant. It was a three-story, round building, and on each floor different types of food were served. The second floor served nothing but different types of pork, and it was to that floor Medina led us. He ordered for all of us, and the first course was pork soup, served in a big crock pot right at the table. It was a great-tasting soup loaded with vegetables and exotic flavors—and it was also loaded with the pig's ears, snout, tongue, and—the Pièce de résistance—two eyeballs, floating right on top, keeping an eye on us. Get it? It was definitely one of the more visually interesting meals I'd ever had. Medina had ordered it purposely to test me out. He started dipping in with the serving spoon and filling Tony's bowl with the soup. When he picked up my bowl, he made a special point of dumping in one of the eyeballs for me.

Right away I saw what he was doing, so I pushed my chair away and stood up, picked up my soup spoon, and scooped up the eyeball with it. Then I raised it up in a mock-toast, looked down at Medina, and said, "*Muy* fucking *bueno,* Medina." With that, I swallowed the eyeball (no, I'm not joking, I really did it).

Medina eyeballed me (no pun intended), clearly surprised. He hadn't thought I'd have the guts to do that. He promptly stood up, spooned up the other eyeball from *his* bowl, saluted me in the same fashion, and swallowed it. This little culinary dare was all that I needed to win Medina's respect, and we became good friends soon after. I often look back at my life and all the rather crazy situations I've found myself in, like this one, and I really believe that the Lord gave me the gift of being unafraid of what people might think of my actions, and the ability to react in just the right way to whatever outlandish thing I found myself facing.

We finished our scouting, and by this time Rudy Ugland was gathering horses for Bronson to ride. As we were getting set up, though, our horses were hit with a highly contagious virus that affected the kidneys and liver. Luckily we hadn't sent for our wild horse herd yet, so none of them were exposed. We called in veterinarians to treat the affected animals, and though we lost four of them, we were lucky we didn't lose more.

During all of the prep time for the film, I met with a real estate agent whom I'd had looking for a three-bedroom residence close to the area; I wanted a nice place for Yvonne and the boys to stay in. he found what I wanted in a seaside town called Aguadulce. It was perfect, so I arranged for the family to fly in and join me. At this point the boys were eight, six and four, respectively, and were about to have the time of their lives.

The Italian production company showed up and all the actors started coming into town. I was meeting all the Spanish stuntmen that I'd need later on. The wild horse herd was starting to be trucked into the location, too, so there was a lot going on. Rudy and I and some of the other guys started working with the herd, driving it from point A to point B for the roping shots I was going to do.

Sturges wanted me to come into Almeria one day to meet with the heads of each department in the production company, as well as Charlie Bronson. I took Troy with me for the meeting to give him something to do. The propmaster had set up a long table with all kinds of props, such as lariats, chaps, spurs, canteens anything else Charlie might want in his department. At the end of the table there were six different Bowie knives; Bronson would pick one of them to wear on his belt. Troy made a bee-line for them, like any young boy would, and started picking them up, one by one, and examining them, checking out the quality of steel and the balance of each one for throwing. Even at such a young age, he knew his stuff.

Troy was in a trance-like state as he looked over each knife. Meanwhile, Bronson and the propmaster were working their way down the table, talking about the different items. As they got close to Troy, the propmaster hollered, "hey, kid, move away from there!" Troy, of course, ignored him. He tried again. "C'mon, kid, move it."

Bronson looked over at Troy and said, "what's your name, kid?"

ME AND MY SADDLE-PAL

"Troy Gilbert," Troy answered, without looking up. He was still fixated on the knives.

Charlie asked him which one of the knives he liked the best, and Troy, never glancing up once, proceeded to talk about each knife, telling Bronson if it was a good knife or a bad one. He picked up the last knife and told Charlie that it was the best of the bunch, well-balanced and good for throwing. Charlie said with a smile, "okay, Troy, I'll take that knife."

I'd been observing all this, and, chuckling under my breath, walked over to the table, introducing myself to Charlie. "I hope he hasn't been too much trouble, but he really likes knives for some reason. His other two brothers are the same way."

"So you have three boys?" Bronson asked me.

"Yeah, the Lord gave me three healthy kids."

We started talking and Charlie told me that he'd brought both of his boys with him, as well. I told him he should bring them out to the location so they could meet mine, and he did, which worked out great. They bonded together right away and became good friends.

We started the shoot, and I got busy setting up different pieces of action for it, as well as doubling Charlie. Everything was going great.

When you're in the business and you shoot in a distant location, the production company has to house you and pay you per diem, along with your salary. Each week when I would collect my per diem, I noticed it was always a little short of what I should have been getting. I went to payroll and asked them about it, and they explained that because it was Italian currency being spent in Spain, there was an exchange rate between the Italian Lire and the Spanish Paseda. The auditor telling me this was Italian, of course, and for some reason I didn't believe him. I went to a bank in Almeria and asked. Just as I'd thought, there was no such exchange rate. The company was not only holding back monies they owned *me*, they were doing the same thing with the actors, the director, and most of the crew, which really pissed me off. We're talking about a lot of money being cheated away from hard-working people. I went to the director and told him about it, and he

CHINO

said he'd check it out, but he didn't really have the time so I ended up mentioning it to Bronson. He in turn told his secretary about it, and found out that my suspicions were true. He came to me one afternoon and said, "hey, Mick, meet me at the studio tomorrow morning and we'll straighten this matter out."

The next morning, when we were supposed to have been on location, Bronson and I met up at the studio. When the production manager saw me and Charlie, he hustled out of his office and approached us. "Mickey, Charlie, *porque,* why are you here, and not shooting the movie?"

Charlie told him why, all right, and he denied it, of course. Charlie said, "Nino, you can deny this all you want, but until you return all the per diem money that you've kept from everybody, Mickey and I are not going to work." Bronson's words were firm and blunt.

The shit really hit the fan, then. The production manager begged us, "*please* go back to work. I will get this taken care of right away."

Later that day, in the afternoon, two vans from the payroll department showed up at the location, set up tables, and one by one paid everyone off, including our director, Charlie, and me.

A few more weeks went by and I got a call from the production manager, calling me to a meeting with him at the studio. *This* was sure to be interesting, I thought. I walked into his office. He got up and gave me a phony smile, shook my hand, sat down and told me what he wanted.

They were paying three dollars a day, per horse, for the herd we were renting. We had two hundred head at six hundred dollars a day, so it came out to forty-two hundred bucks a week. We had contracted their use for eight full weeks. In total, the production would spend over thirty-three thousand just on this herd. The manager wanted me to talk to John and get him to agree to only use the herd for three weeks. If I could talk him into it, he said, he'd pay me extra money on the side. After he'd told me all this, he got up and walked over to the liquor bar he had in the room, and poured two drinks, as if he wanted us to toast to our little sneaky proposition.

I took the drink, clinked glasses with him, and as he started to lift his to his mouth I said, "here's to you, Nino." I then proceeded to pour my drink all over his desk and walked out. As I was going down the studio stairway, I didn't think I'd ever felt better in my life. Doing the right thing is always just that—the right thing. When I got back to the location I told John and Charlie what had happened, and they shook their heads in disgust, but laughed at what I'd done. Afterward, John fired Nino, and that was the end of the "on-the-side" propositions on *Chino.*

The company sent another production manager to Almeria to take over the show. His name was Carlos, and when I met him, I could tell he'd been told about me, and I could see by his eyes that he was forcing himself to be nice. He got to be pretty annoying to me because sometimes when he would come out to the set, he would come up behind me and, with the palm of his hand, slap me across my kidneys. The first time he did it, it startled me and I spun around. "Hey, Carlos," I said.

"*Hola,* Mickey, how are you, my friend?" We talked for awhile and that was it. A few days went by, and then, *whack!* It was Carlos again, pulling his sneak-up-and-slap routine on me again. We talked about upcoming stunts I would be doing.

The next week, he did it again. This time, I spun around, pointed my finger at him and said, "Carlos, don't ever walk up behind me again and slap me in the kidneys like you've been doing, understand?"

"Ah, Mickey, Mickey, you're a big, tough stuntman, eh?" he replied.

I told Carlos that I didn't like the fact that he came up behind me to play his little game, and that if he wanted to punch me, he should come up in front of me and do it.

Carlos nodded. "*No problema, no problema,* Mickey," he said with a smile. That was that…until the next time he did it, which was also the last. One day I was out on the set and Jill Ireland, Charlie's wife, showed up to watch the filming. With her was their secretary, their agent and their maid. Jill spotted me and called me over to introduce me to everyone. We'd been talking for about ten minutes when, out of

CHINO

nowhere, *whack,* there was Carlos again, once again sneaking up and slapping me in the kidneys.

I spun around and snapped a sharp right punch straight into Carlos's heart. He dropped to his knees with his hands across his heart.

I bent over, my hand on his shoulder, and sort of apologetically said, "Carlos, I've told you never to do that to me again. Don't you remember?" Still on his knees, he nodded his head, his hands still over his chest. "Are you alright?" I asked him. I looked at the ladies and shook my head. To my surprise, they all had their hands over their mouths, covering their smiles. I looked back down at Carlos. "Come on, Carlos, let me help you up."

I got him to his feet, and he walked off. I apologized to the ladies and asked them why they were laughing under their breath. Jill told me that Carlos had done nothing but give them problems after problems. I told them that he'd really had that coming, and I was sure that was the end of it.

I told Jill that my boys and their boys were having the time of their lives and that they'll never forget being in Spain and going through different experiences there.

When I was traveling looking for horses, I came across two different owners who each owned an unbroken black three-year-old filly. I asked them not to get friendly with either filly, because I had a scene I could use them for. It was a sequence where Charlie's character ropes a wild black horse out of a herd and takes it home to break it. In the scene, after he thinks he's broken it, he unsaddles it and turns it loose in a corral. As he's walking away with the saddle, the horse turns its head toward Charlie, charges him, and bites him on the shoulder. Putting it all together made for an interesting sequence, and here's how I did it:

Rudy Ugland was training a black horse to attack a dummy that the prop man furnished; it had a pole running through it that fit into a base plate to hold it upright. We clothed it with the same wardrobe that Charlie would wear for the scene. I was training another black horse to rear up and strike out with its forelegs, and also training it to fall and lay still on command. Along with all that, I had the two

ME AND MY SADDLE-PAL

unbroken black fillies kept separate in a pen that I had forbidden anyone from going near, except for feeding purposes. These would be the horses that I would use in breaking corral work.

After a couple of weeks, the biting horse and the falling horse were ready for filming. The breaking corral was about thirty-five feet in diameter with a snubbing post, which is a training device, in the center. We set up cameras in different spots around the corral, then brought up one of the unbroken fillies. With my hair sprayed and wearing a glued-on mustache, I was a good double for Charlie. We were going to put Charlie in as many scenes as possible, of course, but right then it was all me.

They rolled cameras, and Sturges hollered "*action!*" I opened the gate and walked in with my rope in hand, heading toward the filly. As I took a few more steps in her direction, I uncoiled my rope, making a loop. The horse turned and bolted away from me, going along the corral fence. Swinging my rope, I stepped in and roped her neatly around the neck, jerking the slack out of the rope and making it tighten around her throat. Quickly she threw up her head and leaped into the air, and that was my cue to tie her to the snubbing post. I kept her running in one direction around the post, which wound her closer to it.

While she was fighting the rope, she was jumping, rearing and kicking, and she was so frightened that she urinated a few times. We cut the film and gave her a rest, and I had the wranglers bring in the black horse I'd trained for rearing, striking and falling. I put that horse in place of the filly, snubbed close to the post. Rudy was out in front of the horse with his training whip. Sturges rolled cameras again and hollered "*action!*" and Rudy makes the horse start throwing its head around as I slipped a halter on him and tied the lead rope to the post. All the while the horse is rearing and striking out with its front hooves. I stepped in and slipped my lasso from its neck, then took a piece of cloth and laid it across his eyes, tucking the ends into the halter to hold it in place.

At this point, Rudy stopped working the horse, so it started to settle down. At that point we got some tight shots of Charlie saddling the horse and cautiously swinging up into the saddle. Then it was time for my ride, once we led Rudy's trained horse away, ready to bring in the next horse.

Two other wranglers have caught, saddled and blindfolded the second unbroken filly—and believe me, it wasn't easy. They brought her into the corral and snubbed her to the post, tying a quick-release knot with the lead rope. There was a horse and wrangler on either side of her, and I got up behind one of them, slipping off of the back of the wrangler's saddle and setting myself down onto the filly's back. The cameras were rolled, and as she was jumping around, I reached down and released the lead rope, got set and tore the blindfold off of her.

That's all it took—she jumped out, whinnying, kicking, lunging and rearing, tossing her head all the while. About ten seconds went by, and then she reared up so high that she lost her balance and fell straight over backwards. I quickly leaned to one side, and as she landed, I rolled away from her.

This is where I had them bring in the falling horse. They took the filly away and led him back in, and I got up on him. Once they rolled cameras, I spurred him out and made him fall to the ground, staying in the saddle as he did so. At that point we were both laying on the ground on our left sides. We held the horse there so that Charlie could take my place. Remember, this was a gentle horse who'd been trained for this purpose; Bronson had no problem with it—in fact, he enjoyed it. He got down and slipped his left leg under the horse, still holding onto the halter rope. I was at the horse's head, holding him down. I told Charlie that when the horse stumbled up, he needed to stay in the saddle and spur him out of the camera frame. He followed my instructions, and it worked just perfectly.

Next, the two wranglers brought in the saddled filly again, penned in between them. I slipped into her saddle again to finish the sequence, and she finally wore down. I put Charlie on the gentle horse again, the one trained to rear and fall, and he hollered to Vincent Van Patten, who was in the scene watching all of this go down, to open the corral gate. Vincent swung the gate open, and Charlie rode out into the desert.

ME AND MY SADDLE-PAL

In the scene, Charlie was supposed to have been riding the horse all day, and we filmed him coming back to the corral. Rudy had trained the horse to walk slowly with its head almost dragging on the ground, and they'd sweated and lathered the horse up to look like it had been ridden hard all day. Charlie rode it back into the corral and unsaddled it, slipped the halter off, and picked up the saddle, beginning to walk off.

Now came the shot of the horse biting Bronson's shoulder, so we brought in the horse Rudy had trained to attack the dummy. We finally finished the sequence off, and everything worked really well. We were all very pleased with the sequence because, as you can see, there was a lot of preparation for this sequence. Many movie-goers don't realize the amount of work and time involved in something like this—all of the training and switching of different horses that end up looking like the same one on screen. All that work paid off, and it was all worth it.

The Sting, Blazing Saddles and *Earthquake*

※

Around 1972 I got a call to double Robert Redford once again, this time on a film called *The Sting*, which would be a big one. Redford's co-stars were (who else?) Paul Newman, and Robert Shaw, and was directed by George Roy Hill, who'd also directed Redford and Newman in *Butch Cassidy and the Sundance Kid*.

Newman and Redford truly enjoyed working together, and had a rapport going that those working with them could see. The audience could see it, too, which made them really enjoyable to watch.

I didn't do a whole lot on *The Sting;* all of it was interior stuff shot in a studio, but it was an important film in my career because Redford was still requesting that I double him, which was a good sign that I'd continue to be successful.

The next film I worked on was Mel Brooks's comedic western, *Blazing Saddles*. The film starred Gene Wilder. I got the job through Al Wyatt Sr., the film's stunt coordinator, who knew me well and therefore knew what my capabilities were. I really enjoyed working with Al, who along with my father-in-law was one of the top coordinators and second-unit directors in the business at that time. Al introduced me to Gene Wilder, who I instantly liked; he was a really neat guy. He'd never really needed a double before, so it was a new experience for him. When I doubled him, I took pains to mimic the rather goofy way he walked or moved in the saddle. He liked that, and liked me, so I ended

ME AND MY SADDLE-PAL

up working with him on other films, such as *The Frisco Kid* and *Silver Streak*.

I enjoyed working with Mel Brooks, too, and we did some crazy things on the film. I mainly did horse stunts on *Blazing Saddles;* falls and jumps. Slim Pickens, who was portraying one of the townspeople, was also working on the film; he was a former rodeo clown and I knew him from rodeos. He'd done well in the movie business; he was handy at pretty much anything he was asked to do and he was a likeable guy. *Blazing Saddles* was a hell of a lot of fun to make and even more fun to watch.

A couple of years later I worked on a Universal picture called *Earthquake,* starring Charlton Heston and Ava Gardner. There was a lot of action in it. One scene involved a dam breaking and flooding the city when the earthquake hits. To stage this sequence, dump tanks were used to create waves of water going down the street. Each tank held about five thousand gallons of water and was mounted on a swivel that would create the rolling motion needed to form waves. The water would spill down a huge slide pointed in whatever direction the filmmakers wanted it to go—in this case, down a city street. They also had two or three other dump tanks ready to go in case they wanted to increase the volume of water. I was one of about twenty or so stunt people that was going to be in the street and be hit by this wall of water, which would be coming at me pretty fast. When it hit me I knew it would pick me up and take me along with it, and I knew I needed to let it—fighting against it would do no good.

One of my best friends and fellow stuntman Bennie Dobbins was also going to be in the scene, and as we were getting set up I saw him getting into a vest that had a cable hooked up to a post in front of one of the buildings. "Bennie," I asked him, "what are you doing?"

"I'm going to cable myself to this post," he said, "so I can kind of hang here, and wave my arms and scream, you know, that sort of thing."

I was immediately concerned. "Bennie, that's not a good idea. You're going to have all of that water hitting you and trying to force

THE STING, BLAZING SADDLES AND EARTHQUAKE

you along with it. Besides that it's going to have all the debris in it from all the buildings it's taking out—what if that stuff slams into you? You could get hurt. I think you should just go with the flow, man."

"Nah, this'll be great," he told me enthusiastically, gesturing to the cable.

I didn't agree, but I could see he had his mind made up. Shaking my head, I went back to my mark.

They dumped the tanks, and that water hit us like a ton of bricks. Some of us must've been carried a good hundred yards down the street by its force. Once we regained our footing we started walking back up the street again, and I saw people crowded around the post Bennie had cabled himself to. He was half-conscious, and he had an impressive cut over one of his eyes, and another on his cheek on the opposite side. I rushed over, helping unhook him from his cable.

"Bennie, are you all right?" I asked.

"Yeah, I think I'm okay," he said weakly.

I wasn't so sure—I didn't like the look of that cut. This was a night shot, so it was about one in the morning. "Instead of having the medic look at you, I think we ought to take you to the hospital," I told him. Everyone else agreed, so I drove him over to the hospital and took him to the E.R. I was allowed in with him, and I watched as the nurses began to clean the cut out. They told us the attending doctor would be in soon to stitch him up.

The wound really looked bad to me, and it was right over his eyebrow. I was concerned that it might scar really badly, so I suggested calling in a plastic surgeon to place the sutures, instead of the attending E.R. doc. Bennie agreed, and so did the hospital staff—the attending doctor didn't appear to really want to do the stitching—that's how bad the cut was. I called Bennie's wife and let her know what was going on. Then I waited with Bennie for a good hour or so until the plastic surgeon arrived.

Right away, the surgeon examined the cut, and showed me how deep it was—you could see Bennie's skull. Then he grabbed some forceps and started picking small pieces of debris from the *Earthquake*

ME AND MY SADDLE-PAL

set out of the cut. As he worked, I could tell he was getting mad. He demanded to know who had cleaned the cut out when I'd first brought Bennie in. The nurses were scared to answer him, and rightfully so, because he took them to task for the poor job they'd done cleaning Bennie's wound.

When he returned to his patient, he palpated the cut on Bennie's cheek, and glanced down at him. "You know, your cheekbone is broken, Mr. Dobbins," he told him.

"It is?" Bennie replied.

"Yes," the doctor said. "Have you been conscious this whole time?"

"Yes, I have," Bennie said.

"That's quite amazing," the doctor said. "I would've expected you to be completely knocked out. I'll have to repair the cut to your eye, and then I'll have to rebuild your cheekbone. It's going to take a lot of work."

Bennie was in the hospital for about a week, and the injuries kept him out of work for quite awhile. His eye never quite looked the same, though, and when he *did* return to work he had to be very careful to avoid re-injury. I always felt badly for him; he was such a great guy, and a great stuntman. This unfortunate incident was yet another example of the risks people in my industry take—and another example of what can happen if you don't think your stunt through. It's also an example of the power that water can have, and how people don't realize its strength and the potential it has to damage whatever's in its path. I ended up giving some advice to the other stunt people on the set that day who'd never ridden the water from a dump tank before; I told them to keep their feet in front of them as best they could, and warned them that the water would have control, not them.

As a stuntman, if you're working with one of these tanks, you no longer have control over the stunt once the water is dumped, so it's important to be as safe as possible and to avoid taking any risks that might make an already dangerous stunt into something downright deadly.

The Great Waldo Pepper

Early in 1975, I received a call to double Redford again, this time in a film called *The Great Waldo Pepper,* directed by George Roy Hill, who I'd worked with on many other occasions, as you might recall. The film was an adventure/drama about a biplane pilot, played by Redford.

The production had already finished shooting all of the wing-walking stunts, which I had been offered but turned down, because it was one of the few types of stunts I'd never done before, and I knew that all the pilots wouldn't want to work with a novice. Besides that, I never took jobs that I hadn't practiced extensively; I had to feel confident with the skills needed for the stunt.

So, I came into the production at the time they were shooting parts after the point where Redford's character, Waldo Pepper, and Bo Svenson, who played Pepper's rival Axel Olsson, had been grounded from flying. At this time, Svenson's character came up with the idea for the two of them to go to Hollywood and become stuntmen, talking Redford's character into it and hoping they both could make some good money.

There was a scene where the two of them were on a balcony, and Svenson throws a roundhouse punch at Redford, knocking him over the balcony. Redford falls about fifteen feet and crashes into a table where people are sitting. As the two of them are looking down, sizing the situation up, Redford says to Svenson, "why don't I throw *you* over the balcony?" to which Svenson replies that Redford is the better double for the actor.

I call this type of stunt an "ass-buster." I went to George Roy Hill and asked him if we could cover the table with a tablecloth so I could put a cardboard box, 24 by 24 inches square, under the table to help cushion my fall. He said no, so I had the effects guy score each leg of the table by sawing halfway through them, so that the table would break into pieces when I hit it.

Thank God for my gymnastic abilities! I knew I had to hit that table flat on my back to distribute my weight evenly. I went up on the balcony and got ready. All to soon, I heard "*action!*"

Bo threw the roundhouse, and I snapped back into the air, pivoting my body in the air so I'd fall flat onto the table. *Crash, boom, bam!* went the table, and I'll tell you, it was like that table was never there. I smashed into the floor beneath it and did *not* want to get up. It hadn't really knocked the wind out of me, but son of a bitch, did it hurt! I got up as quickly as I could bring myself to, and walked outside, quick. Once outside, I squeezed my eyes shut and screamed as loud as I could, then rolled my neck around, rotated my shoulders and twisted my hips back and forth. Fortunately, nothing was broken, I was okay, but *man*, did I hurt!

Just then, Bob Redford came out the stage door, shaking his head. "Are you okay, Mick?" he asked me.

"Yeah, I'm fine," I told him, taking a deep breath.

He smiled. "That's the wildest, wickedest thing I think I've ever seen you do," he told me. "Everybody in there can't believe you just got up and walked away from it!"

One of the assistants came out to join us right then and told me the director wanted to see me, so we went back inside. When we got in there, everyone on the crew burst into applause.

I went up to George Roy Hill, and he said, "do you want the good news or the bad news, Mickey?"

"I don't want *any* news," I said dryly, trying to ignore how much my body hurt just then.

THE GREAT WALDO PEPPER

"Well, the good news is that was a fuckin' *wild* shot," he said, clearly pleased with the job I'd done. "The bad news is that nobody sitting at the surrounding tables reacted to it—so we're going to have to do it again."

I stood there for a minute, looking at the floor, then took a deep breath. I glanced over at Bob, and then, eyeballing him for a minute, I asked, "are you sure *you* don't want to do this?" Everyone laughed, and I did, too. "Okay, let's fix the table like we had it before, and get this over with." I looked around at all the people who were on camera, put my hands together as if in prayer and said silently to them, *please, please,* please *react when I hit the table!*

As I prepared myself for another take, I pretty much had it figured out how I was going to twist myself in mid-air to land flat on my back again. "*Action!*" I got airborne and hit table perfectly. The only thing wrong with this take was that sudden, bone-jarring stop when I hit the floor.

"Cut, cut," George called. "Perfect! Are you all right?"

"Yeah, yeah, I'm all right," I groaned as Redford helped me up.

"I don't see how you can do that, twice, then just get up and walk away from it," Bob said, brushing me off. "That has to have hurt you."

"You know why I can get up and walk away from it, Bob?" I asked him. "Because I have legions of angels with me, all the way down."

That all being said, throwing myself fifteen feet down to land flat on my back on a table, then a floor, was not something I relished. Boy, was I glad that I only had to do it twice!

The Wind and the Lion

I got a call from my buddy Terry Leonard in the mid-seventies inviting me to work on a film he was doing the stunt supervision on called *The Wind and the Lion,* starring Sean Connery, Candice Bergen and Brian Keith, with the film's writer John Milius doing the directing as well. *The Wind and the Lion* is a period epic which takes place in Morocco in 1904, during a time of conflict with the most powerful nations in Europe. Sean Connery's character, the Berber brigand Mulai Ahmed er Raisuli, is leading an insurrection against the Sultan, and he kidnaps Candice Bergen's character, American Eden Pedecaris and her children in a bid for ransom. Terry said he wanted to bring a few guys over to Spain for the stunts, and I was more than happy to oblige when he asked me to be one of them.

I hopped on a plane with Jim Sheppard and Larry Randles, and we headed for Spain.

One of the stunts Terry wanted to do involved jumping a horse through a garden window during the kidnapping sequence. The window was about eight feet high and twelve feet long. We planned to use breakaway glass, of course, but Terry was having difficulties—he couldn't even get the horse to go near the glass, let alone jump through it.

"You know, Terry, we should've trained him with some cellophane first," I pointed out, referring to a trick I'd use on other films to get horses comfortable jumping through break-away glass. The horse gets used to walking through slits cut into the cellophane, so that when he's asked to go through glass, he doesn't spook and shy away from it.

"No, no, I'm gonna do something else," Terry said. "I'm going to get a Ping-Pong ball and cut it in half, and we'll paint it to look like a horse's eye, but I'll use it as blinders and make him go through."

I fought back a laugh. "Where the hell did you come up with an idea like *that?*" I asked.

He shrugged. "Sometimes, you've gotta do what you've gotta do."

Terry did exactly what he'd said, running the horse blind at the window, holding his head up high with the reins so he wouldn't trip along the way, but the ground was not flush with the window—it was a little lower on the ground side than the inside, so when the horse landed after jumping through the glass, he stumbled and fell a bit, Terry going off over his head because the horse couldn't see where he was going. In the end, Terry got the shot he'd wanted to get, but that sequence always bothered me a bit, because with all the things that stunt coordinators go through to get the results they want on camera, it seemed to me that there would've been a way to get it that was easier on, and safer for, the animal.

Having gotten the shot he wanted via his rather unconventional Ping-Pong ball method, Terry moved us on to another stunt. They'd built a fortress on the beach for the film, and the fortress had huge ramps built into it used by horse-drawn caissons to move cannons up into position at the ramparts. There would be a battle sequence filmed here, of epic proportions.

One of our stuntmen, Larry Randles, had just finished participating in a live-action Wild West show back east; his part in the show had been performing drag stunts (coming down out of his saddle and being dragged behind or alongside the horse from his stirrup). He did three drags a day, six days a week, for about a month, and by the end of it he was a pro at being dragged. So, naturally, Terry decided to use him for a drag stunt in this film—he'd be riding with a group of Arabs and be shot out of his saddle, then be dragged along by his stirrup. I went up to him with a suggestion.

ME AND MY SADDLE-PAL

"Hey, Larry, why don't I ride along in that group you're in, and I can have a cable attached to your horse's bridle, so if something goes wrong, I've got a safety line in place to help you out."

"Oh, no, no, that's okay, Mickey," he told me. "I've done hundreds of these. Hell, I did 'em three times a *day* back east. I'll be fine."

"I know you've done them a lot, Larry, but it doesn't hurt to be safe," I pointed out. "Besides, you'll have other riders all around you—no one will see if I've got a cable on your horse's bridle. Or, I can have a cable on the d-ring of your saddle, too, and ride behind you, so that if something happens I can release the whole saddle from the horse, and you along with it. Why take the chance?"

He waved me off again. "I'll be fine, Mick. I know what I'm doing," he insisted.

When they went to film the drag, I glanced through the cameras they had set up and noticed a problem—with the way they were filming it, and with the cluster of other riders around Larry, the drag wouldn't be caught properly on camera. Larry would simply appear to have fallen off his horse in the charge, and perhaps get caught up in his stirrup just before he went out of frame.

I went to Terry with my concerns, but he didn't share them, but it bothered me that all this hard work was going to be put in by Larry and the results weren't going to be what he and Terry envisioned. I had an idea.

When I'd worked on the pervious Charles Bronson film, *Chino*, also filmed in Spain, I'd trained several horses for that show that were all still in the area with a Gypsy wrangler I knew named Medina. I contacted him and asked after a few horses in particular—a little bay I'd trained for drag stunts, and a fleet-footed red roan I could rope off of. I told Medina I planned to have Larry on the bay, and I'd ride the roan as an outrider, ready to ride to Larry's rescue if something went wrong. Medina brought the horses over after a couple days of shooting some battle sequences, and we got ready to do Larry's drag.

Larry was outfitted with a special trip cable coming up from his boot that went up his pant-leg and attached to his wardrobe, that he

THE WIND AND THE LION

could use to release himself from the unit hooked to the horse when he was ready to stop being dragged along. I cautioned Larry that he was in for a different experience than the drags he'd been so used to in the states, because the surface he was using was different. "You're in sand, now, Larry," I said, "not arena dirt. The sand will be going up into your eyes while you're being dragged, and you've got all that loose Arab clothing on, so it's going to be harrier than all those drags you did in the Wild West show. I'm not trying to scare you or anything, but I want to be ready in case something goes wrong."

"I'll be fine, Mick," he kept telling me. "I got it."

I told Terry I was going to ride out off camera and keep an eye on things. Terry called *action,* and Larry came down off his horse.

He landed on his side first, then popped over flat onto his face. Now he was being dragged full-speed with sand going straight up his nose—God only knew what *that* felt like, but I'm sure it wasn't pleasant. After a moment he hit another little rise in the sand and flopped onto his back, still being dragged at full-speed. He was well out of the camera-frame now, so I took off to help.

Everyone was charging toward the fort, Larry's horse included, and as I rode up and leaned down to grab the bay's bridle above the bit and rescue Larry, I noticed something a little alarming; Larry's horse was heading straight for one of the forty-foot wooden pilings that were leaning in against the fort's walls. These things were like telephone poles. I was more concerned about getting ahold of Larry's horse at the moment, though, and I finally grabbed the bridle and pulled the horse's head into me as we headed for the piling. Unfortunately, Larry had popped to the left, and he went on one side of the piling, while me, my horse and *his* horse all went on the other, with the drag unit running between us.

You can imagine the wreck *that* caused. The whole rig tore out of the saddle, and Larry was badly injured. He ended up with a broken leg, a broken collarbone, and a concussion—he was out like a light. We got an ambulance in there and they hauled him off to the hospital, and once the day's work was finished Terry and I went to see him.

ME AND MY SADDLE-PAL

Larry was a bronc rider, he'd been busted up before, so this didn't put too big a damper on him, but it *did* take him out of working on the film, of course. The minute we walked into his hospital room he looked at me and shook his head. "Why the hell didn't I listen to you?" he asked.

"Because you've done a whole bunch of these, and you think nothing can go wrong," I told him. "I don't care how many times you do a stunt, there is always that *once* that it's not going to work. I don't care how experienced you are, either—it happens to all of us. It's happened to *me*. You get comfortable—and get careless, 'cause you think it's gonna be just like every other time you've ever done it before. That's what happened here. But you've *always* got to think of your safety."

"You're right," he sighed.

"How're you feeling?" I asked him.

He shrugged. "I feel okay. Pain pills help. I'm just sad that I can't perform on this picture any longer. I suppose you'll be shipping me off soon, huh?" he asked Terry.

"Yeah, Larry, I'll have to. I can't keep you on salary if you can't work, so we'll need to get you home once you're on your feet." That was the end of Larry Randles on *The Wind and the Lion*.

I still had a lot of work to do, though, and so did Terry and the rest of the guys. The big battle charge sequence was a busy one for me; I can't tell you how many horse falls I did. These were done with toe-tappers.

A toe-tapper is a getup made of interconnecting cables that allows the stuntman riding the horse to precisely control the timing of the horse's fall. The horse has to be shod to wear one; cables are run down the back of each foreleg (taped to keep them snugly in place), and then run between the shoe and the horse's hoof, sticking out in front of the hoof, with a washer placed to prevent the cable from pulling back through. Cables are attached together between the horse's two front legs. From the cables that are tied together, there's a single cable that continues up alongside the horse, that the rider can attach a handle to. Then, at the moment the rider wants the horse to go down, he pulls up on the toe-tapper and holds it. This pins the animal's front feet up against its body, so it goes down on its knees. The cables are never seen by the camera, so it's not obvious to the audience that the horse is going down on purpose. To the movie-goer, it looks like natural fall—and it looks exciting and adds a great element of drama to any battle or chase sequence involving riders on horseback. The toe-tapper element was something we invented as up-and-coming stunt guys to take the place of older getups like the running W my father-in-law had invented, and it worked really well.

The battle sequence was so big and had so many different riders involved that I really had to stay on my toes and pay attention to the way Terry was coordinating all the different stunts. One of the stunts he had me doing was a saddle-fall, where it was going to look like I'd gotten shot out of my saddle during the charge. I was to fall to the right when I did it. A problem arose, though. One of the other stuntmen was going to fall a horse to the left at just about the same time and in the same position. One of our other guys, a Spanish stuntman and stunt coordinator by the name of Juan Maján, whom I loved working with, was immediately concerned about this. Juan was always keeping track of any potential dangers in the stunts we were performing, and he came to me right away.

"Mickey, if he falls that horse to the left as you're going off your saddle to the right, you're gonna get crushed. The horse is gonna land right on top of you."

"I know, Juan," I said. "I'm gonna talk to Terry and see if I can be on the other side of him. That way I can fall freely to the right, and he can fall freely to the left without danger."

I went to Terry and told him what the problem was. He started to wave me off, to tell me I could stay out of the other guy's way, but I was insistent. I wanted to *finish* this movie and get paid for it, not end up going home early—and going home hurt—like Larry. "Besides, Terry," I said, "what difference does it make if we do it the safer way? You've got all these horses in here as it is. You think the public's gonna know we switched it?"

ME AND MY SADDLE-PAL

He gave in. "Okay, okay, you're right. Go ahead."

I had to do this with Terry quite a bit, change things around to make them more feasible, but I never was shy about speaking up. In my business, if you notice something potentially dangerous and you keep your mouth shut, you could pay for it later—both literally and figuratively.

One of the big horse scenes we did on *The Wind and the Lion* involved explosives going off around us as we rode. The special effects guys rigged up metal casings about two feet in diameter and about one and a half to two feet deep and filled them with pieces of cork. When they hit the buttons and detonated them, the cork created a dramatic look as it exploded. We could see where the explosives were placed, so when we got near them, we'd activate the toe-tappers on our horses and fall them as the "bombs" were going off to look like we'd been blown off our horses by the explosives.

During this charge we were carrying flags, and each flag was attached to a tall staff. When you're riding a horse that's wearing a toe-tapper, you need one hand for your reins and the other to operate the toe-tapper. You certainly don't have a free hand to carry a staff. I made it easier for myself by cutting the staff on my flag down so it was only a foot or two long, that way I could carry it with my reins and have my toe-tapper hand unhindered. Jim Sheppard and some of the other guys followed suit and cut theirs down, too. But our stubborn stunt coordinator, Terry, left his whole. When I asked him how he intended to manage it and the horse and the toe-tapper, he told me he'd stick the end of the shaft in his boot.

"But that's dangerous," I said. "When you fall, that thing's gonna whack the hell out of you. Just cut it down, save yourself the risk."

"Nah, it'll be fine." He waved me off.

"Okay, Terry," I said with a shrug, and mounted my horse.

We did the charge, all of us falling and rolling on cue. When the dust cleared and the shot was done, I heard loud groaning coming from nearby. I looked around and saw Terry laying flat on his back, the shaft of his flag laying across his collarbone—which was broken. I went over to him.

THE WIND AND THE LION

"How'd that shaft in your boot work out, Terry?" I asked him, unable to resist needling him a bit even though I knew he was hurt pretty bad.

"I think it's broken," he moaned.

"Of course it's broken. You've gotta go see the medic, get it set. Told you you should've cut your staff down."

"Oh, shut up!" he retorted.

Terry kept working on the film, but after that he just coordinated the stunts, he couldn't perform any of them himself like he had been doing. Up until that point he'd been Sean Connery's double, but after that injury I took over that job.

Another interesting thing that happened on *The Wind and the Lion* involved our director, John Milius, who was a great guy and a pleasure to work with. He loved all of us stuntmen and he wanted to try his hand at a stunt. He got Terry on board with the idea, and they dressed him up like a Foreign Legion officer who'd be shooting at the Arabs charging into the fort on horseback. His plan was to portray being shot and go tumbling down the sandy embankment next to the fort, out of control, and land right at the cameras.

I came up with a joke to play on him, and I got all the cameramen and the other stunt guys in on it. I told them I knew John was going to go big on this stunt—he wanted so badly to do it. But I told everyone to act like he hadn't done a very good job—even if he had. So John went and did the stunt, and it was *great*. We couldn't have done it better ourselves. But when John got up, brushed the sand off his costume, shook it out of his hair and spat it out of his mouth, and looked to us for approval, we all kept our faces serious.

"Well? How was it?" he asked eagerly.

We all glanced at each other. "Well...it kind of looked like you were trying too hard on that tumble down the sand bank, John," I said, and Terry nodded. The cameramen all put their two cents in, too, telling Milius they though the shot hadn't looked that great.

His face fell. "Really? I thought I did a pretty good job," he said, crestfallen.

ME AND MY SADDLE-PAL

"We should do it again, John," Terry said.

We got everything all set up again, and *bam*, here comes John, tumbling wildly down the embankment, going for broke. Again, he stood up and looked at all of us. "Well?"

We tried to keep the joke going, but we couldn't hold in our laughter. John looked at us all like we were nuts. "What's going on here?" he asked suspiciously.

"You did *great*, John," Terry chuckled. "The first one was perfect. In fact, none of us could've done it any better."

"Why did you say it was so bad, then?" he asked, totally confused.

"You were so keen to do the stunt, John," I said through my laughter, "so we wanted to see if you'd do it again!"

"You *assholes!*" John said, shaking his head, but he was a pretty good sport, when all was said and done. That memory still makes me chuckle to this day. I'm good at what I do; I do my work well, but I like things to be light-hearted, and I *do* enjoy a good joke.

⁂

Terry had his wife with him on the shoot, and she liked to keep him home at nights, which was fine, but he was under a lot of pressure, working hard, and I got the idea that he should come out one night with me and the other boys for a few drinks—just guys, no girls allowed. We weren't planning on getting too wild, but we wanted some "guy time." I knew Terry's wife Jan, whom he'd nicknamed "The Bomber," wouldn't be on board with that at all, and I knew we'd have to come up with a plan if we wanted Terry to come with us.

"Here's what we're gonna do, Terry," I said slyly. "I'm gonna call you up tonight and pretend I'm Juan Lopez at the production office. I'm gonna tell you that John needs you down there tonight to go over some shots. You'll make a big deal about needing to stay home with your wife, but then you'll give in and say you're coming down."

He laughed and agreed to it, and at about seven that night I called

Terry's number. His wife answered, so I put on my best Spanish accent and sprinkled my sentences with just enough Spanish words to be convincing. "Oh, hello, Señora Leonard, this is Juan Lopez in the production *oficina*. Is Señor Leonard *aqui en la casa?*"

"Oh, hello, Juan, just a minute." She went to get him.

He got on the phone. "Who is this?" he asked.

"Who do you think it is?" I asked, in my normal voice. "It's Juan Lopez. Now play along with me!"

"Oh, Juan, does it have to be tonight? I was hoping to spend the evening with my wife."

"I'll meet you at the Buffalo Bar at seven-thirty," I told him, chuckling.

"The meeting's going to last *how* long?" Terry asked in dismay, his voice loud, so his wife would be sure and hear. "Two *hours?* Well, okay, I'll be there."

"You'd *better* be there, buddy," I said. "Is Jan buying it?"

"Yeah. I'll be there," he repeated, and hung up.

She didn't catch on, and Terry joined us that night with no repercussions. We had a great time knocking back a few beers and shooting the breeze. I never did find out if Terry's wife ever found out what he was really doing that night.

Rooster Cogburn

By the mid-seventies I'd done stunts in a whole lot of Westerns, so when you think about it, it's pretty fitting that I ended up working with The Duke himself—John Wayne, the actor who is likely associated more closely with the big-screen Western than any other in history. In 1975, Universal Pictures released *Rooster Cogburn,* starring not only Wayne, as the marshal Rueben J. "Rooster" Cogburn, but screen legend Katharine Hepburn, as well. The film was directed by Stuart Millar and was a sequel the John Wayne classic *True Grit.* The stunt coordinator on the film, Jerry Gatlin, needed about six of us to go up to Grant's Pass, Oregon, to do some action sequences for it.

We had to get fitted for costumes, of course, and I gathered up some of my own pieces, chaps and things, to take along before I went—it was not uncommon in those days for those of us who'd worked on a lot of Westerns to have things we were comfortable in that looked good in those types of movies. We'd bring them along to the costume department, and the costume designer would decide if we could wear them or not during the actual film.

I met up with the rest of the stuntmen at western costume, and as we sat around for awhile in front of the big mirrors after we'd gotten into our outfits, waiting for our stills to be taken, one of the actors, whose name I won't reveal, walked in and asked if we were working on the film. I told him we were, and that we would be doing stunts in the film.

ROOSTER COGBURN

It's no secret that there is a lot of ego in Hollywood, and some of the more visible people in the industry, like the actors and the studio big shots, aren't shy about letting theirs show. It takes the hard work of *everyone* involved in the production of a movie just to get it made—not to mention making it into a great movie. Sometimes movie stars can lose sight of that and forget to think about all the contributions made by folks behind the scenes, like the stuntmen. I've always been turned off by ego and entitlement, and this particular actor showed me both of those things thirty seconds after I'd met him.

He was a big guy, about six-four, and he had an air of cockiness about him that came out right away in the first conversation we had with him. He was from New York and he'd done quite a bit of acting back there, but *Rooster Cogburn,* he informed us all, would be his first Western. They'd liked his look, he said, and had called him in for the film to play the leader of the outlaw gang that would square off against John Wayne. For some reason it seemed to be important to him that me and the other guys knew he was playing the *leader*, because he told us twice. I wasn't impressed.

"Okay," I said, wanting to roll my eyes, but I didn't. "Are you here to get fitted?" I asked him, and he nodded. "Well, the head wardrobe guy is in the back, his name's Lester," I told him helpfully, "and he'll get you all fitted up. You know what?" I said, "with your size, you'd look good in all black."

He raised an eyebrow at me. "You think so, huh?" he asked, checking himself out in the mirrors. I could tell he was imagining how he'd look.

"Well, yeah," I said. "You know, like Black Bart, and all those guys in the old Westerns. Lester will fix you right up, just tell him you saw us all out here."

When the actor came back out, he was dressed in all black, just like I'd suggested—black boots, black pants, black shirt, black vest. All he was missing was the black hat. I asked him about that as he turned this way and that, admiring himself, and he told me Lester had taken his head measurement, but he'd have to have the hat made.

"But it'll be black," he added. "You know, you were right, I *do* look good in black."

"Oh, you *do,*" I said earnestly. "You look like a million bucks!"

Behind me, the other stuntmen were glancing at one another, and I could tell they were trying not to laugh. I could almost hear what they were thinking—*what the hell is Gilbert doing here?* I turned back to the actor.

"There's a prop guy here, too," I said enthusiastically. "You should ask him for a black holster—or maybe even two of them, so you can have one gun on each side. Then you can draw them both at once, like this." I stood next to him and mimed a quick draw. He was nodding, clearly liking the idea. Off he went to talk to the prop man about his two black holsters.

While he was gone, Gary McLarty, one of my stunt buddies, gave me a look. "What are you *doing* to that guy?" he asked me, laughing.

"Oh, I haven't even *started* with him," I said slyly. "Just you wait till he comes back out here."

Out he came, a black holster on each hip. The holsters were empty, I noticed. "Where're your guns?" I asked. "Didn't he show them to you?"

"Oh, he didn't have them here with him, but he said they're really nice," Jordan said.

I looked him over. "I was thinking, while you were gone," I told him. "You'd look good in chaps, too."

He repeated the word, pronouncing it like the British *chap*. I explained that it was pronounced "shap," and told him what they were for. "Go on back to Lester," I suggested, "and tell him to put you in some black batwing chaps. They'll have big silver conchos up the sides, and man, with your height, you'll look fantastic!" Off he went.

As soon as he was gone, the other guys started chuckling. "Mickey, you're going to *kill* this guy!" they told me. "It's going to be a hundred degrees up in Grant's Pass when we're filming!"

"Yep," I said, grinning at the thought of him being taken down just a peg or two. "When he steps out of wardrobe in all his black shit, with

ROOSTER COGBURN

those huge chaps on, he's going to start sweating like a pig, and those two guns'll be *really* heavy on his hips."

Sure enough, out comes the actor in his huge, black, batwing chaps. Lester had figured out what was going on, since the guy kept coming back for more stuff. The actor was from New York, so Lester knew he didn't know anything about Western wear.

Once there were no more black additions for me to helpfully suggest adding to his costume, he finished his fitting and got ready to leave.

"Well, we'll see ya up in Grant's Pass," I told him, and he nodded.

"Okay, thanks for all the suggestions," he said, and left, leaving us chuckling. Lester came out and gave us a knowing look.

"What the heck are you boys *doing* to that poor guy?" he asked.

"Well, we just wanted to give him something to remember us by, once we all get up there in that heat," I said innocently. Lester shook his head.

We went out to Grant's Pass, and when we got there we all said hello to John Wayne, who knew us and liked us by then (we'd worked with him before). Then, along came the actor from the costume fitting, dressed to the hilt in all of his black outlaw regalia.

Well, most of it. He'd forgotten the batwing chaps. Lester came running out of the wardrobe trailer, holding them up. "Hey, wait! You forgot your chaps!"

He put them on, and then faced the rather momentous task of getting onto his horse while wearing them. The bulky, heavy leather made it hard to mount up, and it took him several tries. He finally got up there, though, and started the shoot. By the end of it, he was really feeling the heat, like a flower wilting under the sun's rays—we could see him fanning his face and pulling his black neckerchief away from his neck. I had to give him credit for working all day in that getup. The next day he came out in the outfit again, only no guns, and no chaps. Once again Lester came running out after him, holding the chaps out, but this time, the actor refused.

"The chaps are too hot; I don't want to wear them."

"But you've already started with them on," Lester protested, concerned about the continuity of the costumes in the finished product.

"I'm going to the director," the actor replied. "I don't want them on."

Lester relented, but then the prop master came out with the two heavy pistols. "Here are your guns," he said.

"I don't want those on yet," he said. "They're so *heavy!* Don't you have some rubber ones, or something, that are lighter?"

The rest of the stuntmen and I were overhearing all this and cracking up over it, and every day it went on a little further; the actor was sick of the part and sick of his wardrobe. I was never sure if he made the connection that I'd suggested all those things knowing full well what would happen, but maybe he'd feel just a little less entitled the next time he did a Western—if he ever did another one after this.

During the filming of *Rooster Cogburn,* I worked with John Wayne's stunt double, Chuck Roberson. His close physical resemblance to the Duke led to a nearly thirty-year career as his double. He was a good guy who was pleasant to work with, and on this shoot I ended up learning an interesting trick from him.

Nearly every evening I would see him walking past my hotel window, heading toward a phone booth nearby, and I always wondered why he was using a phone booth when he had a phone in his room. About the third or fourth time I saw him do it, I figured something was up, so I went downstairs to investigate. I hung back a little so he wouldn't see me, and I noticed that he had something stuck into the rotary dial of the phone. I saw him twist it a certain way and pocket something, and then he started heading back toward the hotel after he'd finished his phone call. He saw me there and stopped short, looking like a kid caught with his hand in a cookie jar.

"What are you doing, Chuck? Why're you always on the pay phone when you've got a phone in your room?" I asked him with a laugh, peering at the thing in his hand that he'd stuck into the phone's dial. It looked like a piece of wire that was mostly straight except for a forty-five degree angle at the end. "What is that?"

He gave me a sly smile. "It's a safety-pin," he said, showing it to me. He'd unwound it and bent it into its present shape.

I was puzzled. "Why the hell were you sticking a safety-pin into the telephone dial?" I asked, totally lost.

His smile got even slyer. "There's a trick I know to make free phone calls on a pay phone," he said. "I'll show you if you don't let anyone know you saw me doing it."

I had to see *this*. "I won't," I promised. "Let me see."

He explained to me that there was a magnet inside the phone that would release the coins the caller had deposited back into the coin return, and the safety-pin, when inserted correctly and twisted a certain way, would move that magnet and send the coins back to the caller after the operator had put the call through. "So a call that costs you two dollars will cost you zip," he said proudly.

I started laughing. "That's *great*, Chuck!" I told him. I passed the trick on to Gary McLarty, and from then on, wherever we were, we never paid for a single phone call we had to make on a pay phone.

<hr />

There was a U.S. Forestry Service employee on set that could get us access to different locations; he also was around to make sure nobody started a forest fire with a cigarette or something of that nature. He had a pair of breeding Labradors, and the female had recently had a litter. I told him I'd love to take a puppy, and he told me he only had one left—a little female. He brought her out to me one morning, and I liked the look of her—nice shiny black coat and big paws. I agreed to take her, but the Ranger had to keep her during the day while I was

ME AND MY SADDLE-PAL

working. That didn't last for too long, though, because I got an idea one day when I saw Katharine Hepburn on set.

Katie, as we all called her, was a wonderful, unique person, and she got to know all of us pretty well. When she wasn't working on the movie she'd take her fishing gear and head down to the river; she loved the outdoors and fishing was one of her favorite pastimes. I thought it might be nice for her to have some company while she fished, so I told her about the puppy and asked if she'd like to take her fishing with her the next time she went out. She was delighted, and for the next few days I sent the little pup out with Katie when she went down to the river. After about three days I told Katie that we had a name for her, finally.

"Well, what is it?" she asked.

"Katie Hep," I told her, smiling.

She laughed and told me I was crazy, but she also said with a smile that she approved of the name. From then on, Katie Hep the actress and Katie Hep the dog were great fishing buddies.

Besides the puppy, I had another interesting side-project while making this film; My buddy Gary McLarty, one of the other stuntmen, had started a little antiques business while we were staying in Bend. We brought our trucks and horse trailers, and, working out of the hotel we were staying in and using our stage names (he was Emmett, I was Hambone), we put out ads in the local paper seeking antiques to purchase and take back to L.A. to sell later. We paid the switchboard operator at the hotel to take any calls that our ads generated while we were out working on the movie, and then on the weekends we'd go pick up whatever folks wanted to sell. We had fun when we did that, getting dressed up in beat-up boots and overalls and putting tobacco in our cheeks—we had to look the part, after all, because we figured with names like Emmett and Hambone, that's what folks would be expecting. We ended up with quite a haul, too—beautiful old oak furniture, antique pot-bellied stoves, turned glass, and lots of really beautiful, really unique items.

We met some unique people during our buying adventures, too.

ROOSTER COGBURN

One day Gary and I were out exploring, and we came across a vacant farmhouse. We glanced in the window and caught sight of a man inside—and he was about the *only* thing inside. I waved at him and he came to the door. I gave him a story about Gary and I moving up to the area (I told him we were building a cabin by the river), and that we were looking for furnishings for our place.

"Do you have any old furniture you'd be willing to part with?" I asked him.

He shook his head. "Fact is, my wife's just left me, and she took all my furniture. She really cleaned house—left me with nothing. I don't even have a bed to sleep on," he drawled, gesturing to the empty house. I felt sorry for the poor guy, so I offered him an antique brass bed we'd gotten during one of our antique-hunting adventures. "Then at least you'll have a bed," I told him, and he thanked us profusely, clearly grateful for the kind gesture.

We kept buying more stuff, and in the end the horse trailer wouldn't cut it—I ended up renting a U-Haul for all the antiques I took back to California, and the antiques-buying adventures of Emmett and Hambone created quite a side-note to my stunt work on *Rooster Cogburn*.

Breakheart Pass

In 1975 I got a call from Don Guest, a production manager I'd worked with several times before who was a friend of mine; he was interested in having me do some stunts on a film called *Breakheart Pass,* a western starring Charles Bronson. They were filming in Lewiston, Idaho.

"I've got a sword-fight stunt for you to do," he said. "I'll need you and one other guy. We'll fly you out here for a day's work on this show, then fly you back."

"Sure, Don, let me call Terry Leonard," I said, "and I'll call you right back."

I called Terry, and his wife answered. Terry was a car enthusiast, and she told me he was just loading up his race car, getting ready to take it out and practice with it for a couple of days. "I'll go catch him," she said, and set the phone down. A few minutes later, Terry came on the line, and I told him I had a job for the two of us, a sword-fight on horseback.

"I figure we'll go up there in about a week or so, Terry, if you're free," he said.

"Sure, Mick, I'm free. That sounds fine."

I told him I'd finalize things with Guest, then hung up and called the production manager back. "Terry's free," I said, "so we're all good."

"Great! You know, I think they might be ready for you a bit sooner, though. Can you come in three days?"

BREAKHEART PASS

I knew I'd have to hurry to call Terry back if I was going to catch him before he left. I hung up quick with Don and dialed Terry's number again.

"Has he left yet?" I asked his wife urgently.

"He's just pulling out of the driveway. Hold on, I'll run and catch him."

When Terry came back on the line I could almost hear the puzzled expression he must've been wearing. "What is it, Gilbert?" he asked.

"I just talked to Don again," I told him, "and he wants us there in three days. I needed to make sure you were free that soon."

"Yeah, I'm free. Tell him it's fine."

"Okay, thanks." I hung up and dialed Don again. "We're fine, Don," I said. "Terry's good in three days."

"Okay," he said, "but you know, Mick, now that I think about it…" *Oh, you've gotta be kidding me!* "Can you two be ready to come out tomorrow?"

"Oh, for the love of God, Don!" I said in exasperation. "Let me call Leonard again…"

Terry hadn't made it back outside yet, I guess, because he came to the phone right away after his wife answered, once again. "For God's sake, Gilbert, what the hell is going *on?*" Terry asked me. "This is the third time—"

"I know, I know, but Guest keeps changing his mind. Now he wants us there tomorrow," I said hurriedly. "It's such a quick thing, Terry. We'll be in and out of Lewiston before you know it, and home the next day."

"Okay, okay," he said. "I'm not going to bring my stunt bag with me, or anything, if it's that quick."

"Neither am I," I told him. "We don't need anything. I'll call Don back now, and then you'll hear later today about the flight. I'll see you at LAX in the morning."

"Okay." We hung up, and I called Don *again,* and we were on a flight bright and early the next morning.

When we arrived in Lewiston, we were met by a driver whom I'd met before. He told us we were going to head to the hotel for lunch, and then he would take us out to wardrobe to get fitted for our costumes. After lunch he drove us about an hour out of town to the big tent serving as wardrobe for the film.

Jimmy George, one of the costumers, met us and pulled our sword-fighting costumes from the rack; he already had our sizes since he'd worked with us before. We took them and started to head off, but Jimmy stopped us. "Whoa, you're not done yet," he said. He proceeded to pull out Cavalry uniforms and Indian costumes, after that.

"Wait a minute, Jimmy," I protested, darting a look at Terry. "We're not doing all that! We were told we were just going to double the two actors for the sword-fight!"

He chuckled a little and kept handing us the costumes. "Well, these are your costumes for the time you'll be here," he said.

"But we're only going to be here for a day," I argued. "Just the sword-fight."

"Well, go ahead and take these, anyway," Jimmy insisted, which I thought was odd. Now I was starting to get a little worried, but we did as he said.

They put us on a train next, costumes in hand, to be taken out to the area where the set was. It was around twenty-five or thirty miles away from where the wardrobe tent was. As we went, I caught Terry's eye. "Are you starting to suspect anything, Leonard?" I asked dryly.

"Just a little bit," he replied, just as dryly. "It's sure not turning out the way you described it to me!"

"I know," I said.

We arrived on set, and the minute we stepped off the train, we were met by Yakima Canutt, an old-time stunt coordinator. "Boy, am I glad to see you boys!" he said, shaking our hands enthusiastically. "Now I've got someone who can do all these horse falls!"

"Wait a second," I said again, repeating what I'd told Jimmy George back at wardrobe. "We're not going to be here for more than a day. We just signed on to do the sword-fighting scene."

"Oh, no, now that I've got you out here, I need you for way more than that. You got your wardrobe all set?" he asked us with a grin.

Terry and I looked down at our collection of costumes, then at each other, and started laughing. *This* was going to be interesting! "We didn't bring any of our pads and equipment we need," I told Canutt, but he waved me off.

"We'll borrow some from the other stuntmen. I've got a whole bunch of them out here." As he spoke, the other guys all came over and greeted us enthusiastically, telling us they were glad we were there.

"Well," I said to Terry as we got into our first costumes, "I guess we're in for it!"

We completed our sword fight, or "click-clack," as we call it in the industry, in about an hour, then moved on to other things. We did horse falls, somersaults off of horses, feigned getting shot off of horses—you name it. All told, we were there for about a week and a half, which we turned out not to mind at all, since we were making about twenty-five hundred dollars a day in pay. Every day we had to borrow some other piece of protective equipment, it seemed, and I don't know how many times we hit the ground, but we just laughed about it, because it really did turn out to be a good job for both of us.

They were shooting in hundreds of acres of potato fields, where they grew the big Idaho potatoes. The production had struck a deal with the potato farmers to use the fields for shooting. We'd been working for three or four days with nice dry weather, when, overnight, we had a snow-storm. We took the train back out to the location the next morning, and of course, everything was white and snowy. This would be a problem for continuity—the landscape would suddenly look very different than it had in all the other footage we'd gotten.

Our director, Tom Gries, looked around for a minute, then turned to all of us. "You know what, boys? Let's just start all over with the stunts," he said.

Terry and I looked at each other and burst into laughter.

"What?" he asked. "What's so funny?"

"Nothing. Long story," I said through my laughter, shaking my head. We got moving and started doing all the same stunts over again, in the snow, this time. Which would've been great and all—if the sun hadn't come out right in the middle of it and melted all the snow. Gries looked around again and said, "well, let's just pick up where we left off before, when it was dry."

You're seeing a pattern with this film by now, I'm sure.

It ended up snowing again, so again we had to pick up where we'd left off with the snow. I guessed money wasn't an object with this production, because they just kept us going on and on, both in the snow and dry ground, because the sun came out again and dried everything up for a second time. Leonard and I really didn't care too much, because when all was said and done, we were laughing all the way to the bank.

Eventually they had more footage in the snow than not, so to finish they shipped out boxcar after boxcar full of Perlite, a white, flaky fertilizer. They had tractors spreading it all over the fields to stand in for snow. It turned out to be terrible for the studio, though, because it ruined the potato fields. The farmers who owned the ones they spread it on couldn't make a crop for several years because of it, and the studio ended up having to compensate them for it. It was a high price to pay for fake snow.

Towards the end of my time on the shoot there was a stunt they wanted me to do involving an actor named Doug Atkins, who was playing the role of a mountain man named Jebbo in the film. Atkins was a former pro football player-turned-actor, and he was a massive guy, standing six-foot-ten and weighing in at almost three hundred pounds. He'd once been a defensive end for the Chicago Bears. In the scene we were to share, I would ride up on horseback and shoot him point-blank in the chest. His response would be to look down at his chest, then rush at me like a bear on the attack and hit my horse in the neck. I would be riding a falling horse, so when Atkins hit him, I'd fall him to make it appear as if Atkins had knocked him over.

Doug was a real gentleman—I guess you could say a gentle giant. I met with him and explained how the stunt would work—he would be wearing a squib that would blow when I fired a blank at him, and I would be on a trained falling horse that would go down on my command when I jerked his head around just so. I told Doug to hit the horse lightly but to try to make it look like he was really punching it hard. "When your fist comes down, I'll fall the horse," I told him. Something made me thing he didn't really understand what I was going to do, but he *said* he did, so I told him we'd rehearse it once, without me actually falling the horse. We did that, and it went smoothly, so we got ready to shoot the scene for real.

I came riding in and fired off my shot, and the squib on Doug's chest blew dramatically. He looked down at it and then back up at me, letting out a growl of rage, and rushed at my horse, bringing his fist down to its neck. As he did so, I snapped the horse's head to the side and *bam!* Down we went.

Before I could get up and let the horse up, I heard Doug cry out, "oh, my God! Are you okay?" he was on his knees, leaning over me.

"*Cut!*" the director yelled. "Doug, what are you *doing?* You're not supposed to do *that!*"

Distressed, Doug looked over at him. "Yeah, but I knocked his horse down—I wanted to make sure he was okay!" I started chuckling. "No, no, Doug, this horse is trained to do this! If I cue him the right way he goes down, just like he did. No one's hurt, the horse is fine, I promise."

"Oh, my God, I thought I'd killed the horse and made him fall on you!" Atkins said, still pretty freaked out. He was such a teddy bear, such a kind, gentle man, that the thought of hurting the horse or me made him terribly upset.

"No, it's okay," I soothed. We had to do it again, of course, without him trying to make sure I was okay after he did it. It came out just fine the second time, but I always remember shooting that scene with gentle Doug. It goes to show you that certain people can be brought onto a film sometimes because they've got the right look for the part, but they won't have a clue as to how we do action sequences in the industry. I've run across instances like that a lot during my career.

ME AND MY SADDLE-PAL

One of the last sequences I was involved in during *Breakheart Pass* was a scene on the train as it's moving, in which I play a Cavalry officer shot by an Indian coming onto the train at the caboose. The director wanted to be in the caboose filming out toward the next car, which I was coming out of. The Indian would shoot me and the impact would sort of spin me around a bit in the open space between the two cars. There were some steps and a railing there, and I suggested to Gries that I could fall down the steps as I got shot. He pointed out that the train would be going over a trestle during the sequence. The trestle was built over a five-hundred foot gorge.

"That's okay," I said, "it'll make the shot look even better if it is."

I've always said, both to my sons and fellow stuntmen, that no matter how many times you've done a similar stunt, you should *never* get overconfident and think that just because the stunt went okay the time before, that means it'll go just as well the next time. I've said it over and over again, you've got to take precautions in this business. But did I listen to my own advice? No. When I spun around and fell down the stairs, I fell farther than I thought I would, and had I not been a gymnast and physically strong to boot, I would've fallen into that five-hundred foot gorge, and that would've been the end.

As I was hanging there, the first thing that came into my mind was how stupid I was for not cabling myself for safety. I swung with my feet to get some momentum and managed to pull myself back up. I was being filmed the entire time—Tom Gries and the crew thought it was great, and that I was doing it all on purpose. As I made it back up onto the train at last, I told them to cut.

"Good God, I didn't know you were going to do all that!" Tom said.

"I wasn't," I told him. "I was saving my ass. It was really stupid of me to take it as far as I did," I admitted.

"We really thought you were gonna fall," he told me soberly.

"I'm sure you did—because I almost *did* fall!" I said.

I told Terry about it on the way back from filming that day, and he said, "that's not like you at all, Gilbert, to take such a risk!"

"I know," I said. "I got careless." I learned a lesson from that day and carried that lesson with me from then on; that's why I've always pounded my "beware of overconfidence" philosophy into my sons' heads over the years—I never wanted them to have a moment like I did, that day on the train. I guess that was one of the biggest things I took away from my work on *Breakheart Pass*.

The Return of a Man Called Horse

Whenever I am asked which of the stunt sequences I'm most proud of having done during my career, I always reply swiftly that the buffalo hunt from the 1976 film *The Return of a Man Called Horse* is it—and I give the same answer when asked which film presented the biggest challenge to me. It's the one that always gets the same reactions when I show it to someone: "wow, that looks amazing!" and "how'd you *do* that?"

Well, I'll tell you.

The film is the second in a trilogy and starred actor Richard Harris with Irvin Kershner directing. The plot involved a British aristocrat named John Morgan, known as Horse to the Sioux, who had become a member of a Lakota Sioux tribe called the Yellow Hand during the previous movie. Harris' character has returned to England by the opening of the second film, but recurring nightmares of his tribe being slaughtered cause him to return to South Dakota, where he finds that many of the warriors have been killed and that the women and children who were spared are starving.

I got a call that they were interested in using me on the film, and was given the script. Then I met with Kershner, who would turn out to be a wonderful director to work with, and with Sandy Howard, the producer.

I envisioned a buffalo hunt sequence for the movie—but not a

THE RETURN OF A MAN CALLED HORSE

simple "sneaking-up-and-shooting" kind of sequence. I wanted to do an epic scene with the warriors and Harris on horseback, running in amidst the herd and shooting buffalo with arrows and spears, and, in Harris's case, a rifle. I didn't want to just show the Indians and Harris on horseback, firing their weapons at the running buffalo; I wanted to show the follow-through as well—the animal going down, the arrows or spears looking as though they had actually pierced the animal's skin. It would lend an air of authenticity to the film and show the way real hunts were conducted by American Indian tribes. The problem was that nothing like that had ever been done before, and making it look realistic without seriously harming the buffalo would be extremely difficult. It presented a real challenge to me as the stunt coordinator—I would have to invent a way to do this, and do it safety, for both the stuntmen and the buffalo.

I started thinking, and that old trusty gift I'd always seemed to have for problem-solving once again helped me out. I came up with the idea of using a special rigging called a "running W." This is a unit that my father-in-law Joe Yrigoyen had dreamed up years ago in the days of classic western movies. The rigging was used to trip and fall horses moving at a full gallop. I'll give you a description of how a running W is set up, and how it works. It's very complicated—but then, so is riding among fifteen hundred wild buffalo.

The first thing I did was make up one-inch wide straps, eight inches long with heavy buckles attached to each one. I covered them with buffalo hide so that they couldn't be easily seen once the buffalo was wearing them. These straps were used to buckle around each front ankle on the buffalo, and there was also a small ring attached to each strap (which I'll refer to as "hobbles" from now on). The hobbled buffalo would also be wearing a three-inch wide leather strap wrapped around the buffalo like a saddle cinch, also covered with buffalo hide, that buckled with a three-inch heavy-duty buckle. On the strap there was a four-inch ring that the strap runs through; the ring set tight against the buffalo's belly, just behind the front legs. Now comes the important part—to make all this look real.

ME AND MY SADDLE-PAL

Riveted to the strap that went around the buffalo was a three-by-four-inch metal plate that had a small piece of threaded pipe welded to it. This threaded pipe unit would sit low behind the right shoulder of the buffalo. I cut arrows in half and attached units to the arrowhead end that would screw into the threaded pipe on the harness. I did the same thing with a spear. When the arrow or spear shafts were screwed into the harness, they appeared to be protruding from the live buffalo, half-buried in their bodies.

When a buffalo wearing this unit was running amongst the herd, the cut-off shafts were hidden from the cameras because the cameras would be placed on the off-camera side of the animal. The only time the camera would show the arrow or the spear would be when the buffalo was tripped—the weapons' shafts would show when the buffalo would tumble to the ground.

Now came the actual act of tripping the buffalo. I'd put them in a squeeze chute (a narrow pen just wide enough for one buffalo to stand in and run through) so I could work with one at a time without being pawed or kicked. Once I had one in the chute, I'd attach a cable from the belly ring and run it down one of the front legs, thread it through the ring on the ankle hobble, then back up the same leg, back through the belly ring. From there it would continue down the opposite leg, come back up again, and go through the belly ring one more time. From there it would go to me—I would hang onto it while mounted on horseback so I could follow the buffalo from aways back while it ran. With the cable in my hand, I'd be ready to trip the buffalo at any time.

We shot the film on location in Custer, South Dakota, in the midst of vast prairies filled with rolling hills. We had our buffalo herd there, but when I rode out into it with the ranch manager I realized pretty quickly that I'd have to fix a potentially dangerous problem before we could start shooting.

Many of the cows in the herd had calves, and they were all on edge because of it—we got charged repeatedly. Mother buffalo are protective of their young and will do whatever they need to get any perceived threat as far away from their little ones as possible. I knew we couldn't work with the herd like that—it was too risky for us, and wouldn't look right on camera, either. I decided to cut all the cows and calves out of the herd and put them in a separate pen so that they would be spared the stress of us working in amongst them, and we would be spared from their protective aggression. Once this was done, our working herd was composed of approximately fifteen hundred males.

I went with the second unit director, Mickey Moore, to scout out a location to use for the hunt, and we found a flat canyon that was about half of a mile long that would work perfectly. We had an insert road built for the camera car to photograph from.

During my days in the rodeo profession, the stock contractor at the rodeo grounds would train the roping cattle to run from one end of the arena to the other. At the far end of the arena was the catch pen, where the cattle were housed, fed, and watered. At its other end were the loading chutes that the cattle would be released from. I figured that arrangement would work just as well with buffalo as it did with cattle, and I translated my rodeo experience to this sequence for the film. I had my crew build a huge catch pen at the bottom of the canyon where our filming herd of fifteen hundred bulls could be housed, fed and watered. At the other end we put holding pens with a squeeze chute at the release area. Each day we herded the buffalo up the canyon to the holding pens, and I would leave them there for about an hour before releasing them and herding them back down the canyon to their catch pen. This practice continued ever day for a week. On the last day we spooked the herd so they would charge down the canyon to their catch pen instead of going along at their own pace.

I picked out ten big bulls, and each one was put into the squeeze chute and fitted with the hobbles and the belly-strap. They wore the units in the days leading up to the shoot so they would be used to the feel of them, and run normally with them on. The wranglers and I had also worked with the chosen buffalo to get them used to being in the chute. I fell back on my rodeo experience for all of this, working with the buffalo just like they were regular cattle. Pretty soon we had them trained to go into the chutes, and they were used to being handled by the time principal photography got going.

When we were ready to try out my idea, we herded the ten 'target buffalo" that were wearing the running Ws up to the canyon and into the loading chute area. Then we moved the rest of the herd up into the holding pens that stretched out behind the loading chutes. Then I loaded one of the harnessed buffalo into the squeeze chute and laced the cable through the belly ring and down the legs, then back up, just like I described. I took the end of it and tied on a rope, so I could dally the rope around my saddle horn when I stopped my horse—this would trip the buffalo.

We screwed one of the shortened arrow-shafts into place on the harness, then got up on my horse, which was standing in another chute about twenty feet behind the buffalo. Stuntman Gary McClarty was playing the part of the Sioux that would "shoot" this particular buffalo, and he was on *his* horse in a third chute opposite me, on the other side of the buffalo's chute. On *'action!'*, the cowboys stationed behind the big holding pen with the rest of the buffalo would fire pistols into the air to spook the herd and get them running down the canyon. When a few hundred bulls ran by the chutes myself, Gary and the strapped-up buffalo were in, I hollered to release the chutes' gates. As the buffalo ran, Gary and I would take off, too, after giving the buffalo a good head start. At the same time, the camera would be running on the opposite side, close in on the Sioux warrior with his bow and arrow. At my signal, the warrior would fire, and I would dally the cable and trip the buffalo. The camera would see it go down, the arrow shaft in its side.

We got everything set up and gave it a go—and to my relief and satisfaction, it actually *worked*. Moore loved it from the very first time we did it. I was thrilled—this was what it was all about, taking the audience to a place they'd never been before, and a place they'd never go in real life.

We ran the shot again, this time with Richard Harris's stunt double,

THE RETURN OF A MAN CALLED HORSE

Terry Leonard, acting as the hunter. The rifle-smoke was my cue this time; upon seeing it wafting out of the gun's muzzle, I'd trip the buffalo Leonard was aiming for. In the meantime, close-up shots of Harris shooting the same gun were captured, to insert into the sequence during editing. This is often done on all sorts of films to prevent any danger to the actors. It was too risky to have Harris himself near a two-thousand pound bull buffalo, of course, but we could sure as hell make it *look* like he was. This go-round was a big success, as well.

The entire shoot was going *great*. I was in my element, and the crew was overjoyed. It's always a plus when things go smoothly on a movie set, and it's even more of a triumph if things go well when you're working with animals—especially a whole herd of them.

There was still one more challenge to meet. I wanted to try the shot again with a Sioux throwing a spear at a running buffalo instead of shooting an arrow. This would be trickier, since we were dealing with a bigger, longer weapon. This was the biggest shot I'd envisioned in the whole sequence and I prayed it would go as I wanted.

Bob Orison, the stuntman portraying the spear-wielding Sioux, got on his horse and got his spear ready while I set everything up. I'd had a larger piece of pipe welded into the harness used on this particular buffalo and screwed half a spear-shaft into it. Then I got into my saddle and took up the cable.

We got going, and Bob readied his spear, drawing his arm back and aiming for the buffalo. When he threw it, though, he aimed it just right so that it fell toward the ground instead of the animal. Keeping Bob well in frame was essential, so that it would not be obvious that the spear he'd thrown had missed its mark. As he let it go, I tripped the buffalo, and the camera caught a great view of the buffalo falling in a cloud of dust, the spear shaft protruding from it. It looked *incredibly* realistic, and could not have gone any more smoothly than it had.

I wish we had done a behind-the-scenes documentary on the entire thing, so that we could have captured a visual record of how everything worked. To this day, I am incredibly proud of that buffalo hunt, and how well the things I saw in my mind's eye came to fruition on film.

ME AND MY SADDLE-PAL

My love of stunt-coordination came together with my talent for problem-solving, my talent for working with animals and my background as a rodeo professional, and it all paid off tremendously. When it was all completed, I remember looking up to the Lord and thanking Him for helping me design and film this great sequence. *Thank you, thank you, thank you, Lord.*

The buffalo hunt may have been my biggest achievement on this particular film, but it wasn't the only thing I did in it. In a pivotal scene, the enemies of the Yellow Hand attack them, and I wanted to come up with a way to show the women of the tribe defending themselves and their children with weapons other than rifles or bows and arrows.

I knew of a type of throwing weapon called a *bola* or *boleadora*. These are interconnected cords of braided leather, usually rawhide, with weights attached to their ends, used by various cultures to capture prey or running cattle. The user would swing the *boleadora* up around his or her head and release it toward an animal's legs, entangling them and stopping the animal by tripping it. I came up with the idea of having the Yellow Hand women use weapons similar to these to fend off their enemies by throwing them around the legs of the horses they were riding.

To make the horses go down once a *boleadora* had been thrown, I had the stuntmen riding them use what I call toe-tappers. The rider would hold onto cables connected to the horse's front hooves, taking up and releasing the slack as the horse ran. Then, at the cue, the rider would take the slack up and hold it there, pinning its hooves up against its belly as the horse—and the rider—tumbled to the ground.

The problem this scene presented is that throwing a *boleadora* is not easy for a novice—it is a learned skill, just like roping is. The actors and extras were having some trouble throwing them right, so because of my roping experience, we decided I'd dress up like a woman and double for

THE RETURN OF A MAN CALLED HORSE

the different ones doing the throwing. I felt silly and got a more than a little good-natured teasing, but it was the easiest way to get done what we needed to, and sometimes in the film business you've just got to do what you've got to do. In the end it was worth it; this sequence too, looked very realistic and I was pleased with my efforts.

Performing a horse fall for The Return of A Man Called Horse. *I'm in the cloud of dust. –M.G.*

As I mentioned, this was 1976, and on this and other films I worked on, right on down to *Young Guns II*, the practice of using trained falling horses, or tripping them, was common in the film industry. I *never* hurt a single horse I tripped—we made provisions to keep them safe and comfortable. If I'd thought in any way that I was causing them harm, I would not have done it. But to some movie-goers, some of the horse-tripping or falling scenes looked *too* realistic for comfort, and outcry over animal welfare issues gained a steady following until the industry could no longer ignore it. The American Humane Association started catching up to people like myself and Terry Leonard who were known for such stunts, and even though they knew we were not hurting any horses, they had to shut the practice down and it is now banned

ME AND MY SADDLE-PAL

in the film and television industry. It's worth noting that I had a good rapport with the American Humane Association; I knew most of their people who would come out an monitor the treatment of animals on movies I worked on. I always abided by their guidelines.

Return of a Man Called Horse opened some interesting doors for me, though because of the horse-tripping issue they were doors I sometimes couldn't go through. When Kevin Costner was preparing to film his epic western *Dances With Wolves,* someone connected with the production contacted me. *Dances* contains a dramatic buffalo hunt sequence as well, and he wanted to talk to me about how I'd done the one in *Return.* He thought the scene was wild—he actually thought we'd really shot buffalo in it. I quickly corrected him and explained how I'd coordinated the scene and what methods I'd used.

He wanted me to help with their buffalo hunt, but I had to be honest with him. "I think I went over the top a bit when I did that movie," I said, "and the humane groups are all over me. There's *no* way you'd get away with filming your hunt the same way we did on that picture."

He saw my point and agreed with me; they'd have to use fake buffalo for the ones that were killed. I told him that's what he should probably do, because I knew the AHA would be there to make sure all the buffalo, and the horses, were treated well. They had a copy of *Dances's* script, so they knew exactly what scenes were going to be included in the film. "Take my advice," I told him, "and use animatronic buffalo on tracks for the ones you're killing, because you don't want to get anyone thinking you're hurting any animals."

I didn't end up working on *Dances With Wolves,* though of course I would have loved to. I did see the film, and I could tell they ended up doing exactly that—using fake buffalo that moved along on tracks with the camera. It looked great and is a memorable part of the movie, but I couldn't help thinking that it didn't look quite as epic as the one we did on *Return of a Man Called Horse.*

Silver Streak

As I've mentioned, I always enjoyed working with Gene Wilder. One film I did with him was a 1976 comedy/thriller flick shot in Canada called *Silver Streak,* in which he co-starred with actor/comedian Richard Pryor. The main thing I always remember when looking back on that particular film was that I very nearly bit the dust while making it.

The film centers around a murder that takes place on a train traveling from Los Angeles to Chicago, so much of the action took place on a moving train. There was a scene in which Gene Wilder's character has to uncouple the engine from the rest of the train. Besides coordinating the stunts on the film, I was doubling for Gene.

I had them weld a bar onto the train's staircase that I could hold onto while I was reaching around to uncouple the train. I positioned Alan Oliney, who was doubling for Richard Pryor, on the staircase with me and had it appear that he was holding onto me and allowing me to stretch around and uncouple the two cars.

Unfortunately, I didn't take into account when I was planning and executing the stunt a metal flag that ran along the track, about three feet from the ground. I was leaning out on the train as it was going about fifty miles an hour, reaching to uncouple the cars, when something—something *hard*—hit me right on my butt. It hit me so hard that it ripped me out of Alan's grasp. I stretched way out—but I didn't fly off the train, because I hadn't let go of that metal bar I'd had them weld on as a handhold. I went flying around, over the coupling, and hit smack against back of the car I was trying to uncouple from the one I'd been on.

They had the cameras rolling, of course, and from their angles they saw my body go flying, but they didn't see where I'd hit. They thought I was a goner, because they thought I'd gone right under the train. Even Alan hadn't seen where I'd ended up.

I wasn't under the train, thank God, but I *was* standing on top of the coupling, balanced precariously and wondering what the hell had hit me. The crew was yelling to stop the train—emergency!

Though you probably wouldn't think so, train work is by far one of the most dangerous activities for a stuntperson, because you have absolutely no control over this several hundred-ton vehicle—which is attached to a bunch of *other* several hundred-ton vehicles—that is often traveling at very high speeds when you are executing your stunt. I knew of plenty of bad accidents in the industry that involved train work—in fact, you might recall that I myself was involved in one just the year prior to making *Silver Streak,* on *Breakheart Pass,* when I nearly fell off the trestle during the train sequence in *that* film. I even knew of one stuntman who had literally gotten both of his legs shorn off during a train stunt.

The train came to a stop, and I hopped off the coupling. Everyone was stunned—and more than a little freaked out; they all thought I'd kicked the bucket. I told them in no uncertain terms that only my gymnastics training and my Saddle-Pal had kept me from doing so.

We did the shot again and I stayed well out of the way of that pesky metal flag, so we got it that time. Later on in filming we shot the big train crash. This was staged at the Burbank Airport, where we converted a terminal into a big shopping area. I imagined how great the end result would look, with all of the people in the terminal scattering and running for their lives as the train barreled through.

I was in for a disappointment, however, because one of the producers told me I didn't need to worry about having actual people in the terminal when we got the shot. He said he was worried about safety, and about them following directions, so he didn't want to chance it.

SILVER STREAK

I protested vehemently. Now I saw the shot in my mind's eye once again—and it was as boring as hell, with no people in it. I worked on him and eventually I got him to let me bring in about thirty stunt people. I rehearsed them thoroughly without the train present until the movements they were supposed to make were second nature. That worked well, and the final shot went great.

Something else that happened during the filming of *Silver Streak* took place in Vancouver, when Alan Oliney, a few other stuntmen and I decided we were going to have a party for the crew. We were staying in condos there, and I was staying on the eighth floor of one of these places. I think of the craziest things sometimes...

I went to the prop department and borrowed a full-sized dummy; then I went to wardrobe and got some clothes for it. We dressed it up and took it up to my room, where the party was being held. I sat the dummy down in a chair and stuck a cigar in its mouth, and there it was when people started showing up.

"Gilbert, what the hell...? What the hell are you doing with that mannequin?" they all asked me, with furrows between their brows.

I shrugged. "Eh, I just thought I'd have someone here for you guys to talk to about the movie," I said, gesturing to the stiff in the chair. Later on, when *I'd* gotten a little stiff from a few beers, I called my guests out to the balcony and informed them I was going to fight the mannequin, which I'd brought out there with me. I screamed a few things at the dummy as if I were really angry with it, then socked it nice and hard, and *bam*! it went sailing over the balcony to the street down below as I tossed it off.

A few lights came on on our level as other people in the condo wondered what the hell was going on, while the poor dummy lay splayed out in the quiet street below (for the record, I'd seen that the street was not a busy one, so I knew there was no chance of me endangering any drivers when I threw the thing off the balcony).

"I can't believe you just *did* that!" everyone exclaimed around chortles of laughter.

"Eh, we'll have something to talk about when we're on set," I said slyly.

"You just ruined that dummy," one of them pointed out.

"I'll pay 'em for it," I assured them.

Meanwhile the propmaster, who was at the party but not on the balcony, called from inside, "what did he just do? Where's my dummy?"

"I threw him over the edge," I explained, grinning.

He came out and looked over, and when he saw the dummy he said, "Oh, my God, *Gilbert!* What are you *doing?*"

"Oh, I'll pay you whatever he costs," I said, still laughing. "It was worth it."

I gave him two hundred and fifty bucks—but there was more to come. In short order, the police showed up at our condos, sirens wailing. The cops got out of their car and were standing over the dummy, inspecting it.

"He guys, *party's over!*" I exclaimed. "Everyone clear out of here, or they're gonna know it came from this floor!"

Everyone cleared out, leaving me alone in my little apartment, waiting innocently for the police to show—but they never did, and I never knew what happened to my friend the dummy.

Our Winning Season

In 1978, I received a call from Joe Ruben about a film he was directing entitled *Our Winning Season,* a drama about a high school athlete starring Dennis Quaid, Scott Jacoby and Deborah Benson. The stunt would involve cars—one of my two areas of expertise in the stunt world; the other, of course, being horses.

Ruben wanted to meet with me and discuss ideas for a scripted scene in which two high school kids have been drinking in a drive-in theater, and challenge each other to drive out onto the roadway and play the age-old game of chicken.

"I really want to make this scene *exciting*, Mick," Ruben told me during our face-to-face conversation.

"Well, just running their cars head-on at each other, and dodging around each other will get pretty boring to watch," I told him. As I spoke I was already thinking. How could I take this from *boring* to *wild?*

I came up with an idea that I thought would fit that bill and leave some change left over. I told Ruben to imagine the road running alongside the theater. The boys would line up, facing each other, about two hundred yards apart. Shooting out of one of the cars, the camera would look down the roadway toward the other car, and off to the left, you would see the drive-in, all lit up. We would film passes at each other, each car barely missing the other. On each pass, the speed would get

ME AND MY SADDLE-PAL

higher and higher. On the third pass, the car headed toward the drive-in would veer off to its left just as it was about to hit the other car head-on, zooming through three-foot-high grass.

"I figure we'll have to go about seventy or eighty miles-per-hour to hit a ramp we'll have there," I told Ruben, "and the car will go sailing up through the theater wall and crash through the movie screen, landing inside the theater. What do you think?"

The director looked at me, smiled and shook his head slightly. "Did you just come up with that off the top of your head right now?" he asked me.

"Yeah. So what do you think?" I pressed.

"Well, to be honest, I think you're crazy," he said, his smile getting bigger. "Where would we find a drive-in to use for this stunt?"

"We couldn't *find* one, Joe," I told him, "we'd have to *build* one."

Ruben loved the idea. We presented my plan to the studio, and they loved it even more. I got together with Art Brewer, our special effects man, and we found a spot at the Atlanta Speedway, and a framing crew that could build the theater under our supervision. They constructed the theater set in the parking lot of the speedway, so we had to make our own roadway alongside it. We brought in lots of bushes, shrubs and even some small trees to create the effect we needed.

The theater we constructed was the same size as any real drive-in, and along the front there was a huge neon sign that read "Star Lite Theater" and a marquee that lit up. Way out in front of all that we had them build a ticket booth, and about seventy feet in front of that I had them build my ramp that I'd use to do the jump. The theater wall had a section in the middle that was about twelve feet wide from top to bottom, covered with drywall. It was through this section that I'd drive the car during the stunt. Finally, I had a area running alongside the theater that I could use to abort the jump if anything went wrong; as with all my stunts, I put safety first. The whole project took about two weeks. Once all the construction was done, it was time for me to start testing.

I figured on going about seventy-five miles per hour during my test, and the ramp was set up to get me about twenty-five feet in the air at that speed. I called Joe Ruben and the studio heads to come out to the set one night and see it all lit up; when they did they were amazed.

"How do you know you're going to go through the right spot in the wall. Mick?" Ruben wanted to know. I told them I had the team painting a hundred feet of white line that I'd straddle with the car on my approach.

"You know," Joe said a little uneasily, "I'm getting nervous already, just looking at this."

"Well, you're not the only one," I told him matter-of-factly. Sometimes people think stuntmen are infallible, that they don't ever get scared or nervous. Not the case, I can assure you. If you ever get so comfortable with stunts that you don't ever have a single inkling of nerves, you're letting your guard down too much and opening yourself up to an accident that could get you hurt—or worse.

I called up my good friend Freddy Waugh (of limbo night in Mexico fame, if you'll remember), and asked him if he'd like to take a wild ride with me as my passenger. He said "great!" and we flew him back to Atlanta.

The night arrived to do the jump. We set up eight cameras total, three out front and five inside. Four cameras would shoot at high speed to slow the stunt down on film. I didn't want to rely on using a walkie-talkie alone, so we'd set up a signal at the area where my abort road was. There would be a red light on until I was ready, at which time I'd signal by blinking my headlights on and off. When the light turned yellow I'd know they were rolling the cameras, then when the light turned green, off I'd go.

Here we go. Freddy and I were in position, seat-belted in head-to-toe, the mustang idling, the red signal light in view. I blinked the lights on and off, then glanced over at Freddy. "How're you doing, Waugh?" I asked.

"Shit, Gilbert, when you told me you wanted me to take a wild ride with you, you really meant it!"

Just as he finished speaking, the light turned yellow. "Cameras are rolling," came a voice over my walkie-talkie. I revved up the engine, and the light turned green.

ME AND MY SADDLE-PAL

"Here we go, Waugh!" I shoved my foot down on the accelerator.

We were almost up to sixty when all of the sudden, out of nowhere, a blanket of fog settled down over the theater, seriously impairing my view. The red light went on, and Freddy and I heard "cut, cut, cut!" over the walkie-talkie. I just had enough time to veer off onto the abort road and shut down.

Freddy and I unbuckled, took our helmets off and got out of the car as Joe approached. "Holy shit!" he said, "I can't believe what just happened! That was like a message from above!"

The fog became too thick, so we wrapped production for the night. The next evening, we tried again, setting up just as we had the night before.

Pretty soon Freddy and I found ourselves back in that car, helmets on, strapped in tight. The yellow light came on. "Here we go again, Waugh," I said, throwing him a grin.

"No shit, Gilbert," he deadpanned. The green light came on, and we took off.

We were about two hundred yards from our take-off point when the whole theater—marquee, neon sign and ticket booth—went black. "Cut!" the walkie-talkie blared. I slowed down and pulled up on the abort road, then we got out and headed for the first assistant director.

"What's going on?" I asked.

He shook his head. "The generators went dead, shut everything down." The small generators for some of the other departments still worked, so we weren't completely in the dark, but obviously we couldn't do the stunt at that moment.

Joe walked up to me, shaking his head and heaving a heavy sigh. "Hey, Mick, I've got to tell you, I really don't like what's happening out here. We've had to stop twice now, and I'm about ready to scrap the whole sequence."

I knew what the problem *really* was. During a film shoot Joe had just finished, a stuntman had been killed during a car chase—so I didn't blame him for getting cold feet.

I faced him, put my hands on his shoulders and looked him in the eye. "Joe, I know exactly where your head is and what you went through on your last show." He actually got a little choked up at that; I saw a tear slide down his cheek. Clearly the accident on his last shoot had affected him deeply and not strayed far from his mind.

"Do you know that I've got my Saddle-Pal with me tonight?" I asked him. He gave me a puzzled look, not catching my drift. I looked up for a minute. "He's up there, Joe, and right beside us. He's always been with me, and what's happened these last two nights doesn't mean a damn thing."

I meant what I said. I'd always been sure the Lord was with me, and I knew that now was no different. He would protect me as He'd always seen fit to do.

We took a break and went to have dinner while the electrical crew worked on the generators. Halfway through the meal, all the lights came back on, and everyone let out cheers. Once we'd finished our meals, we got set up again, determined that this time, we'd pull it off and get it done.

Freddy and I climbed into our car again—but before we did, we went over to Joe and gave him a big hug to reassure him. "We'll see you on the inside," I told him firmly, with a smile.

"Good luck," he told us.

There we were again—racing toward that ramp at seventy miles per hour and approaching my painted line. I straddled it, zooming toward the ramp, right were I wanted to be. Lift-off time.

The car sailed up over the ticket booth entrance and continued upward, crashing through the huge lighted marquee. We were still climbing as the next obstacle came rushing up to meet us—the theater wall. We busted through the wall at about twenty-eight feet, right through the movie screen. I remember that Freddy and I were hollering "Ohhh, shhhiiiitttt!" as we sailed over the parked cars of the those watching the movie. The car came down like a 747, landing perfectly in between cars. In total, we'd jumped that car twenty-eight feet high and one hundred and ninety-five feet in distance.

As we unbuckled, still exhilarated from the thrill of the stunt,

Freddy looked over at me and cried, "what a fuckin' ride! *Yeah, baby!*" We slapped a high-five.

"Thank you, Lord," I said under my breath as I looked up. "Thank you, thank you, thank you."

We climbed out of the mustang, and all we could hear was cheering, whistling and applause from the crew. Joe and his assistant came running over to us, Joe half-crying in relief as he threw his arms around first me, then Freddy. "Oh, my God, that was the wildest damn thing I've ever seen in my life! That was incredible!"

Needless to say, I'd pleased my director.

Jumping the car through the drive-in theater screen for Our Winning Season. –M.G.

When it was all over, Freddy and I drove back to our hotel. Freddy glanced over at me. "Hey, Gilbert, why did you have me fly all the way out here to ride with you when you could've just as easily strapped a dummy in with you?"

I looked at Waugh and said, in a whimpering little voice, "because I didn't want to be by myself when I was doing it!" We both laughed.

What a thrill *that* night was, and I guess when you think about it, it was one of those instances when the "third time's a charm." I've always been proud of that stunt, and happy that I was able to get Joe

OUR WINNING SEASON

over that fear he'd held onto from the accident on his previous set. You can't let fear get to you and take over your life; if you do it'll stop you from breaking barriers, and from truly experiencing life. I was grateful, too, for my Saddle-Pal, and that He'd been with me just like I'd told Joe He was.

The Prisoner of Zenda

I got a call to fly to Austria to do some horse stunts on the 1979 reworking of the film *The Prisoner of Zenda*. It was based on an adventure novel by Anthony Hope, first published in 1894. Several versions of the film had already been made by the time we made ours—six movies, to be exact, and several more on stage and television; this one was unique because it was a comedic version starring Peter Sellers. There were several stuntmen already on board, most of them English with a few Americans as well. I hopped on a plane and headed out there to get to work. I traveled alone at first, but eventually brought Yvonne and our three boys, Troy, Lance and Tim, out to join me.

One of the stunts I was hired to do involved jumping a horse off a drawbridge that's in the middle of raising up and closing. The character is fleeing the castle and just barely escapes in time. I was asked if I thought the stunt could be done. "Sure, it can," I replied, "I just have to find the right horse for it."

I'd worked on a few films in Spain by this time; you'll remember *The Wind and The Lion*; so I thought of the Spanish wranglers I'd worked with over there—I figured they'd have the horse I needed. I contacted one of them and told him what I needed, and he told me they'd start looking.

They found about five horses for me, and I took each one out to a location I'd found that had about a five-foot high cliff. I took turns trying each horse out to see his reaction to being ridden up to the edge of the cliff. If the horse spooked or shied away from the edge, I simply saddled up the next one and tried him out. Finally I found one that was a natural for the job—I backed him up and tried the full leap off the cliff, and he did it perfectly. He would be my main horse. One other horse in the bunch would do it, too, so he became my back-up horse. I had both of them on the set, just in case. When you work with animals it's always good to have something to fall back on in case you hit a snag. I worked with both horses every day for awhile, getting them used to jumping off that cliff.

There was a stuntman working on the film by the name of John Moio who was a very good friend of mine. He liked to rehearse stunts multiple times while doubling for Peter Sellers. I'll rehearse stunts as well, especially when there are other stunt people I'm working with, but when I'm doing specialty stunts by myself such as the one I was about to do, I don't rehearse in front of the cameras. I don't generally like to do them, mainly because people in my business make their money by getting paid for each stunt they do. The stunt is mapped out and a price is agreed upon. If you get to doing too many rehearsals, the stunt starts to look easy, and then the production team starts to think that it is easy, and maybe not worth what they've decided to pay you.

The night we were to shoot the stunt came, and I told them to raise the drawbridge about six feet up and I'd come smoking out of there and do the stunt. The cameras were positioned outside the drawbridge, facing the direction I'd come riding out from. While I waited for a cue to go, I cantered my horse in easy circles, warming him up.

A long while seemed to go by with nothing happening; finally one of the assistant directors came hurrying over. "Hey, Mickey, what's going on?"

I pulled my horse up and looked down at him."I'm ready for you guys, I'm just waiting for a signal that you're ready for me."

"Well...they're waiting for you to rehearse the stunt," he said.

I shook my head. "Oh, no. I don't rehearse stunts on camera. I do my training and rehearsals way before I do the job—not on set right before we film it. I work it out my own way, ahead of time. I'm ready to get this done, so you tell them to roll the cameras, okay?"

"Oh," he said, "Okay. No big deal," he said quickly, backing off. "If that's the way you work, we'll go along with it." He told them to roll the cameras.

I took my run and did the jump, and it worked out really well—in fact, it was a hell of a good-looking shot, in my humble opinion. I went on working on the film from there, doubling a few of the other actors in different scenes. Then, toward the end of my time on the show, I hit a snag.

Another stunt, doubling for another actor, was a forty foot-high fall off a castle balcony. My landing area wasn't the greatest—and that was an understatement. It was an old wagon that was six feet wide by twelve feet long, hitched up to a donkey. I was out looking this situation over one day and I decided I needed someone I could trust to lead the donkey on the right line for my fall. There was a Spanish friend of mine there whom I'd worked with in Spain named Timoteas. Tim was a stunt man by trade but was working as a wrangler on *Zenda*. I met up with him and took him to the exact area on the set where I needed him to lead the donkey. Then I went up on the balcony to watch him lead the wagon and donkey under me. I rehearsed with Tim a number of times until we both felt confident about the stunt. I set some fall pads inside the wagon to break my fall.

A few nights went by and they were ready to shoot the stunt. Cameras were all set up, and the last thing I told Tim was that he shouldn't allow anyone to change his speed or the direction that he was taking the wagon. He agreed, so I went up on the balcony and waited for them to get ready. And I waited...and waited...then waited some more. It started to drizzle. "Hey boys, what's going on down there?" I hollered over the balcony.

An answering yell came floating up. "We're waiting for you to rehearse!"

I raised my arms and shook my head in frustration. "I'm not gonna rehearse, I'm ready to *do* this, right now!" I hollered back. I looked

THE PRISONER OF ZENDA

down at Tim, gave him a thumbs-up, and saw him do the same to me. They rolled the cameras, and Tim took off, leading the wagon like we'd practiced. I timed it just right and landed dead-center in the wagon. After that stunt they finally seemed to get used to the way I worked.

They had a second unit director on the film that was going to shoot some carriage stunts I was going to do, but when I got ready to do them, the director was nowhere to be seen—he didn't show up when he was supposed to, which meant I was stranded there unable to complete my work on the movie on time. This was going to be an issue, because Bob Redford had called me to do some more work for him, and he needed me at his location in two weeks.

I went to the production team and asked after the missing director. "We're not exactly sure where he is, but we think he's up at one of the castles near here," they told me.

"No, I know where he is," I said dryly. "He's got a chick he's running around with instead of being here working." I was beginning to get very frustrated. "I have to be available for Redford in two weeks," I told them. "I can't sit around here waiting for your director to decide he's actually going to get some work done instead of just fool around." I got serious with them. "If he doesn't get down here, I'm going to leave."

"You can't do that, you need to finish this film! If you leave, we're going to report you to the Guild."

"And I'll report you to the Guild for hiring a director that's running around after his own interests instead of paying attention to the movie he's supposed to be making," I shot back, unconcerned about his threat. "You'd better get him down here." It's a funny thing—the AWOL director appeared soon after that, out of nowhere.

"Let's get this thing done," I said, and we got the shots done. Redford wanted me for *The Electric Horseman*, and he was worried I wasn't going to be back in the States in time—he expressed as much when I talked to him after he'd tracked me down in Austria.

"Don't worry, Bob, I'll be back in time, even if I have to hitchhike," I joked, but I meant the part about being back in time. "I've told them I have an obligation to you," I added.

Yvonne and the boys really had a good time in Austria, which was a perk of working on Zenda. When I wasn't working we took trips to Yugoslavia and Germany. When we went to Germany I got pulled over by a couple of German police on motorcycles; I hadn't seen a checkpoint they had set up and so I hadn't stopped. It scared the heck out of Yvonne, getting pulled over like that—they didn't speak English, and I didn't speak German. We were at a bit of an impasse for awhile. Finally, half-joking, half-hopeful, I asked, "*¿Habla usted español?*" The answer was no, as you might expect. Finally I said, slowly, "should we go back?" I gestured to the way we'd come.

"*Ja, ja,*" they said, and back we went. In retrospect I guess we should've had a guide take us where we wanted to go.

The boys really had a lot of fun, though. One day at the castle we were shooting part of the movie at, they played on the spiral staircase, pretending to shoot each other and then falling, sometimes as high as two stories, into pads we used during fall stunts in the movie. I wasn't worried about them falling so far; even at their young ages (all under ten), I'd already had them training on trampolines for quite awhile. I knew they were all going to be stuntmen, even that early—there wasn't any doubt, so I'd done my best to prepare them early, and prepare them well. I was, however, worried about all the crew-members that were hanging around and watching them horse around on our equipment, so I went over and told them to stop. I took them aside and did a little creative explaining so they wouldn't be upset that I was telling them to stop doing something I normally encouraged them to do.

"I know you're having fun," I told them, "but listen. When you guys do those falls like that, with all those people watching you, you make it look easy, because I've taught you how to do it. But they don't know that, and so when I go to do it, and get paid for it, they're going to think it's easy and it's not worth paying me all that money. They're gonna say, 'well, gee, if your kids can do it, then it's not that hard, is it?'"

"Ohhh," they said. "Okay, Dad, we won't do it anymore!"

That was the end of that—and pretty soon the end came of my work on the movie, too, and off I went to make *The Electric Horseman*.

The Electric Horseman

❦

One of the many jobs I did doubling for Robert Redford was the 1979 film *The Electric Horseman,* starring Jane Fonda along with Redford, directed by Sydney Pollack and shot in Las Vegas. In the film, Redford plays a former rodeo champion named Sonny Steele, who has sold out to become the spokesperson for a big business conglomerate. The company makes him wear light-up suits and ride a champion racehorse named Rising Star that has been sedated to make it more calm for publicity events. All of this chews away at Steele, who turns to the bottle for solace, and eventually steals Rising Star to get him away from the company big-shots—literally riding him off into the sunset.

Two things stuck out to me about this job: one, Redford would be portraying a former rodeo champ—right up my alley. Two, Redford's character was a drunk—*not* up my alley. This would be interesting. I traveled to Vegas to get to work.

When I arrived I stashed my gear at the hotel, and went to meet up with the wranglers, who were keeping the horses for the film at the back of the hotel's property. When I got out there I found nobody around, but my attention was grabbed by a commotion in a horse trailer. I walked over to take a closer look.

The trailer had a brand-new paint job and the name "Rising Star" painted on it; this was the equine star of the film, whose real name was

Let's Merge. He was making a fuss, so I opened the feed door on the side to take a look at him.

Instead of a nice, friendly muzzle stretching curiously toward me in hopes of a treat or a pat, I was met by a pair of snapping horse jaws. "Whoa, *you're* a son of a gun!" I exclaimed. "You're gonna get a lesson from me, buddy!" With that promise, I closed the door on him and went back inside. The next morning I met up with the wranglers, all of whom I knew from previous jobs.

"What's the deal with the stallion, boys?" I asked, jerking my head toward the trailer.

"What do you mean, Mick?" one of them asked me.

"Well, I came out here last night to take a look at him, and he damned near put his head through that feed door and bit the hell out of me. Have you been working with him, or riding him at all?"

They shrugged. "Yeah, he's just spoiled," they said vaguely.

I shook my head a little. "Okay," I replied doubtfully. "You *do* know that I have to ride him out of Caesar's Palace and onto the strip, right? I need to make sure he's okay. Does he have borium shoes on, for traction on the road?"

"Yeah, he's got them," they assured me.

I had one final question. "Is this the only horse we've got to make this movie with?"

They glanced at one another. "Yeah. Why?"

"Well," I said, "the way I've read the script, I think we're going to need a double horse. I'm not sure that one horse can do everything we need him to do."

"There's no falling, or anything like that," one of them pointed out.

"Not *yet*, there isn't," I said. "but you know me—I make a lot of suggestions and sometimes re-write stuff. I just think you should start looking around for a double—maybe a nice roping horse that looks like this one."

"Okay, we'll start looking," they promised me.

I told them I'd see them that night, when I would be doing a night shot as Redford, riding the horse out from Caesar's Palace onto the strip.

THE ELECTRIC HORSEMAN

The wardrobe I had to wear for the scene was a blue suit rigged up with pin lights all over it. I had a battery pack for it inside my saddlebag, and when I plugged it in, I lit up like a Christmas tree, from the top of my hat down to my boots. I spoke to Sydney Pollack, our director, whom I loved working with. "What do you want here, Sydney?"

"Just ride from the entrance of Caesar's, right by the fountain, at a nice, easy lope with your lights on," he told me, "and then go right out onto the highway. We'll have it lined with cars. Just keep him at a lope right down the center lane, in between the cars. I'm going to be on a crane about two hundred feet down the highway, shooting up at you as you come at us. Then, when you get close to us, just turn behind one of the cars, lope out this street here, and continue right on out into the desert. That's where we'll fade you out."

"Okay, sounds good." I went over to mount up and found Joe Lomax, one of the wranglers, standing there with Let's Merge. One hand was gripping the bridle at the bit, and the other was latched on to one of the horse's ears. My brow furrowed. "Joe, what are you doing?"

"Nothing, Mick," he said. "Go ahead and get on."

"Why do you have him eared down?" I asked suspiciously.

"You know, he's a stallion," Joe said.

"Turn loose of his head," I said, and Joe did. I went to mount up, and as I put my foot in the stirrup, the horse turned and grabbed me by the left hip with his teeth, snatching me around. That was all it took—I popped him in the muzzle as a reprimand. He had to learn that I was the boss, not him.

"Mickey, what are you doing?" Joe asked me.

"This horse needs a lesson in manners," I replied firmly. "You don't expect me to believe that you've actually been riding him, and working with him! I can tell you haven't been. Anyway," I said, "it's training-time, now." I went and put my spurs on.

"What's going on down there?" Sydney called.

"Be right with you, Sydney," I called back. "Just gotta get some things in order, here." I didn't want to tell him what the problem was; I didn't want to embarrass the wranglers. After I had my spurs on, I got into the saddle and took control of the horse both with the reins and my spurs to show him *I* was the one riding *him*, not the other way around. He had to learn to respect me or this wasn't going to work. After a minute I called to Pollack. "Okay, Sydney, we're ready."

They rolled cameras, and I put Let's Merge into a slow canter as I'd been told to. Right after I turned him out onto the highway, though, he started bucking—I mean, full-on rodeo style bucking. I used my long reins to go over and under, popping him in the flanks and letting him know that sort of behavior was unacceptable. As I did so I was holding his head firm, so he couldn't bolt on me. We kept moving like that, him trying to buck and me popping him with the reins, until we got close to the camera, and by then I'd gotten him into a jittery lope. When we reached the crane I turned him, rode him out into the desert as planned, turned out my lights, and came back, riding over to Sydney. "You ready to do another one?" I asked.

Pollack was sitting on the crane with his chin resting in one hand, looking troubled. "Well, yeah, but I don't think it's going to look very good with you slapping him with the reins like that," he replied.

"I figured you'd stopped the cameras," I told him. "The horse was trying to buck me off."

"Really?"

"Well, yeah! Didn't you see what he did when I turned the corner onto the highway? He was going way up on his front end and kicking out with his back legs."

"Oh, I saw it," he confirmed. "I just figured he was spirited."

"No, he was trying to buck me off," I repeated, "so I needed to give him a little training session. He needs to know who's boss of this outfit—me, not him. But he should be okay now." I told him that while I was out in the little wash in the desert where I'd ended my ride, I'd ridden the horse up and down it for a few minutes, working him and getting him under control. "He's good now," I told him. "So let's get another take, and it should be what you want." I rode back up to my starting position, shaking my head at the wranglers as I went. The jig was up as far as they were concerned.

THE ELECTRIC HORSEMAN

I repeated the scene, and it went like clockwork. Sydney was thrilled—it looked just the way he'd wanted it to.

"Just remember, Sydney, about that first take—on the set, when you're trying to get a shot, is *not* the time to train the horse," I said, "but I had to do it that way, because that was the only time I had—I just got in last night." Then I told him I wanted to speak to him alone for a moment—I had another concern about the horse that I needed him to be aware of, and I didn't want the wranglers to hear.

"Sydney, this horse is crippled," I told him seriously.

"What are you talking about?" he asked me. "That's Rising Star—he's our main horse!"

"I know, but look at this." I gestured down to the stallion's left foreleg and pointed out a long raised area above his knee; it was a calcium deposit. "Watch." I ran my hand down his leg and pressed on the area. The horse reacted instantly, pulling his leg up and fighting me—it was clear he was in pain. "When we get to scenes where you want a full-out run, he's not gonna make it," I said. "Maybe he will for awhile, but then he'll be really bad off. I've already told the wranglers we need to find a double for him, so that's the horse we'll need to use for the more demanding scenes." I explained that we had Hollywood tricks for horse doubles just like we did for human doubles—we could use makeup (in this case, white shoe polish) to paint a white star and/or white socks on whatever double horse we found, if needed.

"All right, but I just can't believe this horse would be crippled like that," Pollack said, upset.

"He's a racehorse," I said. "They run them early—usually around two or three years. Their bones aren't fully developed, so some of them end up with a lot of problems later on. That's why this one was sold when he was—if they'd kept running him, he'd be so broken down he wouldn't be worth anything."

"He cost us a hell of a lot of money," Sydney said.

"I'm sure he did, and you got taken, I believe, but I think we can make this work, still. After all, one of the elements in this movie is

ME AND MY SADDLE-PAL

that Redford's character finds out the horse is injured. Well, you happen to have a horse that really is."

With Bob Redford during The Electric Horseman. *That's me on the right. –M.G.*

We kept working on the movie, of course, and I kept working with Let's Merge, training him to jump three and four-foot fences. There were a lot of sequences where Redford is being chased by police and so forth, and he evades them by jumping fences here and there. One chase scene involved a levy with a road running over it, and Sydney was shooting from a helicopter above me. He'd told me, "Mickey, I want you to really open him up, here, and because you're such a good double for Redford, I can really get in tight on you. So I'm going to be right next to you with the helicopter as you run him."

"Sydney, that kind of running will probably finish him off for awhile," I warned.

"I *need* to get this shot," was his response. He told me he wanted me to run him as hard as I could for about a quarter of a mile. I told him I'd start a little farther back and open him up slowly, and they agreed.

We were going along at a full gallop as best the horse could do; I didn't need to spur him or urge him on much at all. He knew how to run. We got about seventy-five yards away from where I was supposed to pull him up and ride down a little embankment, and I could feel the horse faltering on his left side. I pulled him up and took him down the embankment, then I started walking him to cool him off. By then I could tell he was really hurting. When I put him into a trot he began to limp outright, and badly. The helicopter had landed and Sydney got out; I called to him. "Sydney, take a look at this."

"Oh, my God, what happened? What's the matter with him?" Pollack asked.

"Remember what I told you about his knee?" I said. "Well, this is the result of all that running."

"What do we do for him?"

"We can treat him, but we can't run him like this anymore," I said. "We've *got* to get a double in here, both for me and for Bob to use." I reminded them that the script called for a scene at a rodeo in which a drunken Redford is riding the horse at a lope around an arena, then the horse rears and Redford's character falls off, which would be me doubling him at that point. A double horse would need to be used for that scene, too, after today.

"There are going to be a lot of people in the grandstands during that scene that are ranch people who live around here," I said. "They're going to be able to recognize that the horse is crippled. It's not going to look good, Sydney."

The wranglers finally went out and found a good double for Let's

ME AND MY SADDLE-PAL

Merge, a good roping horse bought from a friend of mine who lived in the area. They had to paint white socks on him, but in the end he looked great, and, more importantly, he was sound.

When we went to film the rodeo scene, we put out advertisements in advance letting people know we were shooting a movie with Robert Redford and we would be filming a scene with at the rodeo grounds that we needed spectators for. We offered all kinds of incentives to draw and hold a big crowd, like raffling off TVs, and we got what we needed, filling up the stands.

Bob wanted me to do all the riding for him in the scene; for some reason he didn't want to even come out of his dressing room, so I put the costume on, got on the horse, and came out of the bucking chute. I was trying to stay about a hundred feet in or so from the arena rail—I was afraid if I moved any closer to the crowd someone would realize I was not Bob Redford, as we'd advertised. I knew that it would only take one person to blow the whole thing—and that if the news spread that I wasn't Bob, the crowd would be angry and rightfully so, since they'd come to see Redford, not his double. I told Sydney all of that when he told me he wanted me to get closer to the rail. "If that happens, you're going to have to get Bob out here. You'd better go talk to him."

"Well, let's just try it and see what happens," Pollack said.

"Okay," I said doubtfully. Dutifully I got back on the horse and went back into the bucking chute. They rolled the cameras, the lights came on, and they announced me as Sonny Steele, Bob's character. I was about twenty feet off the rail, weaving in my saddle so it would look like I was drunk, keeping my left hand up to better hide my face.

As I'd predicted, it didn't work. I got down to the end of the arena and some girl shouted, "that's not Redford!" Pretty soon the whole crowd was protesting. "Where's Redford? We came to see Redford!" They started stomping their feet.

THE ELECTRIC HORSEMAN

I pulled up and went over to Sydney. "You see, Sydney?"

"Yeah, I see."

"I want a police escort out of here," I said, completely serious. "Those people are mad enough to riot, and who knows what the hell they're going to do to me—they might start throwing bottles, or something. So I'll go get Bob, but I want protection while I'm doing it."

He agreed, and I was escorted over to Redford's dressing room. I knocked on the door, said who I was, and he called for me to come in.

"We tried it your way, Bob," I told him, "but some folks in the crowd saw I wasn't you, and they're pretty pissed off about it. You hear that stomping?"

He nodded.

"Why don't you want to go out there?" I asked him. "You got some enemies around here, or something?"

"No, no, it's nothing like that," he said. He hesitated a minute. "I know you're riding that rearing horse..."

"Yeah, but he's just a normal horse until you give him the cue to rear. It takes a special cue to get him to do it. He won't rear on you, if that's what you're worried about—you don't even know the cue."

"Oh," he said. "I just didn't want to look like a joke out there in front of all those people if he reared on me."

"He won't do that," I said, "and even if by some chance he *did* rear, you wouldn't get thrown off. You're too good of a horseman for that, Bob. You ride really well," I told him, and I meant it.

I told him the cue to make the horse rear on command. "You have to take your right foot in the stirrup and slide it up to the base of his neck, then dig your spur in at that spot to make him rear, then you hold on tight with the reins to hold him up there a bit. But you don't need to worry because there would be no reason for you to do such a thing."

He nodded. "Okay." That was all his issue had been—simple as that. Goes to show you that even the biggest star can have their insecurities, sometimes.

"So," I said to Bob, "the only way we're going to solve this problem is if we have you come out there. You're going to have to get into the suit, and everything."

So Bob put the suit on and went out there, and the crowd went nuts, appeased at last. We got the shots of him we needed, then the one of me falling off the rearing horse, so everything worked out okay, in the end.

I had another commitment lined up after *Electric Horseman,* which was a film called *Gorp*. The problem was, *Horseman* just kept dragging on and on, and pretty soon it was past the time I was supposed to report for *Gorp*. The production team for *Horseman* had been made aware of my commitment to the other movie, and finally I went to them and said, "I hope I'm done, guys." It was around eleven at night and we were still shooting.

"We know you have to leave, but there's just one more shot to get tonight," I was told.

I was worried about getting to the new location late. I knew I could take a red-eye to Atlanta that night, but then I wasn't sure how I would get to the location from there if I did—it would be too early in the morning. But I couldn't refuse to do the last scene they needed, so I just got into costume.

I was filming that last scene at the arena when all of the sudden I heard the sound of a Lear jet flying overhead and landing. Redford called to me. "There's your ride to Atlanta," he told me with a grin.

"Well, damn it, that's more like it!" I teased, then thanked them profusely.

"Well, we knew you had to get there, so we're flying you back on a Lear. What the heck." What the heck, indeed! Talk about a nice moment for me! I was so touched that they'd bothered to hire a plane to take me to my next job, when they could've just let me be late. All in all, *Electric Horseman* was a great film to work on—and it's always nice to double for Bob Redford. In case you're wondering what happened to Let's Merge, the horse that portrayed Rising Star in the movie, Bob ended up buying him and kept him until he passed away, eighteen years later.

The Frisco Kid

I mentioned I did a few doubling jobs for Gene Wilder, and one of them was a 1979 western called *The Frisco Kid,* directed by Robert Aldrich and staring Wilder and Harrison Ford. Wilder and I were friends and he liked me to double him, so I got called to travel to Colorado to work on the film.

Aldrich was a terrific director who had made a name for himself in the industry; he'd been at the helm of such pictures as *Whatever Happened to Baby Jane* and *The Dirty Dozen,* among others. When I arrived in Colorado I took the first opportunity to introduce myself to him, telling him I'd seen many of his films and that I respected what he'd done in the industry. One of the sequences Aldrich wanted me to do was a big jump on horseback off a cliff, and I'd come up with some ideas for it, so I presented them to Aldrich right then and there—no time like the present, after all. Aldrich had a sort of nervous habit of chewing absently on the side of his tongue on and off, and he was doing that as I spoke.

I figured the sequence might involve a matte painting to fill in the background of the jump, and I'd spoken to someone about it already who was at the top of the field. In my way of thinking the shot would look great, but to my surprise, Aldrich stopped me.

"Now, you listen here," he said, in between gnaws on his tongue, "I'm gonna tell you something. If I need any help on this movie, I'll ask you."

Taken aback, I put my palms up and backed off, nodding in submission. I'd just been trying to help, after all, and it was in my nature to

ME AND MY SADDLE-PAL

dream up bigger and better ways to pull off the stunts I was hired on to do, but I could see Aldrich wasn't on board with that. I decided to keep my mouth shut, and thus went my first meeting with Robert Aldrich.

Aldrich had a stunt coordinator he worked with frequently whose favorite pastime on set was playing a card game called "pitch" with anyone he could wheedle into playing with him. We were shooting a scene for the movie in Santa Barbara one day, a shoot-out on the beach, and true to form, the coordinator sat playing cards with another member of the crew while Aldrich stood in the distance, walking the actors through the shoot-out. I sat on a driftwood log, watching, and after a few minutes it became painfully obvious that Aldrich had no idea how to coordinate the scene—he was lost. I glanced over at the stunt coordinator—it was, after all, his job to help with this.

Pitch won out over Aldrich, apparently, because the coordinator kept right on playing cards. After a minute I got up and went over to him. "Hey, I think the director could use some help," I pointed out. "You can see he looks pretty lost over there."

The coordinator glanced up, watched for a few disinterested seconds, and then turned his attention back to his cards. "Eh, he'll get it, don't worry about it." I wasn't so sure, but I did as I was told and went back to my log, watching. I wasn't sure why Aldrich kept the coordinator on all the time, if all he was going to do was play cards and not coordinate any action sequences.

The minutes passed and the scene got more and more disorganized, and I noticed Aldrich looking up at me—once, twice, then a third time. I could tell that by now, he knew he was lost, and he also seemed to know he wouldn't get any help from his card-playing coordinator, so he waved me over.

"You ever put anything like this together before?" he asked me.

"Sure, quite a few times," I said. "Looks like you could use some help."

"Well, what would you do, here?" he asked, gesturing to the actors.

"Let me show you," I told him. "I've seen enough of these types of scenes, and done enough of them, to know what you're going for, here." I walked him through the best way to put the shoot-out sequence together, and he liked it a lot. I could tell I'd impressed him, too—so much so that he asked me to help him coordinate the rest of the action sequences in the movie. I happily obliged, of course, and I believed he appreciated it, because he called me personally to work on a film he had in development called *The Last Breed,* to be filmed in Canada. As it turned out, Aldrich ran into some conflicts getting his chosen crew members to the location, so he turned the film down. When he called me to tell me he'd given the project up, he told me he'd given my name to the new director and recommended me for the show.

"I won't do it, though," I'd told him.

"Well, why not?" he asked, puzzled.

"Because I want to work with *you*," I'd told him.

I could tell he was touched by that, and I really did enjoy working with him. I did work with him on his next film, *…All the Marbles,* and I was just becoming his go-to guy for stunts when he up and passed away, but such is life, unfortunately.

But back to *The Frisco Kid.* Concerning that big horse stunt I needed to do; here's how I did it: I had a big set of stairs built that could support a horse's weight; these led up into a greased-up chute called a dump chute, that was positioned over a water tank. The chute would be on hinges, and after I'd ridden the horse up the stairs and into the chute, the chute would drop at a forty-five degree angle, causing the horse to slide right out. A horse's natural instinct is to gather itself and jump when it feels itself falling, and that's what we'd see on camera. I explained all of this to Aldrich, who was skeptical, but agreed to my plan. I got the construction guys to start on the tower that would hold the chute.

I was in the office one day when one of the construction guys came in and told me they were all ready to shoot when we were—they'd gotten the tower done. I went out to inspect it, and to climb around on it, and I was immediately concerned—it seemed far too rickety, and that was with just *me* on it—forget about a two-thousand pound horse. It swayed back and forth as I got on it. I knew there was no way a horse would tolerate it like that. I told Aldrich I needed the guys to cable it off on all four corners to stabilize it, which they did.

ME AND MY SADDLE-PAL

We got everything ready and did the stunt, and it worked very well. One of the horses lost his footing underneath him while in the chute, and he ended up falling rather ungracefully, hind-end first, into the water; I had to sort of dive off to one side to get out of his way. I had long reins on the horses' bridles so I could hold onto them and help guide them once they were in the water. Once the stunt was all put together on film, it looked fantastic, and I was happy with it.

The Frisco Kid was a lot of fun to work on, and the actors were wonderful. Harrison Ford was great to work with, and I always really enjoyed being around Gene Wilder, who was just a neat guy, plain and simple.

Doubling for Gene Wilder during my big horse-jump stunt in The Frisco Kid. –M.G.

The Blues Brothers

In 1980 I got a call from my good buddy Gary "Whiz Kid" McLarty, who was coordinating the stunts for *The Blues Brothers,* staring John Belushi and Dan Aykroyd and directed by John Landis. The company was on location shooting in Chicago, and Whiz Kid wanted me to come on board.

I would say that this particular film was the biggest car job I've ever worked on. We needed a large number of police cars, so the studio made a deal through our transportation department to buy most of the Chicago P.D.'s fleet—which they loved, since they needed to upgrade their older cars, anyway.

Because of all the car stunts in the movie, the stunt department had a lot of work to do. Most of these cars had 350 and 400 horsepower engines—and we needed the power those Dodges put out. Under Whiz Kid's supervision, our special effects department welded special cages in each of the cars that were customized to each type of stunt that the car would be used for. For example, cars had full cages built in them for doing high-speed, airborne flips and cannon stunts; other cars had roll bars installed for stunts that were not so radical. Altogether, we had about eighty to one hundred police cars set up for us.

Let me tell you what a cannon stunt is, and how a the cannons work. There are different sizes of cannons, depending on how large the vehicle is that you're going to blow over with it. A normal cannon would be thick-walled pipe, twelve-inches in diameter and about thirty inches in length. At one end, a round cap, or plug, about one to one-and-a-half inches thick would be welded into it. The plug would have a small hole drilled through it to run wires through.

Inside the cannons were logs or cylinders that were the exact size of the cannon's interior, both in width and length. At the top of the log, a metal plate was fastened. An explosive unit of dynamite was taped on top of the plate, with two wires attached to it. These were used to detonate the dynamite. The log was slid up into the cannon and secured, and the two wires were run through that small hole that was drilled through the cap of the cannon. One of the wires fastened into a button that the driver could use to activate it. The other wire was hooked onto another wire that ran from the hot side of the car's battery. These wires' ends were never hooked together until the car was positioned at its start mark—not to mention until the driver was set up with his safety gear, like his helmet, safety belts, and whatever else made him feel comfortable. Once that was set, the wires would be hooked up to make the cannon hot. It was important that all this preparation be done first so that if the cannon accidentally went off, the driver would already be belted safely into the vehicle.

The canon was welded to the roll cage, with its bottom sitting about one-and-a-half inches off of the pavement. It was welded in an area under the car that was dependent on which way the driver wanted the car to flip and roll. Sounds complicated and dangerous, right? Well, guess what? It is.

The director hollers '*action*,' you get your car to the speed you want, the spot you want, and then, sliding your car sideways, you hit the button. *Bam!* Away you go.

Whiz Kid dreamed up a stunt for the movie that involved a cop sitting in his police cruiser, which is hidden behind a billboard sign on the roadway. A motorhome containing the band The Good Ole Boys goes speeding by the billboard. The cop spots them, and he gasses his police car out onto the road after them. A pickup truck is behind the motorhome, and as the police car pulls out onto the road, the truck brakes and slams sideways into the police car as they both flip over. This is where we used those cannons, one on each vehicle. I was doubling the cop in the police car, while Whiz Kid was driving the pickup. In order to pull off this stunt successfully, it was going to take perfect timing by each driver. We both had to get our vehicles into just the right position, and hit our buttons at the exact same time. Fortunately, we did, and the stunt worked like a charm—better than we'd thought it would.

I mentioned how dangerous cannons can be, and that danger comes when the driver hooks up the button wire to the hot wire. If the wiring malfunctions, it could cause the cannon to detonate right then and there—which is not good, obviously. There have been times when that has happened, so the formula was changed to where the special effects department became responsible for arming the cannons—until one effects man was leaning through the passenger-side window of a car, arming the cannon, and it detonated prematurely. As you might expect, he was severely injured. Whenever *I* did a cannon stunt, I would always make sure nobody was close to the vehicle when I hooked up the wiring—and that's the way it's done nowadays.

Whiz Kid thought up a stunt for forty of us to do in our cars. He picked a sweeping curve that hid a hillside that fell away from the outside of the curve. He had a ditch dug horizontally across the hillside, about ten feet down from the curve. The idea was that we would be going about sixty miles per hour and have our cars drift sideways off the curve. Our front and rear passengers'-side tires would go into the ditch and flip us over. Sounded good to me!

We were lined up about half a mile from the curve at around three a.m., ready to shoot the scene. It was going to be awhile, so Gary told us to relax in our cars. I got out of mine to sit with a buddy, Alan Oliney, who doubled Eddie Murphy in all of his movies. When I got to Alan's car, I found him behind the wheel, sleeping like a log. I mean, he was *out*. I got an ideal and went to every other car, telling the drivers to fire up and quietly drive their cars up to where Gary was a the wreck site. After that, I went to a different channel on my radio so that Alan wouldn't hear me, and told Gary what was up.

We all met up at the wreck site, leaving Alan parked all by his lonesome. Then Gary got on his radio and hollered, "*action,* everybody!

ME AND MY SADDLE-PAL

Action!" Then he kept on talking as if we were all flipping our cars and rolling them down the hillside. "All right, that's perfect, guys! OK, OK...that's a cut! Man, that was *wild!* Is everybody all right?" He let the radio fall silent. We all waited.

The radio suddenly crackled back to life, and Alan's voice came over the static. "Breaker, breaker, hey, Whiz Kid, where *are* you guys?!?"

We started laughing as Whiz Kid got back on the radio. "What do you mean, Alan? Aren't you with us in the wrecked cars?"

Alan's voice, when it came again, was sheepish. "No, I'm still down here at the take-off area."

"Well, come on up to the wreck site," Whiz Kid told him, "and you'd better hustle!"

Well, Alan came driving around to the wreck site, and we all met him there—bent over with our pants down, mooning him as a group. We *do* have to have a little fun, once in awhile.

All of the stuntmen were staying at the Holiday Inn on Lake Shore Drive, and we'd sometimes have a beer after work. One evening Whiz Kid and I decided to check out for the night, and we headed for the elevators. As we entered the elevator and pushed the button for the thirtieth floor, some guy stepped in just before the door closed, and proceeded to push every single button.

"Hey, what the hell are you doing?" Whiz Kid demanded.

"I'm the hotel dick," he said, and flashed his badge at us. "I'm checking every floor."

"Well, not on *our* time, you're not!" Gary replied, and unleashed a straight shot that landed flat on the detective's jaw. He stumbled back into the corner of the elevator and landed flat on his ass. As the elevator reached the second floor, Gary and I stepped out to catch another elevator, laughing. The next morning I met Gary in the lobby, and spotted none other than the hotel dick standing at the entrance, looking everybody over. I slid in close to Gary and put my arm around his waist. "Walk swishy, Gary," I muttered, laying my head on his shoulder.

Gary put his right hand on his hip and started cooing at me, saying something about how he couldn't wait to get tighter clothes on me, as we walked straight past the detective. Once outside, we started cracking up, positive that the detective had never suspected us of being the ones in the elevator with him the previous night.

John Landis wanted to do a huge pile-up of police cars, all flipping and landing on top of each other, completely jamming up an intersection under the Chicago El tracks. We planned to do this sequence in two different waves of cars, both to make it work better and so that we could adjust for better angles. The first wave showed flipping, spinning and crashing, starting the pile-up of vehicles. For the second wave, I went to Whiz Kid and talked to him about installing a pipe ramp to the bottom of a police car that was sitting upside down on its roof. I would come in with the other cars and hit the ramp; doing so would spin me into the air as the crashes kept going on around me. We did the shot and the front end of my car slightly caught the under-part of the structure above. It snapped the rear end of my car under and landed on top of the other crashed cars from the first wave.

When I think about that pile-up of cop cars, and about how everything was done in real time using real, live stunt people for the shots, I shake my head to realize that nowadays it would be done completely with computers. Think of all the work stunt people have lost out on in our business because of CG effects…what a shame.

The big police car pileup from The Blues Brothers—*done for real. –M.G.*

The Workings of the Lord

While working on a movie called *Gorp* in Atlanta, I was working with my best friend Freddy Waugh and another stuntman, Stan Barrett. At that time I was in the habit of running twelve miles a day, rain or shine, and Freddy and Stan would run with me.

One morning we were running in the hills, and I realized Freddy had disappeared. Stan and I stopped and looked back, and there was Freddy, about a quarter of a mile behind us. Concerned, Stan and I waited for him to catch up to us, and when he did we asked him what was wrong—it wasn't like him to fall behind.

"I just don't have it in me this morning," he said.

I knew what was wrong, but I didn't want to say it in front of Stan. Freddy had developed a real problem with cocaine, and it was slowly getting the best of him. I knew he had to kick the habit or something very bad would end up happening. I waited for the right time, then took him aside and started working him over.

I told him that whenever he needed a fix, he should light up a doobie to curb his craving for the coke—the lesser of two evils, I figured, and if he did that he could start getting off the cocaine. "Freddy," I said, "take a good look at yourself in the mirror, man. I mean, *really* take a good look."

"It's that bad, huh?" he asked me.

"I'm telling you, Freddy, slowly but surely, it'll creep up on you."

THE WORKINGS OF THE LORD

Because we were so close to the Waugh family, we felt we could say anything to them, and vice-versa. Yvonne started talking to Freddy about becoming a Christian, and Freddy took it seriously and was able to beat his habit.

At this point in our lives, Tim and Troy were out of the house, and only Lance was still at home. We'd moved to Newport Beach so that Lance, a talented tennis player, could play tennis for Corona del Mar High School. We lived in Newport for eight years, and then, from out of nowhere, a flyer came in the mail about homes in Santa Barbara, California. Once Lance had left the nest, Yvonne and I decided to go up and check Santa Barbara out.

We'd been looking below Newport for places, but they were just too expensive and the area was too crowded. We took off, the Santa Barbara flyer in hand, and got a real estate agent. We found a three-acre ranch-style residence, made a low-ball offer on it, and then headed back to Newport. To our disappointment, our offer was turned down on the place in Santa Barbara. But the Lord works in mysterious ways—and He was about to intervene on our behalf, it seemed.

While all this was going on, Freddy had started giving talks about drug abuse to parents and children, and about six months after my offer on the house was turned down, he happened to be giving a talk in Santa Barbara. He spoke about his own experiences with drug abuse and mentioned mine and Yvonne's names quite often in his presentation. Wouldn't you know it—the family that owned the place we'd made the offer on was there, listening to Freddy's talk. They were interested in Freddy's career in stunts, and after his talk they approached him. They wanted to know if the guy Mickey he'd talked about was trying to buy a house in Santa Barbara.

"Yeah, he is," Freddy told them, "but he hasn't heard anything back, so he's still looking."

On their way home, the family talked it over and decided that since we were such good Christian people and had helped Freddy beat his addiction, they wanted us to have the house. They decided they'd accept our offer and sell us their home.

I always think back on this story and believe firmly that my Saddle-Pal had a lot to do with bringing me and my family—and Freddy also—to Santa Barbara. What are the chances?

The Fall Guy

In 1978 I got a call from Al Wyatt, the second unit director and stunt coordinator on a made-for-TV movie called *Colorado C.I.*. The project was being shot on location in Colorado, and Wyatt wanted to hire me to do some car work, skiing stunts and a few fight scenes, for good measure. I took the job and headed to Colorado.

We started with a car chase along the Continental Divide. I drove the lead car, a Jaguar, and drifted around some big, sweeping turns—drifting being the term for setting a car to sliding sideways while still moving forward, your foot always on the gas to control the vehicle. The day after that scene was filmed, I had the day off, so I went skiing at the local resort.

I was on my third run or so when I stepped out of the chair at the top and happened to notice a semi diesel truck moving along in the distance at the other side of a snow-covered meadow. I asked the first local I came across if there was a road out there, and he told me what I was looking at was the Continental Divide.

As I was skiing, I got an idea—it literally came to me as I was *whooshing* down the slope—and it was a wild-ass idea, at that (as my ideas for stunts usually always were). During the car chase, I'd turn off the main paved road onto a dirt one that would take me right to the top of the ski resort—and then I'd drive the car right down the slope. Wild, right?

ME AND MY SADDLE-PAL

Of course, it wouldn't be that simple; nothing in the movies ever really is. Everything's got to be planned out; 'I's' dotted and 'T's' crossed. We would have to cut in a road off the main one and cover it with brush that I'd plow the car through; that way the viewer wouldn't see the drop-off into the resort. I'd also have to have the car rigged up so that it would glide smoothly down the snow instead of getting stuck in it—I had an idea for *that,* too. But first, I had to run all this by Al Wyatt and the producers, as well as the owner of the ski resort.

That night, I went to Wyatt first, meeting up with him for dinner. After I explained my idea, he was enthusiastic, telling me he'd talk to the producers about it. I went ahead and met with the owner of the ski resort next, telling him I wanted to jump my car off the ridge and land down on the ski slope. He loved the idea, too, mainly because of all the publicity it would bring into his resort.

He and I rode the chair lift up to the top and I showed him the area I wanted to use for the stunt. I was in luck, because he told me that particular area wasn't used for skiing and there would be plenty of snow right where I needed it.

The producers gave the go-ahead, so I had the effects guys start prepping the car next. I asked them to install a skid plate onto the car that covered the entire undercarriage; it would be like riding a huge sled right down the mountain.

Somehow the locals found out about the stunt, and on the day we were going to film it, it seemed like everyone took the day off to come out and watch it.

It worked out better than I thought it would. I hit my ramp, got airborne, and came down for the landing. The Jaguar entered the snow like a swimmer entering a pool from a block—it was completely submerged, and because of the speed I was traveling at, stayed that way for about twenty feet before popping up and continuing down the slope, half-covered now. The skid plate kept me going down the mountain, smooth as butter, and whenever I needed more power I'd just hit the gas pedal. All in all, I traveled about three hundred yards down the mountain. It was a great sequence and a real hit for the town.

THE FALL GUY

After that crazy, wonderful thing, I did some other things for the show, and we were just about finished when Al Wyatt got a call from his best friend Bill Catching, who was also a stunt coordinator. Catching was working on an action-filled television pilot called *The Fall Guy*, starring Lee Majors. The show centered around Majors' character, Colt Seavers, a Hollywood stuntman who moonlighted as a bounty hunter.

Bill told Al that he was having some problems with the stuntman he'd hired to double Majors and that as it stood they couldn't fulfill all the different stunts they had planned for the pilot.

"You know anyone that could do car work, fight work, high falls and other different types of stunts?" Bill asked him.

"As it happens, I've got the very guy working for me right now," Al told him. "Mickey Gilbert."

"I've heard of him," Bill told Al, "but he's a cowboy, isn't he?"

"Oh, yeah, he's a cowboy," Al replied, "but he just finished doing a big car chase for me, and he jumped a car off a cliff into a ski resort. You should call him."

Well, Bill Catching *did* call me, and we talked about *The Fall Guy*. I told him I'd be home in a week and could meet up with him at Fox Studios. When we got together, he walked me to the set within the studio where they'd be filming a scene for the pilot. In it, Lee Majors would be doubling Farrah Fawcett, who had a cameo in the pilot as his ex-wife.

The carpenters were setting up booths, like the kind seen at fairs or carnivals, set up in a horseshoe-shape. In the center was an old farm wagon. Bill explained to me that they wanted to do a stunt involving Lee's character, dressed up as Farrah Fawcett, wig and all. He'd jump a car and land it on top of the wagon—and they wanted the car to stop right where it landed. Majors wouldn't be doing the actual stunt, of course; as his double, *I* would be doing it, which meant I'd have to dress up as Farrah, myself. The things we do to create movie magic!

I wasn't concerned with that, though; what I was worried about was getting that car to stop where they wanted it. There was a car parked about sixty feet from the wagon that I could have them build a

ME AND MY SADDLE-PAL

ramp off of for me to use, but the speed at which I'd have to go in order to land in the right place would create so much momentum that I'd slide right off the other end. "That's going to be a tough stunt, getting the car to plant itself on the wagon," I told Bill. Already I was thinking, my mind working to come up with a solution. Suddenly, I had it.

"I have an idea that I think will work," I told Bill. "This sequence takes place at a fair or carnival, right?" I asked him, and he nodded. "Well, they have watermelons at fairs, usually. If we stacked hundreds of watermelons on the wagon, they would probably stop me from going off the end of the wagon." I explained that I'd gotten the idea from remembering car stunts I'd done in the past where I'd jumped into water; the car always stopped moving forward from the resistance it faced before sinking. I figured that a huge pile of melons would provide resistance in this situation and make it work out how they wanted it to. I talked to Bill about how I wanted the wagon outfitted, we'd have to have a two-foot bed of wood attached around the wagon to hold in the pyramid of melons.

There was another man standing near us while I explained my idea, and when I was done I saw him give me and Bill a look, shake his head in disgust, and walk off.

"Who's that?" I asked Bill.

"The creator of *The Fall Guy*," Bill said with a grin. "He also produces it."

"Well, I can tell he thinks *I'm* full of shit," I said dryly.

Bill laughed. "Well, we haven't had too much luck with Lee's stunt doubles," he told me, "so he's a little gun-shy."

"I know this idea sounds nuts," I said, "but I'm telling you, it will work to stop a car fast, and won't look out of place in the scene, either."

Bill told me to handle the gag, get the type of car I wanted and work with the prop department to set up the melons. The day came to do the stunt, and everything was in place as I wanted it. I was going to drive a Mustang that I'd had the special effects shop set up for me.

I was talking with the director when Lee Majors came over to introduce himself. "Mickey," he said, shaking my hand, "I've heard a lot about you, and I'm really glad you're here for this."

THE FALL GUY

I thanked him and was about to go get ready when Lee called after me. "Hey, Mick," he said, "do you really think this will work?"

I just laughed and waved him off. "Wait and see." I got into position. "*Action!*"

At the director's call, I accelerated, hit the ramp, sailed through the air and plowed into hundreds of watermelons. And damned if it didn't work like a charm. The landing was great—watermelons flying into the air all over the place—and when everything settled down the car was sitting neatly on top of the wagon, right where they'd wanted it. I don't think anyone else has ever used watermelons to stop a car, but in this case, they were just the ticket. As I unbuckled my seatbelt, I heard cheering, whistling and clapping from the crew, and as I was about to climb out the car window, Lee Major's arms were suddenly dragging me from the car. Talk about excitement! He was like a little kid, laughing and giving me a huge bear hug. "You're my *man*, Gilbert!" he was exclaiming.

That was it—a car stunt involving a big pile of watermelons. That got me onto *The Fall Guy*. I hate to think about where I'd be if I'd slid that car off the wagon…

*Jumping the mustang over the cart of watermelons—
the stunt that got me the job on* The Fall Guy *series. –M.G.*

ME AND MY SADDLE-PAL

After the mustang jump into the watermelons, I got another call from Bill Catching, inviting me back to continue working on the series. *The Fall Guy* was slated to be the biggest action show on television, and I was excited about being a regular part of it. I started putting my mind to work, creating different types of action we could use.

The studio had made a deal with General Motor Company; it required that their GMC "Jimmy" truck model be used as Lee Majors' personal vehicle during the show. After doing some miscellaneous stunts on the first episode, I got an idea regarding the Jimmy. I went to Bill and the producers, and told them I wanted to make the truck into an important part of the show—almost like a character in its own right. They were interested, and wanted to see my idea on film, so I wrote a chase scene which involved the truck chasing a Porsche. During the chase, the truck would jump off a cliff to take a short-cut, and then as the Porsche rounded the bend with a long sweeping turn, coming straight at our camera, the truck would come flying out of the canyon, sailing over and land right in front of the Porsche, cutting it off. I must say, the producers all loved it—in fact, they loved it so much that they told Bill and I that they wanted to see the truck flying through the air at some point in every episode.

Of course, the average car is not made to withstand such massive jumps, so every jump I did with the truck usually damaged it beyond repair. Fortunately, GMC wanted to keep that truck in the episodes, as you might imagine, so they kept us well-supplied with a stock of trucks—three, to be exact—to double the original. All three of the doubles were freight-damaged, so the company didn't care about us ruining them. After we were done with them, we'd just send them on back to GMC, and they would send them off to the shredder plants.

The reason I was killing off so many trucks was because in order to balance them properly for jumping, I had to carry an extra eight hundred pounds of weight tied into the rear end of each one—otherwise, the truck would nose-dive into the ground, or possibly even somersault over. The way I had them set up made them look like a dolphin jumping out of the water, nice and streamlined and clean.

THE FALL GUY

Jumping the truck for The Fall Guy. –M.G.

As I'd intended, the truck became a big part of the show; I could tell because whenever I was driving it, kids on the street would recognize it, waving and hollering at me, which always made me smile.

Eventually, after the second season of the show, I went to the transportation team and discussed getting the engine shifted to the back, and underneath; this meant I wouldn't have to carry that extra weight in the back any longer. I also had them install a skid plate that went from the front to halfway back, underneath the truck. Doing so would help deflect wind from the undercarriage.

These modifications worked exactly as they were supposed to—with the engine moved back and the skid plate in place, my first jump with the modified truck was like riding in a glider slicing through the air. No more broken trucks! Now, I felt, I could make it sail higher and farther than before, with no problems.

One day, I had some fun with the truck. I pulled into a gas station and the attendant recognized it. He came out of his office and asked me, "Is this the truck from *The Fall Guy?*"

"It sure is," I told him. "Would you mind looking under the hood and checking the oil for me?" I asked innocently. I unlatched the hood and waited.

He lifted the hood and all I heard was, "*Holy shit!* Where's the *engine?*"

I laughed and told him what we'd done to the truck and why, then waved good-bye to him as I drove off.

Things weren't all roses and sunshine on the series, though. It was a sad day when Bill Catching met me and some of the producers for lunch; Bill told me he was quitting the show due to some personal problems. He wanted me to take over as the stunt coordinator for the series from then on. I didn't like the idea of him leaving; I enjoyed working with him, but I accepted the new position, naturally. Now I'd coordinate all the stunts, while continuing to double Lee Majors.

Along with doing chases with the truck, there were many other types of stunts to do on the series. Almost every episode I'd be flying under helicopters, or some other such crazy thing. One stunt I remember was in an episode where Lee was playing the part like a character out of *James Bond*. He was driving a Corvette convertible in a chase scene and had to abort from the vehicle. The effects team made a front seat where a spring would eject the seat upwards, lifting Lee about eighteen inches, to start the sequence. From there, I would take over, sailing upwards, around fifty feet, latching onto the skid of a helicopter. Right about now, you're probably thinking, how in the hell would you manage *that?* Well, I'd done a lot of working out on the trapeze with my best pal Freddy Waugh, and, of course, we had a trapeze net underneath to fall into. I just figured I'd set up the same net, fly above it in a chopper, and hang from the skid. Then I'd fall into the net—but when it was cut into the film, we'd play that clip backwards, so it would look as though I was sailing upwards, not falling down. Fun stuff, huh? All in a day's work when you're in my business.

Another big stunt I presented to the network was me—doubling for Lee, of course—and another stuntman doing a fight in a Cadillac convertible going sixty miles an hour—while heading straight for an eleven hundred-foot cliff. We were half-standing, half-kneeling in the

THE FALL GUY

front seat, throwing punches at one another. My opponent threw a right roundhouse, knocking me into the back seat, half-unconscious, then turned and saw the cliff coming up fast and bailed out of the car.

Tim was doubling for Doug Barr and was chasing us in a helicopter. It caught up to me, and Tim tossed a rope ladder down to me, yelling at me to get me to come to. I came out of the daze, see the ladder, and, just as the car starts its plunge off the cliff, grabbed the end of the ladder. It was a truly wild shot as the helicopter pulled me out of the Caddy, the car plummeting down in a thousand-foot free fall.

For one episode of *The Fall Guy*, we were working with two lions—one was a gentle de-clawed and de-fanged male named Simba, and the other was a male who could get a little mean at times, named Jumbo. We were shooting a scene where Lee's character is on foot, being chased and ultimately treed by a lion.

I was doubling Lee for this sequence, and of course, because of his nature, I wanted to use Simba as the chase cat. The owner and trainer of these lions was a stuntman named Monty Cox who is known for his talent with big cats, and whom I knew well.

The plan was to have Simba chase me toward an oak tree that I would climb up into. After we got that shot, Monty would put Simba away and come back with Jumbo. That would be the part I wouldn't like.

We had a cable tied off that Jumbo would be tied to that ended about three feet from where I'd be up in the tree. What I wanted was to cut Jumbo into the scene as a double for Simba—Jumbo would be the lion that was climbing the tree, trying to get to me. We set up Jumbo's cage about twelve feet from the tree I'd be in; then Monty cabled Jumbo up and I started teasing him in front of the cage, as we rolled the cameras.

I don't need to explain any further—as they released that lion, I made a bee-line for that tree was up in it in the blink of an eye. Jumbo shot out of his cage and jumped up onto the trunk so fast it made your head spin. Just as I'd planned, he hit the end of his cable about three feet away from me.

When he came to the end of that cable and found he couldn't reach me, boy, that pissed him off even more. He roared and pawed at me, and I have to tell you, it's pretty frightening to look into a mad lion's open mouth as his paws are sweeping at you, claws extended. Lee Majors was watching all this from a distance. The director hollered "*cut*" and then Lee called, "Okay, Mickey, you can come down out of the tree, now!"

I looked over at him and gave him a dry chuckle. "Oh, *sure* I can. Why don't you come over here and grab that cable, and pull him out of my way?"

Everybody laughed. Monty came in and got Jumbo out of the tree and chained up, back where the lions' trailer was; Simba was chained up separately there, as well.

We were discussing our next shot when we suddenly heard three loud, long roars. "Oh, shit," Monty said, "I think Jumbo's loose and fighting with Simba!"

We ran back there and Monty was right. Jumbo *was* loose, and he was standing over Simba, mauling him. Monty grabbed a training cane and started hollering at Jumbo, prodding and swinging at him, trying to get him off of Simba. Jumbo turned and took as swipe at Monty, then ran off, Monty chasing after him.

There was a dried-up riverbed nearby that Jumbo ran down into, Monty still in hot pursuit. I stood where I was, watching. *Monty's so pissed off he's not thinking clearly,* I thought. By then both Jumbo and Monty had disappeared from sight down in the wash.

I sprang into action and jumped into the *Fall Guy* truck, got it into four-wheel drive and took off after them, dropping off the embankment and down into the riverbed. When I spotted Monty and Jumbo, man and lion were engaged in a full-on stand-off. Right then, I knew that Monty was in *big* trouble, because the lion was crouched down, tail lashing back and forth, just like a housecat ready to pounce. "What do you want me to do, Monty?" I called.

"Run the son of a bitch over!" he yelled. "Nail him!"

I gassed the truck, flew past Monty, and hit that lion head-on—I

THE FALL GUY

mean, I *really* nailed him. I felt the *thud* of the truck hitting him, then saw him leap away. He hit the ground running and took off, going further down the wash.

I spun the truck around and Monty got in. "Are you *crazy?*" I yelled. "I can't believe you ran after that cat by yourself!"

He was out of breath still; all he could do was shake his head for a moment. I could tell he was still pissed off. Then he said, "Thanks, Mick, you saved my ass. He was ready to get me, any second."

We went back and locked up the trailer after we'd put Simba into it, securing him into the front section that was partitioned off from the back. We'd put Jumbo in the back part once we caught him.

We took off down the riverbed, searching for the wayward lion, and found him laying down under a tree. He was breathing hard and overheated. I circled the truck and trailer around the tree, facing the back of the trailer toward the lion. Cautiously, Monty and I got out and opened the trailer's gate. When we did this, Simba was visible to Jumbo through the partition, and the lion's training took over. They'd been loaded in and out of that trailer so many times that when Jumbo saw the open gate, and saw Simba already inside, he simply got up and walked into the trailer. Relieved beyond belief, we closed him securely up inside.

I still see Monty Cox now and then on different shows, and we still talk about that crazy day when Jumbo got loose.

The thing that gave me the most joy and was the greatest fun for me on this particular series was getting to dream up all these different gags to do. Fortunately, every time I dreamed one up, the producers and Lee Majors would go for it and let me do it. Lee especially loved it because he wasn't just an actor, he was a guy who could really adapt himself well to any type of action piece. The proof is in all the action shows he'd done prior to *The Fall Guy*.

By the time we got into the third season, I'd taken over directing the second unit, giving me a total of three designated jobs on the series. The show was doing so well that they would let me take my unit to different areas outside of California if I needed to, depending on the type

ME AND MY SADDLE-PAL

of sequence we were doing. This in turn opened up a great opportunity for my son Tim, who was always working on the series. When I was gone, he'd take over the stunt coordination on the rest of the production, hiring all the stunt people and setting up stunts. He was a natural at it and had an easy way of handling people; everybody loved Tim.

I had one hell of a great crew; everybody did more than his or her share. My camera crew, in particular, was exceptional. We would scout the locations we were going to shoot at, and set positions where cameras would be positioned. I always had three operated cameras and two wild cameras working on each shot. My directors of photography, or D.P.s, as they're called, were Jim Roberson and Don McCuaig. Both were aces in photography, but there was something about McCuaig that caught my eye. I liked and respected both of them very much, but I found myself confiding in Don more. Our working relationship on *The Fall Guy* would start off twenty-nine years of McCuaig as my D.P., on every job I did. He became, and still is, a great friend of mine, and is someone I really enjoy working with. To put it simply, he's the greatest, and I love him.

There were dozens of stunts we did for the series, but one in particular remains foremost in my mind whenever I think about *The Fall Guy*. It started out as a stunt and ended up as a miracle.

Every day, I prayed to my trusty Saddle-Pal to keep me and my fellow stuntmen safe; I always thanked Him for doing so. This particular stunt showed that my trust in Him was well-placed—but I have to tell you, it sure put that faith to the test!

I was working on a sequence where I was supposed to drive the truck and sideswipe into a jeep I was chasing. The jeep is knocked off the mountain road we're on and is soon out of control, bouncing down a steep slope. When it hits the bottom, it runs into a boulder and flips over. I scouted the location with my crew and found just what I was looking for, so we got ready to stage the stunt.

Lee Majors had asked me to work with a friend of his who was a stuntman; I'd called him and discussed the stunt, laying out all the particulars to make sure he thought it was something he'd be able to

THE FALL GUY

handle, since he'd be the one flipping the Jeep. He told me "no problem, I've flipped vehicles before,' so we proceeded.

The day of the stunt, I was directing the sequence, so I had Tim double Lee for the part where the truck forces the Jeep off the road. We got that shot without a problem, then began working on the Jeep-flipping part of it. We set up a pipe ramp behind the boulder, out of the camera's view. I planned to have Lee's friend start the Jeep around forty feet up the hill from where the boulder was so that he would have more control of the vehicle when he hit the ramp. I was busy setting up my camera positions, so I told Tim to help the stuntman prepare his safety gear in the Jeep.

I'd determined that the best position for the cameras was about a hundred feet in front of the boulder and down a slight hill. Once I'd set the operated and wild cameras up in their positions, I called Tim on the walkie-talkie and asked him how things were going.

"Dad, I think you should come up here and look this over," came Tim's reply, in between bursts of static. He didn't have to say any more; I could tell something was wrong by the tone of his voice. I high-tailed it up the hill and over to the Jeep.

Lee's friend had belted his lap-strap down as he should have, but he wasn't wearing shoulder-straps. He planned to pull his upper body down onto the passenger seat, where he'd set a safety strap to grab as he hit the ramp. This was *not* a safe arrangement. I gave Tim a look, but he just shrugged his shoulders. "Are you *sure* you don't want to wear a shoulder harness?" I asked the stuntman.

"Nah, I'm fine this way," he told me.

He asked me to get his camera to film his flip for him, which I did, and then I started heading over to my camera crew. As I did I started talking to the Lord, silently. *You know, Lord, I don't like the way this guy's setting himself up. He's not going to be able to see what's going on in front of him. You've always told me that if things don't look right, either fix it or don't do it.* My gut was telling me something bad was about to happen.

I got over to my camera crew and hollered a new instruction. "Okay, guys, we're moving the cameras."

Roberson and McCuaig looked at one another, their brows

ME AND MY SADDLE-PAL

furrowed. "What?" they both asked, puzzled as to why I'd want them moved. I told them that I wasn't comfortable with the stuntman's set-up, and I felt we needed to move the cameras for the sake of safety. I could tell they had more questions, but they did as I asked.

It was time to shoot, so I walked over to the position where I'd just moved all the cameras from. Talk about stupid, huh? After all, I'd just moved the cameras away from there for safety. I guess out of habit, I wanted to get the best shot I could, not thinking of the danger I'd put myself in if something went wrong. Tim told me the stuntman was in position, so we rolled the cameras as I crouched down with the stuntman's camera.

"Action!" I called.

The Jeep came flying down the hill and hit the ramp—but it hit it the wrong way. Instead of hitting just inside the front tire, as it was supposed to, it hit the ramp's dead center, which caused the Jeep to jump the boulder instead of flipping over it.

I was looking through his little camera at the time. "Shit, he hit wrong," I remember muttering. I took the camera away from my eye—only to see the Jeep's grill, headed straight for me. I started to push up and get out of the way, but my feet slipped out from under me.

Everything happened fast after that—to fast for me to truly remember anything after the grill and the bumper, headed straight for my body. I only had time to raise my arms in front of my face before it hit me, dead-on.

The next thing I knew I was waking up with my fellow stuntman, Gary McClarty giving me mouth-to-mouth resuscitation. I think Gary scared me more than the Jeep did.

"What the hell?" I mumbled. "Gary, what the hell are you *doing?*" I turned my head and spit a few times. I was really, *really* dizzy.

Gary raised his head and called out, "he's alive, he's alive!"

"What the hell is going *on?*" I demanded. "Of *course* I'm alive! Help me up," I told him.

He shook his head and told me to lay still. "Don't move until we check you over for broken bones," he warned.

THE FALL GUY

"Why?" I kept asking. "What happened?" Gary told me that the Jeep had ran me over, tumbling me over and over underneath until one of the back tires ran over my legs. I was still groggy and mumbled, "the Jeep…oh, yeah, we've got to do the Jeep stunt."

"No, no, Mickey, you've already done the Jeep stunt, and it's the wildest thing we've ever seen!"

I collected myself a bit, came around a little, and realized what I needed to do. I moved my neck from side to side as I lay there, then worked it around in each direction. After that I lifted each leg and scissored both of them to check my lower back and pelvis. I took a few deep breaths to check my ribs.

By this time, a lot of the crew had gathered around. I looked up and said, "hey, guys, I'm all right. Help me up!"

They were afraid to touch me, apparently unable to believe I wasn't injured, certain I must have internal damage of some sort. "Damn it, someone help me up," I said, starting to sit up.

Once I was standing I realized my tank top had been ripped off of me, and I was bleeding all over my body. It looked liked someone had taken a butcher knife and stabbed me in a dozen places. When I'd gone under the Jeep the bolts that held the axles to the vehicle had been tearing into me the whole time. As I was standing there, dumbfounded, I heard the sound of a helicopter overhead, getting ready to land.

"What's that for?" I asked Gary, still a little dazed.

"It's for you, man. We're flying you over to the hospital in Santa Clarita."

"Wait a minute," I blurted out, "we've got to do this gag."

"You dummy, Gilbert, we've already done it," someone said, as they laughed nervously at me. "Get your ass into that chopper."

While I was being airlifted to the hospital, it started sinking in, what I'd just been through. Right away, I started talking to the Lord.

Dear Lord, I was thinking, *I'm looking at my body, seeing all this torn flesh, but it's nothing compared to what could have happened, and the fact that I survived. I could have been killed or critically injured to the point where I could never do something like this again—but I wasn't. You had to*

ME AND MY SADDLE-PAL

have been right next to me, keeping me safe, like always. I love you, Lord, and I thank you very much for this moment.

I came out of it okay—somehow. For me, this was a miracle in my life, and I hope that comes across to anyone reading this book. For years I've spoken of this incident at churches, and everyone I've talked to all says it *was* a miracle. I'm grateful for it—and in awe of it—to this day.

Above the Law

I was at home in 1988 when I got a call from Steven Segal, a then-unknown actor; he told me he was going to be making an action film called *Above the Law,* and that Andy Davis was going to direct it. He said he and Davis had thought of me when they were discussing who would fill the stunt coordinator position on the film, and they also wanted me to direct the second unit. I had Steven send me the script, and after I read it I met up with Segal and Davis.

I talked to them about making more than what was written out of the action sequences. It was Segal's first movie and if he wanted to be an action star, then they needed to have some really good action sequences in the movie for him to be involved in.

Steven was a soft-spoken, well-mannered man and we got along well while we were prepping the show. Andy wanted to shoot the move in Chicago, which had some great locations for the production to use.

The first sequence we shot was at a location in the warehouse district. It was composed of a big shoot-out featuring Steven running and ducking and diving in between cars while firing off his handgun—not an easy thing to do. He also had dialogue during the sequence which didn't match the soft-spoken guy that I knew. His automatic pistol jammed a few times during filming, and that made matters worse. I felt I knew Steven well enough to offer him some advice, so when the time was right, I talked to him about this being his first movie, and that it

ME AND MY SADDLE-PAL

would establish a viewer opinion of him. Because of the role (rough-talking and hard-fighting), it would likely not be a favorable opinion for about seventy-five percent of average movie-goers.

Since he was a martial artist, I asked him if he'd ever heard of Gene LeBell. Steven looked at me and said in excitement, "holy shit, you know Gene LeBell?"

"He's a good friend of mine, actually," I said. As I've mentioned, Gene was known as the "toughest man in the world," and he knew just about everything there was to know about Judo, grappling and martial arts. He also beat Sumo wrestlers in Japan.

I had an ulterior motive for bringing up Gene's name. He was an easygoing, well-mannered guy who was soft-spoken, and if someone was braggadocious when they went to fight Gene, he would quietly back away and tell them he didn't want to fight. Then he'd take him down—but help him up from the ground and apologize to him. He fought like a gentleman, which I thought would help Steven.

After I finished talking about Gene, I told Steven that that was how I thought he should play his character. For years, Steven had studied martial arts in Japan, and he spoke Japanese fluently, so I knew he was aware of Gene LeBell. I hoped I'd made an impression on him, but as we continued to shoot, his character stayed the same. He kept on me about bringing Gene to Chicago so he could meet him. I called Gene and told him about Steven, and he said it was just as well that he didn't work on the show, and I agreed with him.

We were going to do a big shoot-out in a twelve-story parking structure in Chicago, where the bad guys in the movie had trapped Steven's character. He was to jump in his car and take off, but he would get cut off by two cars blocking his way and trapping him. He would look back and see the other heavies approach him from the rear. The script had him back his car up, throw it into drive, then peel out and plow through the two cars blocking his way.

I changed it, however. In my version, Steven backed the car up and slammed into one of the heavies, impaling him on the trunk of the car. The parking garage had openings all around the structure on each floor that were six feet high and ten feet wide, covered with aluminum blinds. My idea was to replace the blinds in one opening with balsa wood and have Steven's double drive the car, in reverse, through the blinds with a dummy attached to the trunk. We cut a hole in the trunk with a mortar stuck into it, the end of which would go into the dummy's body. I had the car cabled off so it could only go about halfway through the blinds; that way you'd only see half of it sticking through, ten stories up. Then when the rear of the car hit the blinds, the effects man would push a button that activated the mortar, blowing the dummy off the trunk. Because a dummy *looks* like a dummy, when all is said and done, I had a stuntman do a high fall backwards from that height, all the way down to an airbag below. For that job, I called Peter Horack, a stuntman friend of mine who I knew could mentally handle a fall of that type. He was a good double for the actor, as well.

We installed a shallow platform on top of the car's bumper as it was sticking out about eight feet from the building that Peter could stand on. We also bolted two handles to the car's trunk that he could hold onto before he pushed off. This wasn't just a regular high fall, folks. When you can't look down at your airbag during the fall to judge the distance for when you're going to hit, it makes it *very* difficult to do mentally—never mind the fact that you're falling a hundred feet.

I was working with Peter up top at the car as they were setting up the cameras below. "Climb out through the rear window, grab the handles on the trunk and get into position so you can get the feel of this," I told him as I put a safety harness on him. I tied it off so he could get to his standing area, and once he got there he started looking down to see his airbag.

He looked from one side to the other, then back at me. "Mickey, I can't see my airbag."

"I know you can't, Peter, but it's there," I reassured him. "The reason you can't see it is because the car's sticking out about eight feet from the building, and you're a hundred feet up. Trust me, it's down there." I had him come back inside, then turn around and slide out on his belly so he could look down and see the bag. Then I got on my radio

ME AND MY SADDLE-PAL

and told the stunt safety men below that I was going to drop a twenty-five pound bean bag down to test the airbag's position, and I wanted Peter to watch while I did it. Once he was in position to look down, I pitched the bean bag into the fall area. It landed in the dead-center of the airbag.

"Good, good, it hit perfectly," Peter said in relief. I'd known he'd needed a confidence booster before doing the fall, and I wanted to do everything I could to boost it. I asked him if he'd like to go back down and do one last check of his airbag's position and the safety men, and he agreed, so I sent my assistant down with him. I was glad he'd decided to go; I figured he'd needed to get away from the take-off area and relax a little bit before we shot the actual stunt. Once he was down at the airbag, I radioed down and told them I was going to drop another bean bag so he could see it hit from below—this would also boost his confidence. Once again, it landed right in the center of the airbag, further boosting Peter's comfort with the upcoming fall.

They came back up, and I talked to Peter as he took his place on the platform. "Peter, when you push off, be sure and keep your eyes fixed on this car. Don't try to turn your head and look at your airbag, because if you do, your body will follow your head and you won't hit your bag right. Understand?"

He nodded, but to be sure I asked him to repeat what I'd just said. He did, and so we were ready to go.

We rolled the cameras, and I told Peter to take off. Nervously he asked me, "we're ready to go?"

"Yes, we're rolling," I replied. "You can do your stuff."

Instead of taking off, Peter tried to look back over his shoulder. Then he looked back at me and said, just as before, "Mickey, I can't see my airbag."

"I know you can't, Peter," I soothed him, "but it's right where it was when you were down there. It hasn't moved." We'd been rolling the cameras for about thirty seconds now, but I was determined to be patient with Peter, even when he asked me once again if we were in fact ready for him to go.

"We're still rolling, Peter," I said. "We're ready for you to do this."

Something must've clicked in his head then, because he looked at me and said, "bye-bye, Mickey!" Then he pushed off.

He did everything right during that fall—he stayed perfectly flat, waving his arms, kicking his legs and keeping his eyes locked on that car as he fell away from it. He hit dead-center on his airbag, just like the bean bags had done, and it made for a great-looking shot. I must say that there aren't many stuntmen who could've handled what Peter did that day, especially considering that he was falling from one hundred feet. If anyone reading this wants to get a feel for what Peter did in *Above the Law*, lay a mattress on the ground below the back bumper of your car, stand up there and fall backwards…just kidding.

Raising a Family of Stuntmen

I can't tell you how wonderful it's been to share my life not only with my beautiful wife Yvonne, but our three boys, as well.

Since they were knee-high, I'd been teaching Tim, Troy and Lance everything I could, from gymnastics to stunt-work. Being ranch boys, they often got bruised or banged-up, but they never looked for sympathy. Yvonne was always concerned about her boys getting hurt as they were learning the ups and downs of different stunts, but she also knew that they loved learning everything I was teaching them.

In one of my pastures on the ranch, I built a small motor-cross track that they could ride their Honda 70 motorbike on. It had small, short jumps on it so they could catch some air while riding. We also had a sand pit where I'd installed a high and low horizontal bar, a parallel bar, a rope climb and a trampoline. One day I put up a cable that ran from the top of the mountain down into the pasture. All in all, it was a hundred and fifty feet high and three hundred feet long, and it ran at a forty-five degree angle; it's called a long line or zip line. I had a special effects person rig up the pulley slider you hang onto when you're sliding on it, and once it was up and ready, I demonstrated a few times for the boys. Then they tried it. Of course, I'd rigged up a safety harness that they'd strap themselves into when they used it; the other end of it was attached to the sliding unit. The only problem with this contraption was that they had so much fun with it that I couldn't keep them off of it.

RAISING A FAMILY OF STUNTMEN

They would ride with me a lot, and I began to show them the ins and outs of horse work. One day Troy and I went riding when he was about eight years old, and I was chewing tobacco. Troy looked over at me thoughtfully. "Hey, Dad, does that stuff taste pretty good?" he asked.

"It's not bad," I said. "They soak the leaves in molasses to make it kind of sweet."

"Can I try some?" he asked.

Oh, boy, this *should be good,* I thought. I handed him the pouch. "Just put a little between your cheek and your gums, but whatever you do, don't swallow the saliva it's going to make in your mouth. Just spit it out."

I swear, I wish I'd had a movie camera with me, once he did it. He shoved a tobacco leaf into his mouth, moved it around, and within a very short time started spitting continuously. I looked back at him, trying to hold back my laughter. "Atta boy, just keep spitting. Don't swallow." By this time, Troy had tobacco juice all over his pant leg and his saddle. When I looked back again, he'd started throwing up off the side of his horse.

After he finished he looked at me and said weakly, "I think I swallowed some of it."

"I don't think you did—I *know* you did," I said. We rode over to the river so he could wash up, and then we rode home. He told Yvonne the story. She looked at me and shook her head.

"You and your boys."

Yvonne and I would take the boys on locations with us all over the world, and that alone was a great education for them. About the time I started working on *The Fall Guy* series, Tim had already been working stunts with me on a few other shows. *The Fall Guy* was a great start for him; he was a perfect double for Doug Barr, the second lead, and it would enable him to get himself established in the business. We would always hire from twenty to thirty stunt people for each episode, so it didn't take long for Tim's name to climb up into the business.

At that time, Troy was going to Questa College in San Luis Obispo, and Lance was in junior high in Canyon Country. During the second

ME AND MY SADDLE-PAL

season of *The Fall Guy,* Troy had a day off and drove down to visit Tim, who had just bought a home in Redondo Beach. Troy called me from Tim's house to say hi, and while we were talking, he happened to be sitting at Tim's desk. On it was a stack of residual payments from the show's first season. His curiosity got the better of him, and he asked me about the payments.

"Dad, Tim has all these documents that say 'residual payment statement.' What are those?"

I explained that Tim received payments from all the first season reruns of episodes he worked on. Troy's amazed voice came through the line, "holy Shit, there's almost sixty-thousand dollars worth of checks, here!"

"It's probably just the statements you're looking at," I told him, but he told me no, that the checks were still attached. I told him to get Tim on the phone, of course, so I could get on him for not depositing his residuals, and while I did that Troy evidently started thinking. He thought about making money doing something he wanted to do, which was stunt-work, of course, and he wanted my opinion about going into the business—which meant that he'd take a break from college for a bit.

"Dad," he told me earnestly, "I don't want to sit at a desk and work with computers for the rest of my life. I just don't think I'll be content if I do that."

I told him that if he wanted to get into the family business that his grandfather, his father and his brother were all in, now was the time, because my work on *The Fall Guy* provided the perfect opportunity. I told him that once he'd finished his semester at Questa, I'd bring him down and start him working on the series. He was a natural at stunts and could do anything I asked him to—and do it *well.*

His first stunt was flipping a truck over. Before we rolled the cameras, I told him, "Okay, Troy-Boy, stay calm and stay focused on this gag. Think of safety first and concentrate on what you have to do, right from the very start, and keep concentrating until the finish. After you take off, if something doesn't look or feel right to you, abort the stunt. Always remember that film is cheap, but you've only got one life."

RAISING A FAMILY OF STUNTMEN

Everything went perfect on that stunt, and it turned out to be a hell of a shot. At the end of the day, I paid out the stunt adjustments to each stunt person. The amount paid would be determined by the type of stunt and how dangerous it had been. I got to Troy, and I asked him how much he wanted for the stunt.

Being a novice, he had no idea about the prices of stunts, or the value of his talent. Tim was standing nearby, laughing, and Troy asked him what *he* would charge for the truck flip. Tim stepped up close to Troy and said, slowly, "twenty-five hundred dollars."

Troy's mouth dropped open and he looked over at me. "He's kidding, right, Dad?" he asked.

I chuckled at him. "Just because you knew how to do it, and had fun doing it, doesn't change the danger of it or lower the risk you took. It also doesn't change the value of it."

I told the boys that when I first got started, doing stunts came easily to me and was exciting and fun, but to put it into perspective, is it worth it to break yourself up over the money you make? There's always that chance. "I don't care how qualified you are at doing different stunts," I told them, "don't ever think you're being over-paid just because you're performing a stunt you find easy to do."

Lance came along into the business about two years after Troy; my best friend Freddy Waugh got him started on some shows he was working on. He told me that Lance was one hell of an athlete and an excellent stuntman. Lance's first big movie with me was *Renegades*, with Keifer Sutherland and Lou Diamond Philips. I took all the boys with me to Toronto to work on that film, and they played key parts in the big car-chase scene that I wrote and directed—one of the best car-chase scenes I'd ever done.

Over the years they've continued to work with me, as you will read, and my grandson Cody is a stuntman now, too—so with three generations of Gilberts in stunts and my father-in-law and brother-in-law before me, I guess you can truly say that stunts run in our blood in this family.

Renegades

✦

In 1989 I headed to Montreal, Canada, to work on a film starring Kiefer Sutherland and Lou Diamond Phillips called *Renegades*. One of the executive producers, Joe Roth, had called me about the project and brought me in to meet the director, Jack Sholder, whom I liked very much. I took all three of my sons with me to work on the film, which would have a lot of action sequences for us to work on. Troy would double for Keifer Sutherland, whom he'd doubled before, and Lance and Tim would double various other actors on the shoot.

The car chases and action scenes in the film were big ones, so I needed to hire a lot of local Canadian stuntmen. Fortunately Sholder gave me a long leash to put together whatever I thought would work well for the show. I started scouting locations, and one day I took Sholder with me.

There was a big dirt parking lot we used for the crew's cars, the camera vehicles, and any other cars associated with the production, and I had Jack drive me there in his car. When we got there, I told him to park and we'd take my car—I'd drive.

He got into the passenger seat and as I slid into the driver's, I told him to buckle his seatbelt. He was always asking me about the crazy things stuntmen like me were able to do in cars—making them slide, spinning them around, that sort of thing. So today I looked over and asked him, "hey, Jack, you wanna learn how to do some of that stuff?"

RENEGADES

"Yeah, that would be kind of fun," he said.

"Okay, let's go check out some locations." As I said it, I'd slipped the car into reverse without him seeing it, and then I shoved my foot down on the gas pedal, sending the car into a backwards spin and surprising the hell out of Sholder. Then I did a reverse 180 and now we were going forward again, ready to pull out of the parking lot.

"How'd you like that?" I grinned at him.

He was beside himself with excitement. "Oh, my God, you've *got* to show me how to do that!"

"I will," I chuckled, "but let me take you out to the locations right now."

He liked just about everything I'd found—there would be a chase down railroad tracks that led into the Goodyear tire factory, but one location didn't sit well with him. It was a veterinary office with a roof that sloped out over the sidewalk and was supported by a pillar, with an alleyway right next to it. I thought we could do a gag involving a car driving through there and going down the alleyway, but for some reason, Sholder didn't like it.

"I don't like this area," he told me. "Find somewhere else."

I'd been planning to glass the whole area in and put offices in there, and Troy was going to drive a limo right through it, knocking over desks as he went, before driving out the other side and continuing out down the alley. I thought it would be a great gag, but I didn't say anything to Sholder. Instead, I took a chance and had them build up the set anyway. When it was done I took Jack out again, passing by the now glassed-in area that was dressed as an office, just like I'd planned.

"You see that area over there?" I said casually. "We're going to have a car drive through all of that glass and go through the office, then come out the other side and go down the alley. The cops will turn down the alley, too, and chase it." I said nothing about his rejection of the area before.

"Yeah, yeah, that'll be great!" he said enthusiastically. "It looks like a perfect spot." I smiled to myself—just as I'd figured, he hadn't recognized the area and didn't realize it was the same location he'd rejected at first.

There was a big sequence at the Goodyear factory in which Troy was doubling for Keifer, driving a black limo and being chased by four cop cars. Tim and Lance were driving the lead cars. They were all racing down an alley-way that was just barely wide enough for two cars. Toward the end of the alley was a forty-foot semi truck and trailer where a crew were unloading material.

Inside the trailer of the semi was a ramp that extended from the trailer's loading ramp all the way through the trailer to the other end, at the trailer's rooftop. As Tim and Lance were chasing Troy, Troy swerved around the semi. Tim and Lance, who were side-by side, tried to swerve around it, too, but couldn't fit into the tight area. Tim's car bounced into the buliding that formed the left side of the alley, then swerved back to its right, slamming into Lance's car—which forced Lance onto the semi's ramp. Stunt workers jumped out of the way as Lance's car disappeared inside the semi's trailer.

As Tim's car continued past the semi, Lance's car came bursting through the roof of the trailer, over the cab of the semi, catches air and landed on top of Tim's car, causing a huge pile-up of police cars. Needless to say, Troy's limo got away. Sholder had no idea how I was going to pull it off, but he liked the idea so much that he told me to go for it.

The stunts went really well, and the whole time we were shooting, Sholder kept reminding me that I'd promised to show him how to do the car spins I'd done that day before we'd gone out scouting locations. Finally I took him down to the parking lot again and showed him how to do the various spins, working the emergency brake and the gas pedal in a way that would make the car do what you wanted it to.

"Now, Jack," I told him, "you've got to be careful. You can't just do this anywhere—you're liable to slide into a parked car or something. You need to practice this somewhere safe, like this lot we're in now. It's better to practice on dirt than on asphalt."

"Okay, I hear you," he told me, nodding vigorously. From then on, every morning before we'd get to work on the movie, we'd hear the tires of a car screeching and squealing in the parking lot of the building that served as our offices.

RENEGADES

"Here comes Sholder," someone would say dryly, and we'd look out the window to see him sliding his car this way and that as he drove up. Every time he drove his car, it seemed like, he'd throw it around, practicing the moves I'd taught him.

"You gotta be careful!" I'd tell him warningly, just about every time I saw him.

We moved the production to Philadelphia to shoot a train sequence. In it, Lou Diamond Phillips' character is being chased through the train—and eventually *over* it, since he ends up on top of the cars. In the scene, the train he's on passes into a depot area, where another train is moving past in the opposite direction, going about twenty miles an hour. Phillips's character was supposed to jump from the original train onto the second one. Sholder was down inside one of the train cars with a monitor, watching while I was directing the stunt on top.

Pretty soon it was time to break for lunch, which we were all having inside the train cars. I went down to see Jack and found him sitting with two older people I didn't know, and he had a brown paper bag on his lap. He was eating something out of the bag, and it was clearly something good, from the way he was shoveling it in. He saw me and gestured to the two people he was sitting with. "Mickey, these are my parents," he said, in between bites.

"Hi there, folks," I greeted them. "Nice to meet you." I looked at my director. "What do you think of the sequence so far?"

"It's great, I love it," he said, around a mouthful of whatever-it-was.

"What are you eating, there, Jack?" I asked, raising my eyebrow at him.

"Homemade Twinkies," he told me. "My mother makes them. Here, have one," he said, offering me the bag.

I took one and squeezed it; the filling went running out between my fingers. Looking at Jack, I said, pretending to be appalled, "you've got to be kidding me. You actually *eat* this junk food?" Jack and his parents looked at one another, startled at what I'd done. I reached for the Twinkie bag. "Here, give me another one." Jack jerked the bag away from me, snatching it against his chest like it was a precious thing. I started laughing then, and told his mom not to be offended, that I couldn't help myself under the circumstances. As I left to go back up to the train's roof, I looked back at Jack. "Are you coming up to watch, or would you rather sit there and eat the rest of those Twinkies?"

"I'm going to sit here and finish these," he replied, he and his parents all looking at me like I was nuts as I left.

We finished the train stunts and moved on to a sequence at a big equestrian estate. Lou Diamond Phillips was going to be inside the barn, taking cover from guys who were shooting at him. Eventually the bad guys throw in a molotov cocktail and set the barn on fire. Obviously we weren't going to set the existing barn on fire, so we built our own that we could do with what we liked. In the scene, Phillips would let all of the horses out of their stalls, vaulting up onto the back of one of them and riding amongst the others as they all headed out of the burning barn in a herd.

When we went to film it, an unfortunate accident occurred. As the horses were running out of the barn, one of them got bumped by another, causing him to swerve against some two-by-six fencing that was connected to the barn on the side that ran alongside the driveway. The impact caused the fencing to pull away from the post it was anchored to, and the horse was impaled by one of the two-by-sixes, right into his chest.

I yelled "cut!" and everyone ran over to the injured animal, who was down by that time, the two-by-six embedded about a foot and a half deep into his body. We got ropes around him and managed to pull him free of the fence-rail, but we knew he was bad off—we could hear his lungs gurgling as he breathed. I knew the injury was fatal when I heard that, and I also knew the poor animal was suffering.

We didn't have a veterinarian on-site, but there was a cop who had a pistol. Shooting the horse would be the quickest way to end its suffering. I asked the police officer to do the deed for the horse's sake, but he wouldn't do it, so I offered to do it myself if he'd let me use his gun. He refused to let me. I pleaded with him, telling him it looked to me like the wood might have punctured the horse's heart or lungs and that it was obvious he needed to be put down immediately, but the cop wouldn't budge. Before I could convince him to change his mind, the horse died on its own.

It was a freak accident, one we would've had no way of predicting or preparing for. The horse would've had to hit that fence just right for the rail to impale him the way it had. I remained upset that the police officer had refused to let me use his gun to help ease the horse's passing, but there was nothing to be done about it.

As far as directors went, Jack Sholder was a great one for me because he pretty much gave me free rein to do what I wanted to do with stunts, but he was also really gullible as far as what he thought stuntmen were capable of doing. We were going to film a scene in which Keifer Sutherland and Lou Diamond Phillips were going to jump from a rooftop during a foot-chase scene. I'd found a parking garage with a flat roof to use for the sequence. To the left of it was a four-story building with fire escapes on its sides, and to the right was another building about six feet away from the one we'd have them jump from. It was just a small ways for them to jump in reality, but I told Sholder I'd chosen the location because we could shoot from underneath and make it look higher-up than it really was, using tricks of the camera to make it look more dangerous.

Sholder thought I was going to have them jump from the four-story building—*really* jump the whole way. I couldn't believe he actually thought that someone could do such a thing and not kill themselves or at least be severely injured. To test whether he really was *that* naive, I "volunteered" to jump off the building right then and there, with no airbag. He really did think I could do it, apparently, because he let me climb all the way up there and look down at him.

"You really think I could just jump off this thing, right now, and land safely?" I scoffed.

"Well, you said you could," he replied.

I shook my head and climbed back down the fire-escapes. "Jack, come *on*," I said. "No one could jump from that height and land on a hard surface without being killed, or having a bunch of bones broken!"

He shrugged. "Well, you said you could!"

Naive or not, Jack and I became good friends on that shoot and spent a lot of time together, getting together with our wives. He never did direct any big movies after that one, but *Renegades* was a good action film, and I had a good time working on it.

Old Gringo

In 1989, Warner Brothers released a film called *Old Gringo,* a big-screen adaptation of Carlos Fuentes' novel *Gringo Viejo.* The film was directed by Luis Puenzo and starred Jane Fonda, Gregory Peck, and Jimmy Smits, and it was being produced by a good friend of Jane Fonda's named Lois Bonfiglio. The plot involved an American schoolteacher named Harriet Winslow (Jane Fonda) who travels to Mexico to work as a governess and ends up getting caught up in the Mexican revolution of 1818.

When the film was starting production, I got a call from the studio telling me they were interested in using me for the stunt coordination. They told me to come and get the script so I could read it and break it down, and then we could discuss what I thought about the project.

After I read the script, I had a meeting with the film's executive producer, David Wisnievitz. I'd prepared a budget for my end of it, and it came to about nine hundred thousand dollars—there were some big battle sequences to coordinate and pull off, and that translated to big bucks. Wisnievitz shook his head when he heard that. The budget allotted for the stunts was only three hundred thousand.

"That's just a figure, though, put in there to complete the budget. You probably put it in there, right?" I asked. He nodded. "Well," I said, "how did you settle on that figure, when you weren't sure what we needed?" I knew he had no idea what staging such large battle scenes would cost, since he wasn't in stunt coordination.

ME AND MY SADDLE-PAL

He shrugged. "That's what's been allotted," he said again.

I told him I needed to level with him, to explain why I'd come up with the figure that I had. "Look, for this to work, I'll need American stuntmen that can handle horses, and Mexican stuntmen that are horseman, as well. You've got some *huge* battles in here, and it's going to need to have a big scope to make it look right. Three hundred thousand won't cut it—you can hardly *start* it with that."

"Well, we'll have to discuss it later on," he replied.

I tried one more time, determined to be up front and honest with him—I believe in being direct. "Okay, but if that's the budget you stick to and you still want me to be the stunt coordinator, you're gonna have problems."

"We'll talk about it later," he said again.

I gave up and proceeded to get in touch with Rudy Ugland, a horse trainer and wrangler I knew who was a good friend of mine. He would bring in the horses for the actors, and the stunt horses we needed.

During my planning I had figured we'd need about fifteen professional American stuntmen, and one stuntwoman, as well as about fifty Mexican performers—some stuntmen and some experienced horsemen.

I got hired for the project, so Yvonne and I packed up and headed to Mexico City, and I began scouting locations. I met the crew and the heads of the different departments that made up the production. There were some interesting people involved; I remember that one of the effects guys had six wives, and something like eighteen children who lived all over Mexico. I was curious how he managed such a lifestyle, and when I asked him he told me he allotted a certain amount of his time per month to each family. I suppose it takes all kinds of people to make a world. Anyway, I met with the Mexican stuntmen and had one of the head ones bring in experienced riders to participate in the film.

The movie was to open with a massive battle sequence, and I began to search for the perfect location to film it. My driver, who was a Mexican native, took me all over as I searched for just the right place. I asked him to think of places he knew of that might work for what we needed to do. After some searching, I found a location known as Prism Canyon. It's a place of incredible natural beauty, formed by water cutting into the canyon walls over millions of years. The canyon walls were around eighty feet high, running for around two hundred yards on either side of a dry creek bed made mostly of rock, and at one end there was a seventy-foot cliff where the river ended and the canyon began. Someone could ride a horse along that river and come to that cliff, and there was that amazing canyon of prisms spreading out before them. I was excited to use the location for a battle scene—it was so unique.

I took some of the other crew out there and showed them the place, and they were just as enthusiastic; they thought it was gorgeous. I told them I was going to get things moving to stage a battle scene there. There was some concern amongst them about the fact that the canyon floor was mostly rock; they were concerned about the danger of the horses slipping unexpectedly, but I told them I'd solve it by hiring some dump trucks to bring in loads of sand to create safe places where I could stage horse falls.

We did this, and I had a sand wash created that was about a foot and a half deep with brush planted into it, and I had other sandy places put in, some higher up, some lower down, so I had lots of specific areas to work with.

Everything was going well. The locations were being prepped, and I was conferring with Jane Fonda and Lois Bonfiglio quite frequently. I got to know them pretty well, and they saw eye-to-eye with me as far as the things I had planned for the production. We often stayed in the same hotels and had breakfast together. My favorite was good old-fashioned Shredded Wheat, which Jane thought looked pretty good—so good, in fact, that she had a whole case of it—twenty-four boxes—flown out to Mexico City from Los Angeles to eat for breakfast while we were all in Mexico. She was wonderful to work with and very agreeable to my ideas for the film.

Around the time Prism Canyon was being prepared for the stunt sequence, David Wisnievitz, the film's executive producer and the one who'd disagreed with my proposed budget, called me in for a progress meeting.

"How's everything going?" he asked.

"Great," I told him. "Rudy's on his way with the horses, and I'm getting all set up at Prism Canyon. I've got all the Mexican stunt people lined up, and everything's great."

It was then that he delivered a blow, telling me I could not bring in the fifteen American stuntmen and woman I needed.

"What?" I asked incredulously. "What are you talking about? This battle's been planned out around those people!"

"Well, we don't have it in the budget."

I reminded him of our meeting back at Warner Brothers, and how I'd told him what I needed to do the job he wanted me to do—and how I'd made it clear that doing so would require more money than the three hundred thousand he'd decided on.

"Not having those American stunt people on the production will help us stay on budget," he argued, "because if we brought them in, we'd have to put them on salary and pay them per diem, and put them up in hotels besides."

"That's just par for the course on movies like this one," I reminded him, feeling like I was stating the obvious. He knew this just as well as I did.

"Well, we're not bringing them," he said with an air of finality.

I couldn't believe this was happening. I sat there for a minute, just looking at him. I knew Wisnievitz fairly well—we played tennis together a lot, and would have a beer together afterward. I'd never dreamed I'd be sitting here across from him like this, at an impasse over this movie. But he did not seem like he was going to budge.

I took a deep breath and closed my script, and closed up the notebooks I kept all my notes for the job in. I put them on his desk. "If that's the way you feel, David, then I'm going to have to bow out of this film, and go get a plane ticket back to the States," I said soberly.

"What are you talking about?" he asked in alarm.

I shook my head. "I can't do this project if I have to do it the cheapest way possible," I told him. "I take pride in what I do, and when I do a film I want to make the scenes I'm coordinating or directing look the best I can make them look. I cannot do that on the budget you want me to. So there are all my notes, you can give them to the next guy if you want." I stuck out my hand to shake his, but he was evidently too shocked to respond, because he didn't take it. I dropped my hand and told him I was just going to go say goodbye to Jane and Lois before I left, and I walked out of his office.

I went to go see Jane in Lois's office, and before I could get there David came charging out of his office after me, calling "Mickey, wait! Come back! Let's talk."

"We just *did*, David," I reminded him. "I don't think there's anything else that needs to be said, here."

"No, no, come on back into my office for a minute," he insisted, so I followed him. I figured he didn't want me saying anything to Jane or Lois about what had happened, because he'd be stuck in the middle. He told me he'd work things out about the budget.

I wasn't very reassured because of the way our last conversation about budget, back in Hollywood, had gone. "David, when I start doing this, I'll be turning in my budget every day, and you will see thousands of dollars being spent to pay all of those stuntmen. I'll be turning that in to the production, and you're not going to like it. I told you I needed a budget of nine hundred thousand back when we were in L.A., and I'll bet you haven't even discussed it with anyone else in the production, have you?"

He sighed. "I'll be honest, Mickey, I haven't."

I shook my head. "David, I've got dates on all my paperwork and on all the budgets I drew up at the beginning. I made it clear what I needed a long time ago. If I need to, I'll turn that all in, because I refuse to be put in the middle of things when the shit hits the fan about this, understand? The budget isn't my responsibility, it's yours."

"Don't worry about it," he said firmly. "We'll bring your guys over, and we'll do what you need us to do."

I gave him a look. "You must have some money hidden around

somewhere, I'm betting," I said. "This isn't my first go-cart race, David; I've been around this kind of thing before." He just sort of laughed. I knew he had the money for what I needed, so I agreed to stay on.

My American stunt people came in, and we were moving things along, getting ready to start shooting. At the fort location for the film, they constructed smaller adobe buildings within the fort's walls, and those buildings housed many facets of the production, such as the makeup department, the hairdressers, prop-makers, the costume department and all the seamstresses, which were local Mexican women. This was so they could keep everyone on set and still use the location to shoot scenes. The audience would see what looked like adobe shops and dwellings that were part of life inside the fort, never knowing that inside them were crew-members making wardrobe and props and doing hair and makeup.

Yvonne was going with me to all the locations so she wouldn't be bored in the hotel all day, and on the day we went out to the fort she said, "I don't know why you don't have me double Jane. I'd be perfect."

I disagreed. "You're too short, and you're thinner than she is, and besides that, I'm not comfortable with you doing stunts. It's too dangerous."

"But it would just be on this one show," she protested. "I could be drawing pay for it, bringing in more income for us, and besides, I *do* look like her."

Before I could reply, one of the hairdressers came out of the adobe she'd been working on and called to me in her Mexican accent, "Hello, Mickey! This is the double for Jane?" as she gestured to Yvonne.

Yvonne gave me a look that said, "see? What did I just tell you?"

I shook my head, both at her and at the hairdresser. "No, this is my wife, Yvonne."

"Oh, my goodness, you look so much like Jane!" the hairdresser gushed. "You are not related to her?"

Yvonne started to laugh. "No, I'm not." She gave me another look.

I rolled my eyes, refusing to bend. Now I had *that* over my head.

Another day I went to wardrobe to give them the measurements of all the stunt people for their costumes, and Yvonne was with me. The costume designer, Enrico Sabbatini, came up to us. "Oh, are you *Señora* Jane's double?" he asked Yvonne. Again, I got the look.

"Oh, no," she replied, "I'm Mickey's wife."

"Oh, my God, you could double for Jane Fonda!" he exclaimed. "You look just like her!"

That was number two.

Then we went to makeup, and the makeup gal came over. "I need to test out some makeup on you," she told Yvonne, "even though you're the perfect double for Miss Fonda now, as it is."

That was number three.

"Look, Yvonne, you're *not* going to double her," I said firmly. "I've already got a double for her lined up who's on her way here."

Yvonne did not end up doubling for Jane, in spite of all the crew members (and Yvonne herself) who thought that she should. I just wasn't willing to risk her safety. I know it was disappointing for her—and I haven't heard the end of it to this day.

There was another disappointment in store for Yvonne during the shoot,

unfortunately. During an off day we decided to go out and see the pyramids, and she and I took bottled water with us when we went. You had to be careful not to drink local water because it could make you sick, and you had to stay on your toes and make sure you weren't getting it in unexpected places, like the ice in your drink.

We finished our bottled water and when we were coming back down, we decided to stop at the Pyramid Bar to have some lunch. We were thirsty, so we ordered some cokes. I asked for mine *sin hielo,* which means "without ice." Yvonne ordered one, also, but she forgot to tell them not to put the ice in.

Our drinks came, and I didn't notice that Yvonne's had ice in it; she didn't either. By that evening, she was *sick*. And the next day. And the next. It must've kept her down a whole week, and people on the crew started noticing her absence. "*Donde es su esposa?*" they kept asking me, and I told them what had happened. Finally Jane Fonda noticed, and she offered to get a doctor in there to look at Yvonne, which I was grateful for. The doctor gave her an injection, and it completely turned around—the next day she was back on her feet again and feeling great.

"So, Yvonne," I asked her over dinner that next night, "how do you want your drinks from now on?"

"*Sin hielo!*" she said immediately, shaking her head, and neither of us got ice in any of our drinks for the rest of the shoot.

∽∾

I heard about something pretty amazing when I met up with the head carpenter to go over a few things I'd need built for my stunt sequences—things to hide cameras in, catchers for pads for the stuntmen to fall into, and so forth. I told him I would make up a list, which he was grateful for; I was asking for things early in the shoot and not rushing him. Then he told me the story.

"You have a driver, right?" he asked me. I nodded. "Well, I have a driver too, his name's Ricardo. You gotta hear this: one morning he was driving me out here, and we stopped at this little convenience store. There was this big sign in one of the windows for some kind of lottery. Ricardo comes running back to the car. 'Hey, Boss, give me twenty pesos!' "What for?' I ask him. 'I'm gonna buy some lottery tickets.' I don't believe in that; I think it's a bunch of B.S., but I gave him the money to get him off my back. So one morning about a week later, he detours to that store again and tells me he's gonna see if we won. 'We're gonna win this, Boss,' he keeps saying. So I'm rolling my eyes, but I let him go in, and he starts jumping up and down and spinning in circles, and he tells me we won. I think he's just bullshitting me, but he makes me come inside and shows me the numbers—and damned if he wasn't telling me the truth—we *did* win."

He told me the winnings amounted to about five hundred thousand American—and this was the late eighties. He told me he'd put the money in a bank in Tijuana and he'd be able to withdraw it in cash as long as he only withdrew nine-thousand-ninety-nine dollars at a time. He planned to live in San Diego and make trips to that bank on the border. He was over the moon.

"That's incredible, man! What did you do for Ricardo?" I asked.

"I bought him a beautiful four-bedroom home in a nice neighborhood outside of Mexico City, and a brand-new car, and gave him some extra cash besides. He's in hog heaven and waltzing around here like he's royalty!"

"That's really nice," I said. "What a great story!"

I'm sure he doesn't think lotteries are B.S. any longer, and I know Ricardo was glad he got those twenty pesos out of his boss that day.

Inside the fort, they'd built railroad tracks along the front of all the adobe buildings as part of the set; the trains would come in to the plaza with loads of supplies, then exit the fort on a so-called 'spur' of track that went through huge gates and hooked up with the track outside. We were going to stage a battle involving the train, where groups of Mexican revolutionaries under Pancho Villa came rolling into the plaza on flat cars, all wearing bandoleros and brandishing rifles.

I designed the battle sequence for this location, and I took the director and Jane out along the train tracks outside of the fort and explained what I wanted to do. There was nothing alongside the tracks except brush, and I told them I wanted to clear everything out with bulldozers and create small hills along the track, like sand dunes, one after another. I would have the revolutionaries on horseback riding alongside the train carrying the men. I took them back toward the fort and looked down at the track, and told them that on a long lens, they could capture "waves" of riders going up and down these little dunes alongside the train. The effect would be dramatic. Added to that was the fact that we'd be having cannons be fired from the fort, trying to ward them off. The mortars would cause big explosions full of flying debris, and horses would be falling, and men would be knocked out of their saddles and off the train. The sand dunes, made of sand that I'd have trucked in, would also serve as a soft place for people and horses to land. I was trying to paint a picture for them, and they must've gotten it, because they were enthusiastic. "This will look great!" One concern they had, though, was how we were going to get everyone into the fort.

I told them that I'd have one of the revolutionaries come running into the fort during the battle and pull the lever that diverted the train from the main line onto the spur that went into the fort through the gates. As he's doing this, he gets shot, and his body lays over the lever. Gregory Peck's character Ambrose Bierce would see this, ride over and throw the body off, trying to flip the lever back so that the train will keep on going down the main line. He can't get it flipped in time, though, so the train comes barreling on through into the fort. Now you have the battle from the outside being brought inside.

I started work prepping the location, getting the bulldozers in there and bringing in the sand to create my dunes. I had plywood "chambers" built into some of the dunes on the downhill side that a camera operator could be holed up in with his camera, to capture the action up close and personal and get some really unique shots of the horses going right down the dunes at a full gallop, or falling down them. The boxes would be sturdy enough, of course, to keep the cameramen safe. I had cameras in other locations, too, to be sure and capture the sequence from enough angles to be able to put together a really amazing piece.

Pretty soon we were ready to get started shooting. The stunt people, including my three boys, were all there and ready, the wranglers were there, and the horses had arrived. We left Mexico City and headed to Pachuca in Hildalgo to start on our battle in Prism Canyon. I laid everything out to the stuntmen, and then I spoke to the effects crew. I wanted them to plant mortars around different places in the sandy wash we'd created at the bottom of the canyon and mark them with flags or trees so we'd know where they were. I also wanted them to bury containers here and there that would be filled with water and dry ice, to create a misty or smoky effect all along the length of the canyon. It would give it a nice eerie look, and the clouds created by the dry ice would swirl around the bodies of the horses and men that fell into them. The rehearsals we did ensured that everybody involved knew exactly were each dry-ice pot and mortar were located—I didn't want horses being ridden over these things during shooting; that would be a safety hazard for the horses.

I had the soldiers up on top of the canyon and the revolutionaries riding through the bottom, and I was confident the scene would look terrific—tons of gunplay, horses falling everywhere through the vapor from the dry ice, men flying every which way. In one part, my son Lance got to do his first high fall. He'd only been in the business for a year or two at this point, and he was pulling out the big guns already. We took him up to a spot about seventy feet high or so, and there was a catcher built with a airbag for him to fall into. He'd be holding a rifle as he fell, but it was a rubber one, so he couldn't hurt himself with it during the stunt.

"What do you think?" I asked him. "Look okay to you?"

"Yeah," he replied, "it's just higher than my trampoline at home."

"Yes, but know where you are in the air, plan out the fall, and you'll do great."

As I mentioned, this was Lance's first high fall, and Yvonne was on location with us. She was understandably apprehensive about the stunt—seeing your son fall seventy feet through the air is nerve-wracking, of course. Yvonne led the entire crew of stuntmen in a prayer for their safety, like she would continue to do every time she was on set with me from then on. It became a habit, and it was a good habit, because it was very comforting to everyone involved.

We started shooting, and the scene was almost like a miniature movie within a movie, because it was so complicated to shoot and there were so many cameras being used from all different angles. It kept going and going on to a climax, which involved my son Troy.

I'd worked out a scenario in my mind; I wanted to see a soldier on the edge of that big cliff where the river met the canyon. I envisioned the horse rearing up and running full-speed toward the cliff, and leaping off. Of course, I could not have a real horse jump off that seventy-foot cliff—at least, not with out a safety line. I told Troy I'd rig up a harness for the horse he'd use out of nylon straps that would run underneath the horse and back up behind the shoulders and in front of the flanks, and come together through the hole in the saddle's pommel, right behind the saddle horn. Attached to rings on this harness would be another line that would go up near Troy's face; this line would be attached to a crane. Troy would use one of the trained rearing horses Rudy had brought to do the big rear, and then we'd use a second horse to double that one; this second horse would be wearing the crane-harness outfit under its saddle.

I told Troy that after he did his rear, he'd switch to the second horse and back him up aways from the cliff's edge. Then we'd hook him up to the crane, and Troy would get him running as fast as he could toward that edge.

The horse's natural instinct would be to plant its hooves and stop when it got close, so the crane would keep him going toward the edge, besides acting as the device that would control the horse's fall. I knew the horse would likely leap when it got to the edge, as most horses naturally do. Once the horse was in mid-air, the descender on the crane would let it down into the canyon, and we'd shoot its descent in slow motion. We would paint the cable out in post-production, of course (this was before computers could eliminate unwanted things from shots, or put things in that weren't there already).

Troy looked at me like I was off my rocker a bit. Clearly, he wasn't so sure. "How the heck did you think of something like *that*?" he asked me incredulously.

I shrugged. "Hey, it's never been done before. So let's give it a go and be the first to do it." Simple.

So, as I always liked to do, I ended up creating and executing a stunt that was the first of its kind. The seamstresses who'd made all the costumes ended up sewing the safety harness for the horse to my specifications, out of nylon that was the same color as the horse's coat. It was also well-concealed by the saddle.

Troy tested out the horse that would be doing the jump, and though at first he didn't want to go anywhere near the edge, but after Troy worked with him a bit, he got to where he'd go within six feet of the edge, which was all we needed him to do. I reminded Troy that the crane would have the horse—and him—on tension the whole time.

The day came when we did the shot. My luck and the Lord must have been with me that day, because it worked *perfectly*. The horse got within about five or six feet from the cliff's edge, and once the crane took him, he gathered his legs under him and leapt right out into the open space, just like I'd hoped he would. As he was in mid-air, his legs were pawing, making running motions, and it looked *wild*. Everyone loved that shot.

Then, after all that work, all that preparation and innovation, what do you think happened?

That battle got cut out of the movie.

I was *devastated*. I'd been so proud of that sequence—it was so intricate and so multi-faceted, and then to have it cut out of the finished product…I was heartbroken. To this day, I think that's the best battle sequence I've ever shot, and that no one's ever seen. But such is the nature of the movie business. Sometimes some of the best things done are the things that don't make the movie, sacrificed for any number of reasons, like running time or giving the actors more screen time, since they're the box-office draw (in this case, it was for running time), and guys like me don't have the final say. I'm glad I could tell you about it here—though of course, it would have been better if you could have *seen* it.

ME AND MY SADDLE-PAL

A worthwhile footnote to that ill-fated battle sequence was that while I was working on it, the head of the studio came out to see for himself what was going on. He loved what he saw; he was impressed by the battle, but he had a question for me that I hadn't expected him to ask.

"Mickey, who gave you permission to spend fifty thousand dollars to put a road in out here?" he asked, pointing to the new road that I'd seen people working on during the shoot.

I was completely confused. "What are you talking about? I didn't have anyone put that road in out here. I just had dump trucks come out and dump sand in over the edges of the canyon to pad the bottom of it. There *were* a couple of guys out here with a tractor and a dump truck, working on that road, but they were going on past us."

"That's where the production built Pancho Villa's hacienda," he said.

"I hate to tell you this, Gary," I said, "but when we came out here we were just following two lines of tire-tracks. None of that was here." I gestured to the road he was talking about. "Who told you my unit spent fifty thousand dollars to put that in?"

"The transportation captain."

I was furious. I knew what was going on here—blame was being shifted from the first unit to the second unit—*my* unit—for spending so much money. I set the studio head straight. "Gary, there were *two* people building that road—one guy with a tractor that was smoothing it, and the other with a dump truck that was dumping granite. Do you *really* think that the transportation captain paid those two guys fifty thousand dollars? That road isn't worth even *five* thousand dollars! You'd better look into it, because I bet you that transportation captain is keeping the rest of that money for his own use." There was no way in hell I was going to let my unit take the blame for someone else's dishonest activity.

Turned out I was right, and they fired the guy, as, of course, they should have.

OLD GRINGO

With the Prism Canyon battle completed, we started to shoot the big battle at the fort. Everything was prepped there as I'd asked it to be, with my sand dunes and pits dug in certain places in the sand for stunt people to fall into. There was a parapet running around the edge of the fort's wall where the cannons were, and I planned to have guys get shot off of it during the fight.

The first part of the battle was the part with the revolutionaries on the train and riding alongside on horseback up and down the dunes. We shot it in pieces, and ended up looking really dramatic and very period-appropriate.

We did our shot with Gregory Peck trying to divert the train, and that went well. But in between the times he was needed, Peck used to sit in the saddle of his white horse and just watch us work. He wouldn't be in the scenes we were working on, but he enjoyed watching the action. I tried to convince him to go back to his trailer and relax a bit; he was in his seventies by this time and I figured he might want to take it easy in between takes. But he always resisted. "I really like watching you guys work, Mick; you guys are really something," he'd tell me, and he didn't want to sit anywhere but on his white horse. So I kept him out of the way and let him watch—he *was* Gregory Peck, after all, and he was a *great* guy.

One day, though, Rudy Ugland, the head wrangler, was standing with his own horse near where Gregory was parked in his saddle when he noticed Peck's head starting to bob—he was nodding off. It went further, and he started to slide right off the horse. Rudy dropped his reins and rushed over to catch him before he could get hurt. He pushed him back up into the saddle. "Greg, are you okay?"

Gregory started laughing. "Oh, yeah, I just nodded off there for a second," he said sheepishly.

Rudy came to me and told me we needed to put a wrangler on Peck to act as safety net for the actor. We wouldn't take the experience of watching us work away from him since he really did seem to enjoy it so much, but we couldn't chance him getting hurt. We charged Mitch, the wrangler who took care of Gregory's white horse on set, with the task of "wrangling" the sleepy Peck, and luckily it all worked out fine. I caught Peck dozing off on several more occasions, just like he had that first time, but Mitch was there to rescue him, so all was well.

The battle was action upon more action, and I had a lot to keep track of. For the interior part of the battle we moved to Estudios Churubusco in Mexico City, one of the oldest and largest studios in Latin America. This would house part of the hacienda that was inside the fort, along with part of the battlefield. It was made up of two soundstages built back-to-back, with a wall separating them. One soundstage wasn't big enough for what we needed, so the crew had some experts come in there and cut a massive hole—around thirty by sixty feet—into the wall between the two. They had to brace everything and reinforce what was left of the wall once they'd cut it, so this in itself was quite the project.

They got it done, and we started shooting in there. I had some stuntmen on horseback that were going to be charging from the plaza section of the soundstage through the glass of the hacienda's huge windows; the glass would be break-away glass.

Rudy and I started discussing how we'd get the horses trained to go through this glass without stopping, which would be their natural instinct to do. We decided we would have construction build us a huge window frame that was ten feet tall and twenty-five feet in length. The construction department supplied us with large rolls of cellophane that we fastened to the window frame; then we set the frame on the stage where we would be doing the actual scene. Once this was done, we cut vertical slits through the cellophane, about four feet apart, so that each horse and rider could go through.

At first, each horse would walk up to the cellophane and sniff it, and then each stuntman would ease him through it. We rehearsed them each day, several times, until they got to where they felt comfortable running through cellophane that *didn't* have slits in it. At this point, the horses wouldn't think twice about going through the break-away glass—they wouldn't know the difference between that and the cellophane.

The day we were going to get this shot, the construction unit set the break-away glass up, and they also set up the cellophane unit in another area of the stage, like we'd used in training. Just before we did the shot, we rehearsed the horses through the cellophane one more time.

All the training paid off and it worked well, and it's an example of how in my line of work, you sometimes can't rush things. You have to take the time to train the animals you're working with, you have to rehearse, and the director has to be patient with you. Otherwise, you might not get the results you're looking for.

I spent quite a bit of time with Gregory Peck when we were making *Old Gringo,* and I enjoyed every bit of it. He was such a wonderful, warm man, and he seemed to have so much fun on the shoots I did with him. At the wrap party, he told me something I'll always remember:

"You know, Mickey," he said, "I really enjoyed working with you, and to be honest I found myself wishing I was just working with you instead of with the first unit, just because it just seems like we have more fun on your watch."

"Thank you Greg. I'll tell you, I *love* my work, but I don't take it so seriously that I feel the need to scream at people and act like I'm a dictator. I just like to have fun and make sure that everyone working with me is having fun, too."

"Well, you're doing a great job on all fronts," he told me, and he made my day, of course. It was wonderful to get such a great compliment from such a legendary actor—who also happened to be such a great guy on top of it. I think working with Gregory was one of the best things I took away from making *Old Gringo.*

We're No Angels (A Wild Ride for Troy)

※

In 1989, Paramount released a remake of the 1955 film *We're No Angels*, about a couple of convicts who pretend to be priests. The original had starred Humphrey Bogart and Peter Ustinov and Aldo Ray; this version starred Sean Penn, Robert DiNiro and Demi Moore. I got a call from producer Joe Roth, whom I'd worked with before on *Our Winning Season*, to take over as stunt coordinator on the film, and I headed out to Vancouver. The location was a huge dam and spillway, and when I arrived in Vancouver I was met by a driver that took me right out there; he told me they needed me out there right away.

I stepped out of the car at one of the spillways; there were six in all, coming off the dam. Each one was fifteen feet wide about two hundred and fifty feet long, dropping at an angle into a waterway at the bottom. All six were open. There were about twelve people standing on the dam bridge, just above the spillways; all of them were looking down and discussing something. I spotted Joe Roth and headed over to him, and he introduced me to the director, Neil Jordan, and the other VIPs with him.

Jordan told me what the sequence there was all about: in the scene, DeNiro was going to dive off the dam side of the bridge, and then be swept under it. From there, he would be swept through a spillway opening, drop into the spillway itself, and fall all the way to the bottom.

WE'RE NO ANGELS (A WILD RIDE FOR TROY)

As we were looking down, seeing thousands of tons of water pouring out and swirling in a rage below us, I already had an idea of how they could pull off the stunt. Jordan had told me they were planning to use a dummy for the sequence, but I said, "why not use a real guy, instead of a dummy?" By this time, there had already been a lot of thought put into this sequence, and yet, nobody had come up with an answer or an idea of just exactly how it could—or would—be done. So when I piped up with my 'why-not-use-a-real-guy' suggestion, they all looked at me like I was nuts (a response, as I'm sure you've noticed, I've often gotten before upon presentation of my sometimes wild ideas), shook their heads, and frowned. I could almost hear their collective thoughts: *what the hell is this guy talking about?*

"A real person?" the director echoed, frowning, too. He sort of stuttered, fumbled for words, and then said, "Well...how in the hell would you do *that?*"

"It's all in the way you photograph it," I explained earnestly. "Would you all have a minute to take a walk with me? I can show you what I mean."

"Where're we going, Mick?" Joe asked me.

I pointed to where I'd gotten out of the car and said, "down there, to look at a side angle of the spillways." I saw them glance at one another; they had no idea where I was going with this, but they followed me down to the spot.

Now we were looking at the tremendous amount of water leaping downwards, and I said, "see that middle spillway? If you shut that spillway off, you could drop a stuntman down it and from this angle, it would look like he's engulfed in water." In other words, the spillways toward the camera side would hide the empty space created by the spillway we'd shut off. What they needed to do was tell the dam operator to turn off that middle spillway, so they could have a better look at what I was talking about.

We did that, and then I told them we could ring a descender unit—a hydraulic unit with a cone-shaped spool set at a horizontal position and a special braking unit on it used to control falls done on a cable—up on the bridge that would lower the stuntman down the spillway. We could make him slide the spillway as fast as the water was moving, only we'd have control of him—we could stop him at the water below, or we could let him enter the water, then pull him back out. The descender unit is built with a frame around it so it can be assembled anywhere; it would be easy to use even for this grand stunt.

The executives and the director listened to my explanation—and liked it. They all nodded their heads, agreeing to try my idea.

"There's one thing that won't work here," I cautioned them. "You can't put a camera out towards the front of the spillways, because then you'd catch that empty space of the one we turned off. You can put a second camera over at the top, looking down and across the spillways. That way you'll have one camera positioned toward the top, and one will be toward the bottom.

When we were ready to give it a go, I brought Troy up to double DiNiro; all they had to do was spray his hair to match the actor's. Then, wee started prepping the shot.

The first thing Troy and I needed to do was dive the water below to see if Troy's entrance spot was clear. It was winter-time, so the water temperature was about forty degrees. We rented some dry suits and got a small outboard motorboat that we would use to get out to the spillways; it would also be used as a safety boat when Troy performed the stunt.

The dam operator turned off the spillways so we could do the dive. Underneath, close into Troy's spillway, there was a huge overflow of cement pilled up with heavy two-inch rebar sticking up out of it. We looked at each other, and I motioned to the surface. We swam over to the spot where Troy would enter the water, and we both agreed that the concrete and rebar was far enough away so that he wouldn't hit it.

We did a test where we hooked up a one hundred and eighty pound weight to the descender, and, while Troy and I were underwater, it was sent down the spillway. They had a mark on the descender to stop it at five feet underneath the water's surface.

The test worked well, so we decided to shoot the stunt the following day. Someone in the production had hired a second unit director to shoot the sequence, whom I didn't think had much experience with camera angles and lenses. I met with him to show him the best positions for the cameras, but wouldn't you know it, he was one of those guys that thinks he knows everything, but actually doesn't know shit from shinola. I left him and went back up to Troy and the special effects team. I had a monitor up there with me, so I could see what he was getting through his cameras.

He had two cameras set up, pretty close to where we'd all previously agreed upon, but the next thing I see is the guy out in a boat, looking at an angle that exposed the empty spillway. He radioed up to me and said, "let's put some water on that spillway that Troy's coming down."

I shook my head, telling him we didn't do things that way.

"But why not? It's a great shot," he protested.

I gathered my patience, but inwardly I was starting to get pissed off at him. "We can't do it that way because it's not safe. Even if there's only three inches of water going down that spillway, by the time Troy gets to the bottom he'll have tons of water coming down on him. So it's out of the question."

He started to get an attitude, demanding that we do what he wanted, but I didn't argue with him. Instead I got ahold of Roth and told him what was going on with the so-called director.

Roth and the *actual* director, Neil Jordan, showed up and explained to the other guy—telling him, of course, exactly what I'd told him and saying they wanted it shot my way. He had some unflattering words for me then—calling me a dick—but to make long story short, we shot it my way after all. It ended up looking pretty awesome when it was done, and everyone was pleased with it.

We did a few more shots with Troy doubling DiNiro, and then his work was finished. I stayed on and worked until the film wrapped—and luckily, never saw that second unit director again.

Problem Child

In 1990 I got a call from a producer I'd worked for several times in the past, Jim Brubaker. Dennis Dugan was directing a comedy called *Problem Child* starring John Ritter, and Brubaker, whom I always affectionately called "Bru," was one of the producers. He wanted me to coordinate stunts for and do some second unit directing on the film, so off I went to Dallas, Texas, to get to work.

I met up with Dugan, who would become a tennis buddy of mine during the shoot, and started scouting locations. Dugan was a jokester—he always had a joke at the ready. I had a few tricks up my sleeve, too, and one day during our location scouting when we'd stopped at a little café for lunch, I showed him and Brubaker one. That's right—another mischief-in-a-restaurant scenario here, folks. You should be used to it by now.

The waiter set down some rolls and butter, and I was reminded of a little table-trick I'd picked up somewhere—I can't remember where. I called it m*antequilla arriba,* Spanish for "butter up." If I folded my napkin just so, and put he butter in the center, I could flip the whole cube up into the air by pulling the ends of the napkin in a certain way. In fact, I could get the cube up so high that I was pretty sure I could get it to stick to the ceiling, and it wouldn't be obvious to everyone in the restaurant.

"Hey, Dugan, Bru, have you ever seen *mantequilla arriba?*" I asked him with a grin.

"No, what's that?"

I told them about it. "I bet I can get it up to the ceiling."

"You can not!"

"I can—and I'll do it while the waiter's here, taking our order. He won't even see me do it!"

They started laughing, picturing what was going to happen. "You're on, Gilbert," Dugan told me.

The waiter came over, and both Dugan and Brubaker were giggling while they were ordering, anticipating my little prank. I snapped my hands apart, the butter went flying, and *splat!* It went right onto the ceiling. Brubaker was laughing so hard he fell out of his chair.

I feigned complete ignorance. "What? Did I say something funny?" I asked, deadpan, shrugging at the waiter when he glanced at me for an explanation as to why both of my companions were giggling like schoolboys.

Brubaker wanted to know how to do the trick, so I said I would teach him. "But," I warned him, "you've got to be careful, because if you have your hands too far towards you the butter will hit you right in the chin—or go right up your nose. It takes a little practice to do it right. Are you sure you want to do it in here?" He said he did.

I got him all set up, and he was all nervous that he was going to do it wrong, but determined to do it then and there, just the same. Keep in mind that the restaurant was about three-quarters full at this point. Brubaker snapped his hands apart, leaned his head back a little to keep his face out of the line of fire, and *splat!* There went more butter, right up onto the ceiling again. Bru cracked up. The other patrons in the restaurant looked at him like he was nuts—he'd done the trick correctly, so it had been so fast that no one had seen him do it and therefore had no clue what was so funny.

"All right, all right, enough of that," I said between chuckles. "Let's get out of here."

For whatever reason, that *mantequilla arriba* trick was a hit and a half with Jim Brubaker; he just loved it, and he was always doing it, wherever he could get his hands on butter and a napkin. Some people can say that they've inspired others to learn a life-skill or follow a career path. Me—I can say I've inspired people to flick butter onto the ceiling with a napkin. Go figure.

Once we were done working on the movie each day, Dugan and I would head back to our hotel, each in our respective cars—the only difference was that Dugan had a driver, and I was driving myself. That led to racing each other to see who could make it back there first. Most of the time I beat Dugan and his driver. One day, we pulled up beside each other at a red light on a four-lane road. Dugan was in the passenger seat of his van, which was right next to the driver's side of my car. Suddenly, Dugan's window comes down, and he hocks a big loogie right onto my windshield, laughing and flipping me the bird. In jest, of course. There was no one behind either of our cars, so I backed mine up, came up behind them, and used my car to edge theirs right out into the intersection. Cars were honking and people were screaming at them. The light turned green then, and I zoomed around them and still beat them back to the hotel.

Dugan came up to me. "You almost killed me!" he exclaimed, but he was laughing so I knew he wasn't too mad.

"Don't *ever* spit on my windshield again, Dugan!" I retorted, but I was laughing, too.

Once my part on the film was finished, I prepared to leave the set for good one afternoon around two o'clock. Dugan came up and gave me a big bear hug, and he told me he had something for me, but it was back at the hotel, waiting at the front desk.

"Oh, *this* should be good," I said dryly.

"No, no, I really appreciate all the good work you've done on this movie," he told me sincerely, "and so I've bought you a little gift."

"Oh, okay, well, thanks!" I said. I went back to the hotel and inquired at the front desk, and they handed me a box, telling me it was from Mr. Dugan. Inside was a really beautiful, really expensive wristwatch. Wow. I was touched and surprised. I took mine off and stuck it in my pocket, then put the new one on, thinking what a nice—and unexpected—gesture this had been.

PROBLEM CHILD

Yvonne and I got on the plane and went home, and that night we were awakened at two a.m. by a strange *dinging* noise which neither of us had ever heard before. By the time we were fully awake and asking each other what it was, it had stopped. Puzzled, we went back to sleep.

The next night came, and once again, the noise jolted us both awake. Once again, it stopped before we could figure out what it was. Finally, when the same thing happened for a third night in a row, I realized that it was my new wristwatch, set out on my nightstand, that was making the noise. Dugan, ever the practical joker, had set the alarm on it intentionally for two a.m., west coast time.

"That S.O.B.!" I muttered, and right then and there got on the phone. It was around four a.m. in Dallas. I called the hotel. "This is Dr. Everglade," I said gravely, "I need to speak to Dennis Dugan immediately; it's an emergency. I need you to put me through to his room, right now."

"Oh, yes sir, right away," the clerk said, and pretty soon the phone was ringing in Dugan's room.

After a few rings, Dugan's voice, heavy with sleep, came over the line. "Hello?" he asked groggily.

"**Ding, ding, ding, ding!**" I said loudly, and waited for a response.

After a few minutes, it came. Still speaking in that bleary, sleepy voice, he said, "it took you long enough!" and hung up the phone.

I saw him about six months later, and he laughed at me. "I still can't believe it took you three nights to figure out it was the alarm on that watch that was waking you up!"

"Oh, screw you," I retorted. That was Dennis Dugan, and *Problem Child*.

Young Guns II

Around the time I finished *Problem Child,* I got a call from a producer named Irby Smith, who was interested in having me work on *Young Guns II,* the sequel to the popular 1988 western *Young Guns.* The film was directed by Geoff Murphy and starred a couple of familiar actors—Keifer Sutherland and Lou Diamond Phillips, among others, like Christian Slater and Emilio Estevez, who was reprising his starring role as Billy the Kid. The cast was a good one; a lot of talented young actors who were fun to work with.

I liked the director a lot, and he gave me free rein to dream up whatever sequences I could for the film. He wanted me to come up with things that were imaginative and different, which, I told him, was my specialty. I've always loved doing things that haven't been done before, and I told him so.

Our initial location scout was a bit of a disaster. The first day, I went with the director, the location manager and Dean Semler, our cinematographer, to look for a location to shoot the first action sequence I wanted to do, and for some reason we ended up out in the desert at a location that was all wrong and that no one in the van seemed to have any idea why we'd come to. Geoff had been asleep in the front seat of the van, and when we stopped there I woke him up to ask why we were there. He seemed puzzled and asked, "isn't this where you're going to do that first action sequence with Emilio and the horses?"

YOUNG GUNS II

"No, it's too flat," I said. "Why are we out here?"

"I dunno," Geoff shrugged. We started the van up again and began driving around as I kept a lookout for the right location to do what I envisioned. When we finally found the right spot, we all went to get out of the van. The side doors were sliding ones, and when the location manager got out of the van, he slid it shut, hard—and cut off one of Dean Semler's fingers right at the first knuckle. I guess Dean had had his hand in the way of the door. He began to bleed profusely, and we had to wrap up his finger with someone's handkerchief to try and stop the bleeding. I looked around and found the end of his finger.

"Here," I said, handing it to him, "we've got to get you to an ER, right away."

For someone who had just lost a finger, he was unbelievably cool. "Eh, I don't need that finger," he said with a shrug.

"Yes you do," I said, trying to make light of the situation. "How're you going to pick your nose?"

He started laughing, then got back in the van and was taken away to get medical attention. He got the finger sewed back on in time, and they did such a good job you never would've known he'd lost it.

Anyway, we kept scouting without him, and about two hours later he came right back out and joined us, as if nothing had ever happened.

There was a sequence I'd planned out where Emilio and the boys ride their horses up to a downhill slope. It wasn't a full-blown cliff, but it was pretty steep. You could get a horse down it, but you really had to hold its head up or it would stumble and fall. I planned out several horse falls on that slope, and a gunshot to a horse, as well; Pat Garrett would shoot one of the boys' horses during the pursuit. I staged it by placing a squib covered with horse hair on the horse's neck.

When we'd scouted out the location, we'd noticed that about three hundred feet below were rock formations known as "tent rocks," so-called because they resemble Native American teepees. They were all different sizes and heights, created by erosion of wind and water over millions of years. It looked amazing and really gave the area an ominous look.

ME AND MY SADDLE-PAL

I told the guys I wanted to walk the area, so I went down the slope and checked the place out. I knew it would look really great on film—we could get the horses plunging down the slope, kicking up dirt dramatically as they went. My instincts were correct and the whole sequence came out really great—in fact, I think it's one of the best dramatic horse scenes (I call them "horse operas") that I've ever shot. It was only about twenty or thirty seconds long in the final cut of the film, but it really looked good.

I'd brought Lance and Troy with me on the shoot, and Lance would ride the falling horse that would be "shot" by Pat Garrett. I placed a large squib on the left side of the horse's neck and arranged to get a shot where the horses are all coming in a group, jumping off a little area. I had a P.O.V. shot in there of Billy Peterson, who was playing Pat Garrett, saying "those horses are as crazy as they are," before shooting Lance's horse right behind the jaw. The squib blew, and Lance had the horse fall. Because of the incline, the falling horses would roll over two or three times before stopping. It all came out very realistic and I was very pleased with how it all looked.

There was a sequence we did in town with a torch-bearing posse coming to lynch Emilio's character. The Kid had already escaped, but other members of his gang were being held by the sheriff, who offered them to the posse instead of Billy. Unbeknownst to the sheriff, the cloaked and hooded members of the "posse" were actually Billy the Kid himself and other members of the gang, coming to rescue Keifer Sutherland, Lou Diamond Phillips and Christian Slater. As they're riding away, the real posse starts riding in.

Now, around this time in production Yvonne had been playing tennis to keep herself occupied, and she'd met the local tennis pro, Bo Gray. She'd become friendly with him and eventually he offered us the chance to rent a guest cottage on his girlfriend's property, a chance we jumped on since our dog had gotten us kicked out of the place we had been staying. Bo had a western air about him and loved the old west, so I offered to get him on as a bit player in the film.

"Can you ride, Bo?" I'd asked him.

"Sure, I can ride," he'd said, but he didn't say it very convincingly.

"You sure?" I asked. "You sound a little uncertain."

"Nah, I can ride," he'd assured me.

I put him in as one of the posse-members in that sequence, coming after Billy and his cronies. I could tell he wasn't a very good rider, so I gave him a few pointers. My main concern was the torch he'd have to carry as he was riding.

"Once you light that thing, whatever you do, *don't* have it too close to your horse's head," I instructed him. "Keep it up and back a little ways. You don't want to spook your horse too much."

"Okay, Mick," he said, but when they got going, he started having trouble; his horse was out in front and out of control. As he came past the cameras, he started reaching down with his torch hand to try and pull the horse up, which of course caused the torch to move even closer to the horse's head and spook him even more. The horse took off down a side street, moving away from our cameras, then took another left, coming back down the main street.

"Bo, throw the torch down! Get rid of the torch!" I was hollering, unable to hold back my laughter as I did so. He looked so silly. Finally he complied and came back over to us, chagrinned. Everyone was chuckling at the absurdity of the whole thing.

Bo recovered just fine from that little fiasco and became a great friend to me; we're still friends to this day.

After the shoot was over, I was working in California when I got a surprise call from Lou Diamond Phillips and Keifer Sutherland. They asked me if I knew where Indian Dunes was—was I close to it?

"Yeah, it's not far from my ranch, as a matter of fact," I told them.

They told me that Emilio was shooting a movie there, and that his birthday was two weeks away. Then they told me they had a rather unusual request for me—they wanted to give Emilio a cow for his birthday, and they wanted me to arrange it.

"You want to give him a *cow?*" I repeated. "As in a milk cow?"

"Yeah. We don't care what it costs, it's a joke we want to play on him. We know you can do it for us, Gilbert."

There was more. They wanted me to make a sign to hang around the cow's neck that said "happy birthday from your bros, Keifer and Lou."

"Okay," I said, laughing. "I'll make your sign up, and I'll call one of my wrangler buddies to get ahold of a cow. I'll have him trailer the cow over to the set on the day of, and maybe have him wait till lunch time. Then he can just walk the cow over to Emilio and put the rope around his neck, or something like that."

"That'll be perfect!" they said.

I called the wrangler and arranged for the prank, and it worked out just as we'd planned. The wrangler walked over, delivered the cow to an astonished Emilio, then walked nonchalantly away as if to say, "here you go, buddy! She's your problem now!" The crew was in stitches. Emilio was laughing, too, but also thinking "what the hell am I supposed to do with a *cow?*" He asked the wrangler that question.

"I dunno, Mr. Estevez, I just got paid to deliver this cow to you. What happens next is up to you." And off he went. He came back at the end of the day, of course, but I'm sure Emilio spent the time in between trying to figure out what he was supposed to do with his new four-legged friend.

I really loved working on *Young Guns II,* in fact it's probably my favorite western I've ever worked on, just for the look and feel of it. We took care with the details and being on those sets and at those locations in New Mexico really took you back to the old west. There were also many great sequences in it that I really enjoyed coordinating and directing, like the horse chase scene. The actors all got along great, the director was pleasant, and my boys all had a good time working on it, so I always look back on it fondly—even if it did get off to a rather interesting start, with Dean losing his finger and all.

City Slickers

In 1991 MGM Studios released a western comedy called *City Slickers*, about an urban man named Mitch Robbins who, in the midst of a mid-life crisis, is badgered into going on a cattle-drive vacation on a dude ranch with his two best friends. The three of them have no idea what they're in for, which made for a lot of humorous situations. The film starred Billy Crystal as Mitch, Daniel Stern and Bruno Kirby as his two pals, and Jack Palance as Curly, the surly trail boss.

I received a call from Irby Smith, one of the producers, asking me to come down and meet Billy Crystal, and the director, Ron Underwood. He'd sent me a script for the film before the meeting date so I would have some knowledge about the plot. A friend of mine, Jack Lilley, was the livestock coordinator and head wrangler on the film, and he'd called me to give me a heads-up on the show, too. Because of all the background I'd gotten, I went to the meeting with some new ideas that weren't in the script.

I met with Billy, Irby and Underwood; Jack Lillie was also present. They asked me what I thought about the film, and I told him one of the most important things to do was to train the herd of cattle, which was about five-hundred head, to move as a bunch. Otherwise, we'd have cattle scattered all over the desert where we were filming. Jack backed me up on this; it just made sense. The meeting went well and I was hired on a stunt coordinator.

ME AND MY SADDLE-PAL

Over the course of filming, Billy Crystal really made an impression on me; he just put his all into the movie. There's a sequence in the film where he and Curly help a cow through a dangerous birth, after which Curly is forced to euthanize the cow. Billy's character adopts the calf and names it "Norman," and the little calf goes on to play an important role in the rest of the movie. Billy really made everything look real and natural in that scene—and all the others, too. Besides his acting ability, he is just a really wonderful person—warm and funny and great to work with.

During the cattle drive, I wanted to create a scene that had a wild look to it. I wanted to find an area along a river that had a steep bank, about two hundred feet or so, that we could drive the cattle down. I went scouting for the perfect location with our director, who found an area he thought would work. "How about this one, Mick?" he asked me.

It was not steep enough, so it was not what I'd had in mind. "No," I told him, "this place is too easy. Let's keep looking." There was no point in doing something, I always figured, unless you gave it your all and did it right. I didn't want to use just any old location—I wanted to find the perfect one.

Underwood shrugged his shoulders and we walked on up the river. Again, he pointed out a spot and again, it was not right. "This looks good," he told me. "We can drive the cattle out of that meadow over there and across the river."

"It's still not right, Ron," I told him. "Look, you know how important the right location is to a scene. Not only will the right location make a scene work, it will also impress your audience. We should keep looking." I was determined to get this right. He shook his head again but kept following me.

We came around a bend in the river and there it was—just what I was looking for. It was a steep slope dropping right about two hundred feet from top to bottom, right into the river. I stopped and pointed. "There it is, Ron."

He looked where I was pointing and raised an eyebrow. "You've

CITY SLICKERS

gotta be kidding, Gilbert," he said. "You want to drive the cattle down *there?*"

"Yep," I replied, "and that's not all. I want to do it in the rain." I'd figured that rain would make the steep bank slippery as hell, with all the cattle sliding down and the stunt doubles on their horses sliding down along with them; a nice dramatic break in an mostly comedic movie. I had my boys on the show with me, and I'd decided I'd have Lance, Tim, and Troy do the riding, along with Brian Burrows, who was doubling for Billy. I'd position them on each side of the herd, driving them down the steep bank and into the river, which was about three feet deep at that location. At the top of the bank there was a flat area where we would build portable fences to contain the cattle in; the fences would funnel into a hundred-foot opening right at the edge of the bank. To make the location even *more* perfect, I saw that there were some old, dead pine trees that had fallen onto the bank; we could use them as barriers to keep the cattle where we needed them while we were diving them down.

Ron kept staring at the spot, shaking his head. "So you want to do it here, and you want to do it in the rain," he repeated wryly. I explained to him why, that it would make the whole sequence look more difficult and thereby be more engaging to the audience.

Ron didn't think it was going to work, I could tell. He felt that the bank was *too* steep. Billy and the other actors, however, loved the idea once we'd shown them the location, so Underwood gave in.

When we brought the actors out to look the place over, I had Tim, Troy, Lance and Brian mounted on their horses to show them how the shot would look. At my signal, they took off for the slope and started their horses down. "You see how the boys are all keeping a tight rein on their horses and keeping their heads up as they go down?" I asked the actors. "That helps keep the horses from stumbling, and that's what I want all you guys to remember when I get you into the scene." I could tell they were getting excited about the sequence and could hardly wait for the day we were going to shoot it.

In the movies you can make weather if God doesn't give you what you want when you need it, so we made it rain for the shoot. The effects guy pumped water out of the river, shooting water up and out about a hundred and fifty feet over the area we were photographing. The water fanned out and looked just like natural rain, a trick often used in the industry. The day before we shot they'd pumped water onto the slope to soften it up, and then on the day of filming, we positioned about thirty head of steers on the other side of the river so the cattle we were driving would go to them, following their heading instinct.

We set up all our cameras, the effects men working the artificial rain setup were in place, and the wranglers were all at top of the slope, ready to spook the herd to help get them started on their way down. My doubles were spread out on top to go with the cattle. The word came—"*action, action, action!*"

From below we heard guns going off, firing blanks, of course, and lots of shouting as the wranglers got the cattle going. All of the sudden, swarms of cattle appeared and started dropping off onto the slope, some sliding and others picking their way down carefully through the mud. Then Tim, Lance and Troy started appearing, spaced out among the herd. At different times, each double would check their horse and rein it in, waving their ropes and keeping the cattle moving down the slope. There were spots in the sequence where, later on, we could insert our actors with some cattle. We did the same thing when we shot that, taking the herd across the river. It turned out to be a great sequence, especially with the rain coming down, and it worked out exactly how I'd envisioned it.

Back to Norman again, the adorable calf Mitch had adopted. After our city slickers got the cattle across the river, they heard little Norman calling out in distress and turned to see him being swept downriver. Mitch spins his horse around and takes off to the rescue, splashing along the riverbank and twirling his rope. To get closer to Norman, he rides in a little deeper.

This set up a stunt I coordinated. As Billy throws his rope around Norman's neck, his horse loses its balance and falls head-over-heels, throwing Billy off into the river. To do this, I had a backhoe dig a pit

CITY SLICKERS

into the riverbed, underwater. The pit was eight feet long and six feet wide, and about three feet deep. This was where Billy's double, Brian Burrows, went to work.

"*Action!*" Brian spurred his horse out into the river, its hooves kicking water up into the air, headed straight for the pit. When he hit it, the horse's legs went out from under him and he turned a summersault, throwing Brian off, just as planned. It could not have gone more smoothly. At this point, we cut Billy in wearing a wet suit under his costume to protect him when he went through some small rapids, and also to keep him warm. We shot him in the river, holding onto Norman, at three different locations. After the first take, I helped Billy up out of the water.

"Son of a bitch, I'm getting cold already," he told me.

"The thing to do, Billy," I told him with a perfectly straight face, "is to pee in your wet suit. Warms you right up and nobody'll know the difference, since you're sopping wet."

He stared at me like I'd grown another head. "*What?*"

I repeated myself, staying perfectly serious.

"You're kidding," he muttered.

"Nope. I'm serious. Sit down in that shallow water and let it go, you know, like a kid in a swimming pool."

So he did as I said, since I was so serious and all, half-closing his eyes before looking at me. "I'll be damned, it really does work!"

I started cracking up laughing. "I can't believe you did that, man! I was just messing with ya."

"*You son of a...!*" He was mad, but it was all in good fun and he knew it, so he forgave me and laughed about it. In the end the footage we got of him in the river with Norman looked great and turned into a wonderful piece of footage for the movie. It was a blast working with Billy and everyone else on the film, and once *City Slickers* was released, it made a lot of money. In fact, it did so well, they decide to film a sequel.

The Last of the Mohicans

1992 would see the release of one of the biggest—and most memorable—films I ever worked on, Michael Mann's big-budget period epic, *The Last of the Mohicans,* starring Daniel Day-Lewis, Madeline Stowe, Russell Means and Wes Studi, among others.

I received a call from Mann's office during pre-production and was invited to come out to Beverly Hills to discuss the project. Upon arriving, I came upon Mann and Tommy Fisher, the special-effects coordinator, coming outside the building as I was going in. Fisher was a one of the best special-effects guys in the business (if not *the* best, in my opinion), and a good friend of mine; I'd worked with him on previous projects. He and his crew, along with Mann, were headed toward Tommy's special-effects truck, which was loaded up with some mock-ups of the 18th century cannons that Mann wanted him to produce for the film's epic fort battle scene. Tommy had mocked the cannons and their caissons up in styrofoam so that Mann could get an idea of their size and shape before he approved the production of the actual props. The director's pre-approval of, then dissatisfaction with props would become a recurring theme over the course of the production, but I didn't know that yet.

"Mickey!" Tommy called, seeing me and greeting me with a grin. "Good to see you. I'm about to show Michael the cannons for the film, why don't you come along?"

THE LAST OF THE MOHICANS

"Sure, Tommy, let's see what you've got," I agreed.

Mann was busy speaking to some people he'd encountered as he'd left his office and didn't notice me tagging along. He'd never met me before, only heard of me by reputation. I kept quiet as Tommy herded us all up to the truck.

The crew began unloading the styrofoam cannons, which were about seven feet long and fashioned from full-scale blueprints that Tommy had drafted and shown to Mann before he'd started in on the styrofoam. One by one, the cannons were set out on sawhorses for the director to inspect.

And he *did* inspect them, standing there with one hand beneath his chin and contemplating them as if the integrity of his film would be made or broken by their appearance alone. I watched, getting the feeling that he was rather hard to impress—and difficult to convince. He pointed out a particular area of the cannon he wasn't thrilled with, something to do with its shape. I saw what he was looking at, but I also saw that the area that was bothering him wouldn't be visible to the movie-goer once the caisson's wheels were in place. I spoke up. "You know, guys, once you get the wheels on the caissons, you won't even be able to see that part of the cannon. It'll be blocked by the wheel."

Everyone looked at me, and Mann's eyebrow rose. "Who are you?" he asked me.

"I'm sorry," I told him. "I was heading into your office when you guys came out, so I tagged along. I'm Mickey Gilbert, and I got a call to come meet with you today."

"Oh," he replied.

"I just thought I'd make the suggestion," I continued, gesturing to the cannon. "It'd save a lot of work, you know, instead of having to redo the blueprints and mock-ups and everything."

Mann looked at Tommy, who spoke up. "I'll go get the mock-ups of the wheels for the caissons," he said, and brought them out. When he set them into place, they hid the offending part of the cannon, just as I'd figured.

ME AND MY SADDLE-PAL

Mann studied them for a minute more, looked at Tommy and then at me, and finally nodded. "I guess that'll be all right," he said.

"Perfect," Tommy said. I could tell he was relieved; the last thing he'd wanted to do was to start over again because of some miniscule detail the director wasn't happy with.

Mann and I went back to his office then to discuss some of the stunt work. He started telling me about how he'd heard of some of my work in the industry, and asked for my opinion on the groundwork he'd laid for some of *Mohicans'* fight sequences. "I've got my actors working with some professional Judo and Taekwondo teachers in Arkansas," he told me. "I'd like you to take a look at some video of what they've been doing over there, and tell me what you think." He set up the TV set for me and went to make a phone call while I watched the video.

If you know anything at all about American Indians or British soldiers and the weaponry they used in the 18th century, you'll likely have a pretty good idea that their combat style was about as far away from Judo and Taekwondo as you can get. This was the Colonies, the future United States—not the far east. I was appalled to see the actors on the video doing overhead kicks and martial arts moves, none of which would have been accurate to the period and place the film was set in, or the people involved. My first thought as I watched was *ridiculous,* and if *I* felt that way, how would the audience feel, when they saw a bunch of Huron and Mohawk braves and British soldiers in full costume and makeup, using these moves in the middle of what was supposed to be the untamed American-Canadian frontier in 1757?

The thing ended and I sat there, waiting for Mann to come back. He did, and asked me what I thought.

"Well, Michael," I began, "I know you don't know me, and I don't know you, but I'm going to level with you."

He nodded. "As you should, that's how I like it."

"You've got these guys using martial arts moves, and you're gonna have them doing it in the middle of these colonial battlefields, and it just *never happened* that way," I said firmly. "These guys didn't know anything about what was going on in the far east! They used tomahawks

THE LAST OF THE MOHICANS

and knives and clubs when they fought, not Judo or Taekwondo, like you've got 'em doing here. I have to be honest, if you want *this* in your movie," I said, gesturing to the television set, "then I'm going to have to bow out right now, because I won't coordinate the film this way. It's just too inaccurate and over-the-top." I knew I was jeopardizing my chances of getting the job, but I had to be honest. After all, my name *would* be in the credits. I sat back on the couch and waited, unsure how he'd take my criticism.

He raised his eyebrows. "You're serious, aren't you?"

I nodded. "I'm *absolutely* serious. I put my heart and soul into every film I work on, but I couldn't do that with this one if you're going to insist on these kinds of fight sequences." I leaned forward a little. "We can get in there and do some really great moves," I told him, already seeing some in my mind's eye. "We can have Daniel duck under a Huron's tomahawk, do a spin and have him slice the guy's torso open as he goes, that sort of thing. But we *can't* have a bunch of Indian warriors doing overhead kicks and circling each other like they're in a Sumo ring. I won't coordinate it, and the audience won't buy it. In fact, if I were you, I'd pull your actors out of there right away, before they waste any more time learning this stuff."

To my surprise, he nodded slowly. "You know, you're absolutely right."

I kept eye contact with him. Crunch time. "So, do you still want to hire me for this picture?" I asked, giving him faint smile.

"I do," he replied. "I like you. I like a guy who looks me in the eye and is honest with me, and the fact that you were willing to turn the film down shows me you're serious about what you do. I want guys like that on my crew."

I was relieved, and I got the job. The first hurdle had been overcome. Fortunately I was blissfully unaware, right then, of the many that were to follow.

ME AND MY SADDLE-PAL

Once hired, I went with the rest of the production team and the crew to Asheville, North Carolina, where we'd shoot the film, and we had our first production meeting, with Michael Mann, of course, doing most of the talking.

Production meetings like these involve the heads of every department (wardrobe, makeup, cinematography, animal-wrangling, stunts, etc), and together we go through the script from start to finish, discussing key elements of the process that will ultimately be used to bring the story to life on the big screen. Right away, the director's vision proved to be a stumbling block.

For those of you who've seen *The Last of the Mohicans,* you'll likely remember the film's opening elk hunt scene, in which Nathaniel (Daniel Day-Lewis), Uncas (Eric Schweig) and Chingachcook (Russell Means) track and kill an elk as it runs through a wooded glen. The three men are supposed to seek out the elk using their tracking skills, follow it as it flees briefly, then take it down by way of a single, well-placed shot from Daniel Day-Lewis's rifle. Mann had his own very definite idea of how he wanted to do that: place a camera between the horns of a live elk and shoot its perspective of the three hunters.

He wants to do what? I thought incredulously. My eyes met Jay Fishburn's. He was the head wrangler on the film and as such would be responsible for handling the animals on the shoot. He looked just as taken aback as I felt. I knew there wasn't any way Mann's idea would work. I'd done work in the past with horses having to wear elaborate headgear, and no matter how lightweight we made it, the horses never felt comfortable wearing it—their instinct was to get it off. We were talking about a wild animal this time around, and I knew, and Jay knew, that the elk would do whatever it needed to do to get the foreign object off of its head, even if it meant breaking its antlers off in the process. It would likely break the camera, too, while it was at it.

I didn't bring any of this up right then, feeling that it was better to approach Mann after the meeting was over. Fishburn and I sought him out at the end and told him our concerns about the "deer cam." I explained my experiences with horses fighting headgear and told Mann

THE LAST OF THE MOHICANS

that the elk would likely react even more strongly than the horses had; after all, horses were used to wearing bridles.

Mann wouldn't hear it. He told me I was being negative. I told *him* I was just trying to be practical. "Look, let us do a test, Michael," I proposed. "We'll carve a fake camera out of some lightweight wood, balsa wood or something, and strap it on between his antlers after we get him into a holding chute. Then we'll let him out in the pen and see how he reacts."

Mann nodded. "Okay, that's fine. He'll get used to it, then, like a horse would."

Both Jay and I knew the elk would *not* get used to having anything strapped to his head, but I had a plan in mind to prove my point. "Here's what I'm gonna do, Jay," I told Fishburn, once I was alone with him after we'd left Mann. "We're not gonna actually *do* what I just told him, 'cause you and I both know the elk won't get used to having a camera on its head. He's gonna rub his head in the dirt or on a fence post to get it off, maybe even break his antlers. So we're just gonna *tell* him we did it, and it didn't work, and I'm going to get on a horse with my little pogo cam and shoot some footage while I'm running under branches and jumping logs, and stuff. It will look the same, and I'll have more control over it than we would if it was shot from a live deer's head, too."

When the opportunity arose to speak to Mann in the midst of his director's flurry of activity, I told him my little white lie, and I also told him my horseback-footage idea.

"Oh," he said. "Well, why didn't you tell me that in the first place?"

I kept my cool and said, "because you were so *adamant* that you wanted the footage shot from the head of the deer..." I waited.

"Well, okay," he agreed reluctantly. "I would've rather had a deer, though."

I was puzzled. "Why?" I wanted to know. "What's the difference?"

"You know how a deer bounces when it runs?" he asked, and I nodded, seeing where he was going with it.

"I can do that same movement with my hand, Michael, with the camera, as I ride. I can do several versions of it, until you get what you like." In my head I was imploring him to see how much easier it would be to do it my way, for the elk's sake and its owner's, and how much better the shots would turn out, to boot.

Fortunately he gave his consent, and so we got the shots that way, sparing the poor elk the trial of having a camera strapped to his head.

I'll bet you can't even tell the difference, can you?

Mohicans contains some incredibly epic battle scenes—clashes between native tribes and British soldiers. Some 250 extras were hired to play Huron and Mohawk warriors, most of them actual American Indians, and just as many, if not more, were hired to play the British troops. Our military technical advisor Dale Dye would work with the British troops, teaching them the proper way to march, to raise and lower their muskets, and to engage in combat the way the British Military did. The Indian extras would be trained at a separate training camp we'd set up about twenty miles away, by the same trainer the actors had been learning their earlier martial arts-type moves from.

I was firm with him—*no* martial arts moves. I wanted big swings with tomahawks, knife-slashes, and scalpings. I told both trainers to go at it and do their stuff—but not to get the two groups together yet. I told them I'd be checking in on things every week or so to see the progress they were making, a deal to which they agreed.

I went to see Michael Mann about the wound effects we'd have to use on the extras and actors. A concern I had was that because the Indians would be dressed in little more than loin-cloths and body paint, we wouldn't be able to use squib effects on them.

The term "squib" refers to a miniature explosive device mounted on a piece of leather and placed under or in an actor's costume and rigged up with a packet of fake blood. When the squib is detonated, the effect produced is a realistic-looking bullet hit, complete with the spray of blood one would expect from a gunshot. Because our Indians wouldn't be wearing clothing, there would be no way to hide the squib and its wiring from the camera's—and therefore the audience's—view.

I had an idea, though, to solve the problem. I told Mann I would have the wardrobe department look for some flesh-colored bodysuits for the stuntmen who would be sustaining major wounds in the battle scenes. "We can place the squib units under the bodysuits and then paint the bodysuits to simulate the look of war paint on bare skin," I explained. "When the squib detonates, you'll see the charge blowing through the fabric of the bodysuit, and it'll look like their skin is actually being torn open."

He agreed to it, and I met with the wardrobe and makeup department. They managed to locate what I had in mind, and we had over a hundred of them shipped in to use on the production. Worked like a charm and looked very realistic, much to my relief, and to Michael Mann's delight.

I began to hire stuntmen for the project, and right at the beginning, I let them in on a key aspect of the film: if they wanted to be in it, they'd need to shave their heads bald, except for a strip of hair left down the middle, because that's how the Huron warriors wore their hair. "I don't want to hear anyone crying about it once we get to work. The shoot will likely last around eight to ten weeks—so make sure you're okay with it before you sign on," I warned each one as I hired him. It turned out they were all fine with it if it meant getting the job ("go ahead, Mickey, shave whatever you want!"), and they all had great fun filming one another as they went under the razor. My sons were doing stunts on the film too—and my son Troy was the only stuntman I was using who got to keep his hair, because he was doubling Steven Waddington's character, Major Duncan Heyward. He had a fine time rubbing that fact in to the other guys. They were all great sports about it and enjoyed the rougher edge their new look gave them, teasing the hairdressers and makeup girls (who often teased them first).

As the project began to pick up steam, more and more scenes were being mapped out and planned, including one particularly momentous sequence: the fort battle. Fort William Henry was constructed at the top of a hill, giving excellent vantage-points for the camera both looking down, where the French and Huron army is waging their siege, and looking up, where the British soldiers are making their stand and defending their fort. Michael Mann wanted Tommy Fisher and his special effects crew to rig up the shrapnel-filled cannons used by the French army in a trench below the fort. When he charged him with this task, Tommy told him mildly, "come on out there tomorrow and we'll show you what we've already come up with." Mann seemed to think Tommy was being too blasé about the whole thing—this was supposed to be *epic*, after all—and he voiced that opinion to me.

I quickly reassured him. "Michael, Tommy is that way about everything, but I'm telling you, he knows what he's doing. You'll see."

In the morning we went out and met Tommy at the fort, and he had air mortars rigged up to fire off basketballs painted black (cannon ball doubles). Mann didn't seem too impressed ("is this it?").

"You're not gonna see *these*, Michael," Tommy said. "These are the inner-workings of the guns—the guts, you might say. These will all be hidden inside cannons, and all the camera will see are those cannons, when you shoot the scenes. Let me show you what they can do." He and his son loaded up a basketball into the cylinder, and when they fired it, the pressurized air shot the ball out like a rocket. It went so high and so far that it went right over the wall of the fort, looking very much like the cannon ball it was representing.

That impressed Mann. Tommy fired off a few more, and told him he could reduce the air pressure so that the balls would be lobbed directly at the fort's walls, if Mann wanted. He demonstrated this a few times, much to Mann's delight. Tommy earned his stripes with our director that day.

The sheer volume of tasks to accomplish during pre-production on this film was staggering, but eventually we got to where we began shooting it, and I was still coming up with solutions to make stunts and injuries such as scalpings look as real as possible—gory, perhaps, but this type of battle *was* gory, and I wanted to show that in a close-up, in-your-face sort of way, so that the audience would feel like they were a part of it. One key scene involves the film's antagonist, Magua (Wes Studi), revealing his true attitude toward the British Soldiers he has been acting as a native guide for. Magua has disguised himself as a Mohawk, the tribe friendly to and tolerated by the British, so that he can get close enough to the British Colonel Munro (Maurice Roëves) to attempt an assassination. During the scene, Magua breaks from the head of the party he has been leading from Albany to Fort William Henry, and begins walking toward the company of soldiers marching at the party's rear. As the camera follows, Magua calmly produces a hidden tomahawk and buries it into the base of one soldier's skull. Making this injury look realistic that close up was worrying Mann, so he asked me to come up with a solution.

I had a sort of prosthetic head and neckpiece in mind that the solider would wear, with a fake tomahawk already embedded into it. The angle and position of Mann's camera lens meant that the fake tomahawk wouldn't be seen as he marched forward. Studi would feign the blow with his own tomahawk, but would stop short, of course, of actually hitting the other man. Then the soldier turned violently when he was "struck," revealing the weapon's handle to the camera, sticking out of a gory, bloody wound. Mann shot it the way I proposed, and it came out looking pretty damned realistic. It was one of many things I ended up designing for *Mohicans* that, fortunately, worked just as I'd intended it to.

Prep for the film continued. Locations were scouted, sets were built. I started work on the massacre sequence. The scene is chaotic, with Wes Studi's Magua and his Huron war party unleashing a surprise attack on the defeated British army, leaving the captured Fort William Henry. Its massive battle, with hundreds of people engaged in combat at once, most of it hand-to-hand. We'd scouted out the location for it, a large grassy meadow sheltered on each side by dense wooded areas.

Snakes were going to be an issue, so we had to have people clear the meadow of bull snakes before we could use it—we didn't want anyone getting bitten. After that was done, the meadow was fenced off and left alone so the grass the snake people had trampled down would return to its natural state. A week or so before shooting, the wooded areas on either side were checked for snakes, too; the Huron antagonists would be lying in wait there to ambush the British soldiers.

We were getting there. I'd found, over the course of checking in with the stuntmen and the extras at the two training camps, that the trainers had them all really hyped up about the intensity of the battle—had them believing they were really going to be fighting each other. The day came when I sent the word out: the Indians and the British troops were going to meet up—tomorrow.

We set up massive tents and brought in the makeup team and the wardrobe department, and I had loudspeakers set up so I could give all five hundred of them or so directions at once. The Indians were in a couple of tents together, while all of the soldiers stayed together in theirs. As I walked around introducing myself to them all, I noticed a real mental separation between the two groups, more evidence at the intensity with which the trainers had driven home the difference of opinion, you might say, between them.

I got on the loudspeakers and directed the soldiers to line up and space themselves about three or four feet apart. Once they'd organized themselves, the effect was striking—imagine all those uniformed British troops, in the formal dress of the era, with the gilt braids on their red coats, and their white wigs under their black tri-cornered hats. It was a sight to behold. I had the Indians face them from about twenty feet away, and it took about an hour to get everyone in place. Now I had a long line of Indians facing a long line of soldiers. The background would be a sea of British uniforms and war paint, white wigs and scalp locks, bayonets and tomahawks, all fighting to overcome one another.

I had a little trick up my sleeve to break the intense tension I'd already felt between the two groups. I directed them to, on the count of three, walk across to the opponent closest to them and first shake hands, then hug each other.

THE LAST OF THE MOHICANS

I could see heads turning as they looked at one another a little incredulously. Eyebrows rose and I could almost hear their thoughts. *What the hell is this guy* doing? But it worked; I had many of them come up to me later on to tell me how much that particular direction of mine had relieved them—the trainers had really worked the idea of going at each other whole hog into their minds, and up until that point I think they'd been more than a little worried about how things were going to go down. The trainers weren't happy about it—they thought I was destroying the attitude they'd spent all those weeks building up. I had to remind them that this was, when you got down to it, just make-believe. The knives and tomahawks and bayonets were just rubber.

That didn't mean, however, that I wanted them to act like they were kids playing in their front yards after dinner. I didn't want them laughing or looking like they were having fun out there. I reminded them to act serious (deadly serious, if you will)—this was a grim, life-or-death clash we were staging. We rehearsed it for a week or so, and pretty quick I saw them making friends with one another during breaks, which was a great thing to see, since they'd all been so tense and stand-offish with one another that first day.

When we shot that massive battle sequence, I kept control over all the chaos through a group system I'd set up. My sons Tim, Lance and Troy, who are all stuntmen, each led a group of thirty or so extras, and the other professional stuntmen working in the sequence had groups of their own. Each group was being directed by the stuntman leading them, and those stuntmen were in turn being directed by me. I'd had everything rehearsed ahead of time, so everyone knew exactly what they were going to be doing when the time came. While we were getting the cameras ready, the entire bunch of them were laying down, relaxing and talking.

Michael told me he wanted to have Daniel Day-Lewis come running through and take out a couple of Hurons on the way (this is the scene where he comes running to save Cora from a Huron warrior who is about to slit her throat). "I'm going to get the cameras set, so why don't you get your people up and ready while I do that," Mann told me.

ME AND MY SADDLE-PAL

"They're ready, Michael," I said.

"What do you mean? They're all laying down."

"They're just relaxing. They're ready, I promise you. We've got this thing down to science."

He raised an eyebrow at me. "They're ready, huh?" he asked dryly, looking around at his two armies laying around talking. "I don't buy it."

"Michael, look," I said. "I will bet you a hundred bucks that before you get your cameras set, everybody will be up and ready."

He looked at me. "A hundred dollars? You're on." He looked at his crew. "You hear that, guys? Get the cameras in here *right now.*"

I got on my megaphone and called everyone's attention. "Everybody up on your feet, we're gonna do this! Just like we've practiced. Get ready!"

You'd think a shot had gone off—everyone was on their feet and waiting for Mann to call *'action!'* in somewhere around thirty seconds. Michael was busy with the cameras at that point.

"Hey, Michael," I called sweetly, "we're ready over here."

He looked around and his brows came together. "What the—you son of a…" I heard him say in irritation. "I'm still setting up the cameras!"

I just gave him a smile. "We're ready," I repeated. "Let's go!"

He let out a breath of frustration, walked over to me, and handed me a hundred-dollar bill. I said as I took it, "aren't you glad I didn't bet you a thousand?"

He shook his head. "You know what, I probably would have taken that bet," he admitted.

We shot the sequence, and all of my hard work—the training, the repetitive rehearsals, the bodysuit idea for the squibs—all paid off. Michael Mann was pleased. Everything looked very realistic and smooth, and the massacre scene went on to be one of the most memorable ones in the movie.

THE LAST OF THE MOHICANS

To get the shots that would make up the final seventeen minutes of *The Last of the Mohicans*'s running time, the production traveled to Chimney Rock Park in North Carolina (not to be confused with Chimney Rock National Monument in Colorado). The final portion of the film is very intense and extremely memorable to the viewer—this is the sequence in which Uncas (Eric Schweig) attempts to rescue Alice (Jodhi May) from Magua and his band of Hurons. Uncas challenges the Hurons, who are moving along a trail at the edge of a towering cliff. The Hurons are going along single-file, unable to spread out because the trail is so narrow. Uncas battles with them one by one, and for the first few minutes he's winning—until he gets to Magua, whose prowess proves too much for the young Mohican. As Alice watches in horror, Uncas's throat is slit and he his shoved from the cliff to his death below. Alice, as viewers will remember, then steps off the cliff to her own death, landing near Uncas.

There were several falls to stage in this section; one of the Hurons is thrown off the cliff by Uncas, still clutching his rifle as he falls. I was directing this scene, and my son Lance would be doing the fall.

We had to build what's called a catcher off of one part of the trail. This is a big, solid platform that's bolted into the rock itself and extends six feet or so beyond the six-foot wide trail and the face of the cliff beyond it. Lance was supposed to fall about eighty feet—not eight hundred, which is what would happen if he missed the catcher. We put an airbag on top of the catcher and inflated it, then tied it down, then Lance and the safety guys climbed up into position.

The safety guys were experienced rock-climbers, and they had to rappel down the rock above the trail until they found an appropriate foothold where Lance could stand before falling. He would hold onto a safety line to keep himself against the cliff until he was ready to go. He was dressed in costume, of course, as the unfortunate Huron, and he had his rubber rifle with him.

Lance had done a few big falls like this before, and he was good at it. He'd had a lot of practice with trampolines, and he looked good in the air. I had plenty of confidence in his ability to do this, and do

ME AND MY SADDLE-PAL

it *well*. But as I looked up at him as he stood there on his little perch, I saw something I didn't like. As I'd always told my boys, and other stunt-people I'd worked with in the past, the danger of becoming comfortable with a particular stunt you've done several times over is that you don't get pumped up over it anymore. You loose a little bit of that adrenaline and this can make you careless. What I saw now with Lance was that he was chatting away with the safety people instead of studying his upcoming fall. I knew that in order for him to hit that airbag properly, he couldn't pitch himself out from the cliff—in other words, he couldn't push off of it and fling his body out into the air. Instead, he would need to simply drop down, staying fairly close to the cliff.

They had a radio up there with them, and I got on it. "Hey, Lance, are you getting ready for this thing, or what?" I asked.

"Yeah, Dad, no problem," he said breezily.

I wasn't terribly reassured. "I want you to drop a line down to me, and I'm going to put a fifty-pound camera bag on it. I want you to toss it down like you're gonna do with yourself, and I want you to hit the airbag with it."

"Okay," he replied, and he did as I said. He hit the airbag dead center.

"You saw that bag hit," I said. "You saw how far out you threw it. Are you sure you can do the same thing with yourself?"

"Oh, sure, Dad."

But I wasn't convinced. He was still talking, still didn't seem like he was concentrating. And I didn't like that. You've got to stay in your toes at all times in this business—or you might not stay *alive*.

We got all the cameras set up, and I got back on the radio with him. "Okay, Lance, are you all set to go?"

"Ready," he replied.

I went out on the very edge of the catcher platform so I could supervise—and, I admitted to myself, act as a last, desperate safety net, just in case. I had a safety guy and another stuntman come out there with me, then I rolled cameras and called *action* to Lance.

Instead of lifting up and dropping, like he needed to do, he pushed off with his feet, just like I'd feared he would. I felt my heart drop. *Oh, my God, I've lost him,* I thought in horror. *He's not going to make it.*

He *did* make it—but just *barely*. He hit the airbag very near where I was standing. Thankfully the airbag we were using had a thicker lip all around it that helped to contain the stuntman falling into it. The lip popped him back into the airbag, saving his life. When I peered in at him, I saw that his eyes were the size of saucers.

"You know what? You almost died, just now."

Still dazed, he replied, "Son of a bitch, I almost did!"

"That's what you get," I told him, shaking my head, "for being overconfident and not concentrating on what you're doing. You are pretty damned lucky, son."

Lance learned a big lesson from that stunt, and so did a lot of other guys who were there that day. You can't ever let your guard down, even if you've done a stunt a hundred times, because the one time you do, could be the time you die.

During filming of *Mohicans,* my sons and I spent the better part of a day filming a scene with the canoes that Hawkeye, Cora, Chingachcook and the other main characters escape in after the big massacre scene. The scene I was directing consisted of stunt doubles in the canoes going over a small waterfall. This scene cuts into another location with a waterfall at the upper entrance to a lake to match the waterfall previously shot with the doubles.

At the second location, we had the actors rowing towards the camera with the waterfall in the background. At the opposite lower end of the lake we had the cameras set up. Michael Mann and his assistant director were positioned at the tip of a huge twelve-foot high boulder to oversee the shots.

What Michael didn't realize was that the place he told the actors to beach their canoes was a part of the lake where the overflow formed

ME AND MY SADDLE-PAL

into a river, and that approximately a hundred and fifty feet down the river was a huge, one-hundred-and-twenty-five foot waterfall. The force of that waterfall was causing a current to pull upon the area we were working in—everything wanted to go towards that massive waterfall. I asked Michael if he could pan (rotate) his camera one inch to give us a little more room to stay out of that current. His response was swift and firm—he wasn't going to pan his lens. Period.

"Okay," I said, "I just hope I don't get in your shot." I had my sons, Tim, Troy and Lance put in catch safety lines along the river below where we were shooting, just in case, but I was also standing there to prevent any chance of the actors being taken by the current and thrown over the waterfall. Because of where I had to stand, I was afraid I'd be in Mann's frame, but the actors' safety was my primary concern.

The canoes we were using were custom-made and they were twice as heavy as a normal canoe. Because of their weight, when the current caught ahold of them, they were hard to control. I told the actors about the current and directed them to row a little harder as they approached their end mark, and we started shooting. About two out of every three takes, I ended up in the shot. Michael made comments about it every time ("you got in my shot that time," and "don't come in so fast!").

The combination of Mann's stubborn refusal to give up total control in the scene and my unwillingness to risk the actors' safety was a bad mix, and it led to trouble. The third time I got in his shot, I was fighting with one of the canoes, keeping it from being swept into the river. I was so involved with the canoe that I didn't hear Michael's comments as he hollered down to me. When I *did* hear him, I glanced over my shoulder to see who he was cursing at, not realizing it was *me*. Of course, I saw nothing but the river.

I turned back and looked up at Michael, hollering, "are you talking to me, Michael?"

"God damn right I am, you son of a bitch!" he hollered back.

Well, that was all I needed to hear. He was too high up and too far away for me to get to him, but I could improvise. One of the actors had

THE LAST OF THE MOHICANS

left an oar near me, and I snatched it up and cocked it like a baseball bat. I was furious that he was speaking to me like that in front of the actors and the crew, instead of talking to me privately. "Well, the hell with you, Michael!" I yelled, and threw the oar straight toward him.

My aim was right on, and Mann and his assistant ducked out of the way as the heavy oar went sailing right over their heads. Had they not ducked, the thing probably would've done some damage, to say the least. When they stood back up, everyone held their breath, waiting to see what they'd do.

"That's a wrap!" the assistant director called quickly, and everyone started scrambling uncomfortably to head back to the parking lot, a good ways away from the location of the scene. I stayed behind with my sons to gather up all of our safety equipment. They wanted to know what I was going to do when I saw Mann again.

"If he tries anything physical with me, I'll do what I have to do, and then I'm going to get on a plane and go home, because he'll fire me after that." My answer was matter-of-fact.

We lugged our gear back to the parking lot and found the crew and the actors already gone—except for a lone stretch limo belonging to none other than Michael Mann. Crap. This wasn't going to go well.

"He's waiting for you, Dad," Lance murmured, darting a look at me. "What are you going to do?"

"Already told you," I said grimly.

They looked at one another. "We're going with you, if you leave," Troy said stoutly.

"No, no, you're going to stay, and take care of the show," I told them firmly. There wasn't time to say anything else—Mann was getting out of the limo and looking my way. Great. I waited.

He looked right at me, gave me a sheepish grin, and threw his arms out to either side of him. I raised an eyebrow. "What's this mean, Michael?" I asked dryly, imitating his gesture.

"You were right, Mickey," he told me, as near to an apology as I'd ever heard from him. He awkwardly held his arms out again. "Let me give you a hug."

ME AND MY SADDLE-PAL

I accepted his apology, a little taken aback. I'd been ready to deck the guy.

I stayed on the shoot, of course; after that little incident Michael became much easier to work with; not just for me but for the entire cast and crew. I guessed no one had ever dared to call him out on his attitude before I tried to take him out with that oar. He never cussed me out again after that, and indeed called me back for work on other projects, as well as remembering me on holidays. It was one of many memorable moments I experienced during the filming of *The Last of the Mohicans*.

Striking Distance

In 1993 Columbia Pictures released a thriller called *Striking Distance,* starring Bruce Willis and Sarah Jessica Parker. The film was directed by Rowdy Herrington, who had also co-written the script. I got a call from producer Hunt Lowry, whom I'd worked with on *Last of the Mohicans,* about coordinating the stunts for the film, so off I went to Pittsburgh to meet with Herrington.

The boys were going to work with me on the film, so I found a place in Monroeville, about thirteen miles from Pittsburgh, for Yvonne and I and the boys to stay. We all had apartments near a big tennis complex, which was great since Yvonne and I were playing tennis at that time. I got to know the tennis pros there, and Yvonne met some new friends, too; she was doing a lot of water aerobics at the time and got invited to help teach one of the classes.

Every morning when I'd meet up with the boys to go to the set, Troy would always be late. Tim or Lance would have to go wake him up, and he'd rush to go with us, still half-asleep. One day I called him on it and told him that if he was late one more time, we'd leave without him. Sure enough, the next morning at the appointed time, no Troy. I gave him about five minutes, and he didn't show, so I stuck to my guns and herded Lance and Tim into the elevator with me.

"C'mon, Dad, let me go wake him up," Lance said.

"No," I said. "He's got to learn, and this is the only way he will."

ME AND MY SADDLE-PAL

Troy eventually did wake up, and found out we'd left without him. Now he was panicked. He caught a cab and went to the set, and we were already shooting. He was terribly embarrassed, but I wasn't going to cut him any slack. "You're in the movie business, Troy," I reminded him. "You've been in it for years now. You need to get it together and do whatever you need to do to be on time for jobs. I'm not going to cut you any slack."

After that talking-to, and that one experience of having to show up late, Troy pulled it together and was never late to a job again.

Pittsburgh was a great place to film a car chase; there were lots of hilly streets to use. I took a location manager with me and started scouting locations for a chase scene; it's the location that often makes the chase and provides the foundation for a great-looking action sequence. I got my ideas going and started writing the scene. Just as I'd gotten through about three-quarters of my scout, Hunt Lowry approached me and told me that they would be bringing in a guy from Sony to create a computer-animated, shot-for-shot version of what I wanted to shoot, instead of using traditional storyboards.

I wasn't keen on the idea, but I couldn't refuse to work with the guy, of course, so I told Hunt to send him on out. When he arrived, I asked him to explain the process of what he was going to do.

"Well, I need to go with you to all of your locations and take measurements of them, and get measurements of every type of car you're going to use in the sequence," he told me. "I also need to know where you're going to place your cameras, and the size of your lenses."

"Wow," I said, a little skeptically, "you can do all that with computers, huh?"

"Yep. I'm going to try," he said.

He followed me around and measured everything under the sun, and when he was done he told me he was going to take everything back to Sony and put it together. It would take him about three weeks, he said.

"Okay," I said, "We won't be ready to do this for awhile, anyway."

He came back as promised, and sought me out. "Hey, Mickey, you want to see this?"

"Yeah, I really do," I said, and he showed it to me. All the cars in the animated piece were in block form, but you could tell what they were supposed to be. He had all my camera angles and proposed shots in there.

"So, you're going to take this back to the director because he wanted to see all this in motion, huh?" I asked him.

"Yeah."

I raised my eyebrow at him. "Tell me something. How long is it gonna be before all the cars in these things are rounded out and look just like real cars, and have heads in them, and everything?"

"Maybe ten years," he told me.

This was very alarming to me. What he was telling me, essentially, was that in ten years or so, the work people like me did with real car chases in movies was going to be cut down dramatically and a lot of our physical stunts, that we all worked *so* hard on and poured so much blood, sweat, and tears into, were going to be done, more often than not, on a computer. This meant income taken away and talent underutilized. Directors wouldn't hire us as much, since they would be able to do practically anything they wanted on computers.

"Well, I don't think it'll go that far," he told me.

"*I* do," I replied bluntly. "You may just be getting this going right now, but it's going to spread like wildfire through this business."

After I was done with *Striking Distance,* I went around and met with the different stuntmen's' organizations, warning them about what I'd seen, and what I was positive was going to happen. "This is real, and it's coming," I cautioned them. "It's inevitable, and it's going to take a lot of work away from all of us." I encouraged all the other stunt coordinators to do their best to talk the directors they worked with every time they got a job to shoot things *for real.* I knew that computers were going to be able to do things that were not possible for us to do in reality—but I also knew that it wasn't going to look the same, and it wasn't going to generate the same thrill that real stunts did. I was glad I'd had a warning, because look what's happened with today's films—all the computer-generated effects are, more often than not, over the top.

ME AND MY SADDLE-PAL

During the filming of *Striking Distance,* I had the opportunity to write some stunt sequences involving boats chasing each other through locks on the Allegheny River. In this sequence, I had Troy and Lance diving the boats, with Troy doubling Bruce Willis and Lance doubling Robert Pastorelli, the film's antagonist. During the sequence they had to jump the boats over the locks, sailing about a hundred feet through the air. This was quite dangerous because of the whirlpool effect created in the overflow areas of the locks—if you get caught in one of those, you can't get back out again; the water sucks you in and tumbles you over and over. Because of this danger, we needed permits, and so I had to go meet with people from the city. The director and Lowry came with me. During the meetings we were shown videos of unfortunate people getting caught in overflow areas.

"Do you really think we're going to let you do what you're proposing to do near these things?" I was asked after I'd viewed about three such videos. "And to top it off, we understand it's your *sons* that are going to be driving the boats?"

"I see what you're getting at," I replied, "but these boats are high-speed boats that are going to be going at least forty-five miles per hour and are going to be landing a good hundred feet or so beyond the falls at these overflow areas. The only thing that could go wrong is if one of them runs out of gas—but here's what I'm going to do. I'm planning to have two big barges equipped with hydraulic pilings that anchor them to the river's floor The barges will be around one hundred feet apart, with an underwater cable tied between them. There will be a four-inch ring that the cable runs through; I'll have a line run through this ring that will be attached to a high-horse-powered safety boat. That line will come back to the safety boat and into a pull-and-release unit. This is so the safety boat can go to its right or left as the ring slides on the cable that's run in between the two barges. If one of the boats we're using for the picture gets trapped in the turbulence at the falls, the men in the safety boat will feed out some line to let their boat get closer to the falls. The safety men will have floating throw-lines and poles for rescuing purposes. Also, the stuntmen, Lance and Troy, will be wearing water safety vests to keep them more buoyant if they get trapped in that turbulent area."

They accepted my safety provisions and gave the production permission to go ahead with the stunt. It worked like a charm, and thousands of people came out that night to watch us shoot it. Despite having been reinforced with plywood for strength, Lance's boat did crack when it hit the water, and it began to sink. I told him to drive it toward land, which he did, and just as it went under Troy drove his boat over there and picked Lance up, so no one was hurt—except the boat.

That sequence was quite a big deal because of everything we had to go through to get permission from the river patrol and the lock engineers and so forth, and because it had never been done before, but I was very happy with it when it was done.

Another big stunt that my son Tim did involved driving a car on a dirt road that ran alongside the Allegheny River, with Bruce Willis, as the river cop, racing parallel to Tim, firing flares at Tim's car. It was a night shot, so the flares going horizontally through the air looked very impressive. In the scene, one of the flares goes through the rear windshield and explodes, lighting up Tim's car, which then goes out of control and flips over and over.

We needed to do some safety work on Tim's car so we installed Lexan, a clear thick sheet of durable polycarbonate material, top to bottom and side to side behind the front seats of the car, which would protect Tim from heat or fire. The effects department also welded in a small canon that Tim would ignite, blowing flames out the rear window.

The back end of the car was billowing with flames, just before Tim hit a special ramp that flips the car over multiple times. I had four stunt safety men, a fire truck and an ambulance all standing by as we did it. The safety men would be the closest to where Tim ended up, so their job would be to put the fire out and help Tim out of the car. The fire truck would have its hoses out, full of active water if we needed them. And the ambulance—well, you never want to think that you might need one, but, just in case, they were there and ready.

I must say, the whole sequence looked great, particularly since it was shot at night, which made everything all lit up look even more dramatic. The best thing about it, though, was that we didn't have to use the ambulance.

One of my favorite car chases that I wrote and designed for *Striking Distance* was a real challenge, sort of a cat-and-mouse chase. Our director loved it once he read it, so now all I had to do was find the different locations for it. Along with our location manager, I went driving all over, looking for and sometimes stumbling onto spots that would fit the sequence. I've found, during my career, that one of the hardest parts of filming action sequences is finding the right locations for them.

The scene involved Robert Pastorelli's car being chased by Bruce Willis's, and I had Lance doubling for Pastorelli and Troy doubling for Willis. As the chase progressed, there were more cop cars that joined in and followed Bruce's car. The lead cop car was driven by my other son Tim. It's a good thing I have so many sons in stunt work; it comes in handy for scenes like this!

I found an old road that dropped off of a hillside road and ran across four single-lane roads as you were driving down it; those crossroads were spaced out about every hundred feet or so. On each crossroad I had the carpenters build jump ramps so each car coming down would fly into the air, then land until it hit the next ramp. What a shot! My cameras were positioned at the bottom of the hillside road, all shooting up with different sized lenses. All the cars were about thirty feet apart, following each other. Lance's car was first, sliding into our frames and turning onto the downhill road. Troy was second, Tim was third, and then the other cop cars followed. It was wild-looking—picture six cars heading down this road, and all are leaping up and down, one after the other, the light bars on the car roofs starting to fly off from the compression of jumping up and landing. This was one of my favorite sequences of the chase.

Another one was what I called the "cat-and-mouse" scene. By this time into the chase, swat teams and cops have blocked the road that Lance is coming down. Lance hits his brakes and does a long slide before he stops. Troy's car, doubling Bruce, along with the other cop cars, pull in and block the road behind Lance. Everyone gets out of their cars, taking positions and getting ready to fire. It looks like there's no way out for Lance—or so they think. During this chase you never see who's driving Lance's car, so it makes it more mysterious. At this point, there's a lot of dialogue going on between Bruce and his character's dad, and one of the police captains. Over a loudspeaker, they're hollering at the ghost car, ordering the driver to "get out with your hands up!"

The ghost car revs its engine like a race car in response, and the captain repeats his order, but again, all he gets in response is the sound of a revving engine as everyone shakes their heads. It happens a third time, but now, as the ghost car revs its engine, its backup lights go on and here it comes in reverse, right towards Bruce and the cops. They unload their guns on it, with bullet effects going off on the rear of the car.

This road we were filming on was under a freeway, and off it its left was a lower parking lot that sat down about ten feet below the road. Lance, still in reverse, swerves and crashes through the fence around the parking lot, landing on top of parked cars. He keeps going, backing off the parked cars to make his getaway. I loved it, because it had everyone shut down from a wild car chase into thinking, "now we've got him," and what happens after waiting and waiting? "Oh, my gosh, here we go again!"

The next part of the chase, and another favorite of mine, happened after Lance left the parking lot. Troy caught up to him, and it became one-on-one. Troy's car pulled up alongside Lance's, and Bruce's dad shot out Lance's front left tire. Lance's car swerved hard to its left, plowing into Troy's car. They both sailed off the roadway, right where a hill dropped off. Then the fun part came. I had two jump ramps set up off the ledge of the hillside, one for each car. Troy's car would be about one and a half lengths ahead of Lance's car when they hit the ramps. They'd be jumping out over a twenty five-degree hillside, becoming airborne before landing, almost side-by-side in the air. The trick was

ME AND MY SADDLE-PAL

for all of my camera operators to let the cars go out of their frame just as they land. Why? Because I had two other cars, each with a cannon in it, to blow them sideways. I picked a spot lower on the hill where it was not as steep. The boys would back their cars up onto the same position they landed in. On 'action," they would speed down the hillside, and at a marker they would slide their cars sideways, hit their cannon buttons, and get ready for a wild ride.

It really *was* a fabulous, wild ride. Each car rolled over three or four times before stopping. When you watch the film, you see the cars flying in slow motion, dropping down and hitting the ground, going out of control and flipping over and over. You'll love it.

I was so proud of my boys for the work they did on that movie. The stunts I had them doing were not the easiest to do and it took a lot of concentration and special abilities to pull them off. If anyone could do it, though, it was those sons of mine—they're the best, and I love them.

There was a lot for me to be proud of in *Striking Distance;* all the car and boat chases turned looking wild. Bruce Willis was great to work with; I ended up working closely with him when I directed the big underwater scene he had for the end of the film. It turned out to be a good action movie—but I'll always remember it for introducing me to CGI, and heralding the approach of the biggest change the stunt industry's ever gone through.

City Slickers II: The Legend of Curly's Gold

City Slickers II: The Legend of Curly's Gold, was released in 1994; the producers were hoping to mimic the success of the first film, since it had been so wildly popular. I got the call to coordinate the stunts again, which I agreed to do with enthusiasm. In fact, I let out a whoop after I'd hung up the phone. "*Yeah, baby*! Guess what?" I hollered to Yvonne.

"What are you so happy about?" she asked me with a smile.

I put my hands on my hips and lifted my chin at her. "I just got a call from Billy Crystal's company to direct the second unit and coordinate the stunts on the sequel to *City Slickers.*"

"Well, yeah, baby, yourself!" she said with a grin, happy that I was happy.

The next day I went down to the company's offices and met with Billy, Peter Schindler, who was the executive producer, and the director of the film. This time around, Paul Weiland took over the director's chair from Ron Underwood.

We discussed the film thoroughly. I mentioned that it would save us some time and some money too if I shot the scripted horse stampede before they brought the main unit out to the location at Moab, Utah. This way they would know where and how they'd need to cut the actors into the shots. Also, by this time, the herd would be trained to run from point A to point B, and wouldn't be scattering all over the place. When I left the office and I knew I had the job, I called my good

ME AND MY SADDLE-PAL

friend and director of photography, Don McCuaig, and told him we had another job coming up.

Don and I headed for Moab and started scouting out the locations we needed. Jack Lillie was back as head wrangler and livestock coordinator and was already gathering up two hundred head of horses for the stampede shots. Don and I found a canyon that zigzagged its way through jagged rocks. It was about twenty feet wide and twenty to thirty feet deep with a sandy bottom, more like a crevice that had just split open than a wide canyon. You could see where the water line had been, about eight feet up from the bottom. It ran for about a mile.

Don and I loved this location, and it was the place we used to film the scene in the movie where Billy's Mitch sees a beautiful white stallion that he playfully chases after, ending up in our narrow canyon. We envisioned this scene like a ballet of sorts, only instead of two dancers, we'd have two horses. Don suggested shooting the whole thing backlit, which I agreed to.

We gathered about thirty wooden stakes and, after walking the canyon two or three times, picked out different spots for the cameras according to where the sun was; Don always wanted the sun behind the object we were filming. At each spot where we'd decided to place a camera, I'd pound in a stake to mark it, and write the time we needed to use the spot on the stake. That way, the sunlight would always be where we wanted it.

It was a beautiful sequence between Billy and the white stallion, and this chase led us into the stampede scene. We shot all that with Billy's double, Brian Burrows, who was a perfect double for the actor; Billy and the rest of the first unit were still in Hollywood, working on a soundstage. Working the way I was gave Billy and the director the chance to view the footage we'd shot in Moab. Now they knew exactly where to cut Billy into the chase.

The stampede scene, with the two hundred head of horses and the wagon in the center really photographed well. Speaking of the wagon, I needed a driver to hide himself inside the wagon and do all the driving blind, so I brought in my brother-in-law Joe Finnegan, who is also a

CITY SLICKERS II: THE LEGEND OF CURLY'S GOLD

stuntman, to Moab to fill that position. Jon Lovitz, the actor who the audience would think was driving, was going to be bouncing around all over the place in the runaway wagon, so we needed someone to actually keep control of the wagon without Lovitz having to do so, and act, at the same time.

By the time the first unit arrived in Moab, I had finished the entire stallion and stampede sequences. I met up with Billy, Paul Weiland and some executives, and we planned out our shooting schedule. Billy told me that Jon Lovitz was very concerned about staying safe in the runaway wagon, but I told him not to worry. Then my impish nature took over and I suggested to Billy that we kid around a little bit with Lovitz; I told him that every time I was around the actor I'd bump into him when I walked by, with my shoulder, and walk off. "That'll get him really worried, if I do it the next two days," I said with a chuckle. Lovitz hadn't met me yet and didn't know who I was, this little prank would really make him nervous.

I did as I'd said, and on the second day, after I'd shoulder-checked him and was moving on, Lovitz gave Billy a wide-eyed look. "See, Bill, I told you. He did that on purpose. That guy doesn't like me."

Billy had his own way of playing along with me and told Jon, "Oh, I'm sure he didn't mean to bump into you."

I was walking away, and I turned and looked back at Lovitz with a serious face.

"Look! See him looking at me?" I heard Jon blurt out to Billy. "He's mean, and he's gonna do something to me, I can tell. Who *is* that guy, anyway?"

"I think he's one of the wranglers," Billy fibbed. "I'll have Jack Lillie, our boss wrangler, have a talk with him. Don't worry, Jon, we'll fix it."

The next day I did it again, but instead of walking away I stopped and faced Lovitz. "He did it *again*, Bill, he's crazy!" Lovitz said.

Billy started laughing then—really cracking up. I started chuckling, too; then I walked up to Jon, put my arms around him, and kissed him on the cheek, telling him about our little joke as Billy introduced

ME AND MY SADDLE-PAL

me. I told him he had nothing to worry about during the wagon scene; my brother-in-law was a pro and we'd keep him safe.

"Just the same," I told him, "if you're worried about anything on this show, you let me know."

Jon did fine during the sequence, and wouldn't you know it—he and I became very close on *City Slickers II*. I ended up working with him again, many years later, on 2001's *Rat Race*.

The Amazing Panda Adventure

In 1995 Warner Brothers released a family/adventure film called *The Amazing Panda Adventure,* about a ten-year-old boy who helps rescue a panda cub from poachers during a trip to China. The film starred Ryan Slater, brother of actor Christian Slater, and Stephen Lang.

I'd gotten a call from the film's director, Chris Cain, and he'd sent me the script. He wanted me to coordinate stunts and direct the second unit, so off Yvonne and I went to Chengdu to get started. We were very excited about the opportunity to visit China and observe another culture.

When we arrived in Chengdu, we were loaded onto a bus with a bunch of other people associated with the film, and we took a fourteen-hour trip out to the Jiuzhaigou Valley. That was a *long* bus ride, traveling along a narrow dirt road that was just wide enough for the bus; a road that often ran alongside a steep eight or nine-hundred foot cliff. On the way out of Chengdu, I spotted a massive row of bicycles—about three hundred of them—all leaned together. The whole bunch of them made up a mass about eighty feet square, and I found out that they all belonged to people working in the city. I wondered how the heck you got your bike out if it was one of the ones in the middle, but I was soon told that people just took the first bike off the row as they came out to go home, until there were none left. Everyone got a bike—it just wasn't necessarily the bike they'd ridden in on. It didn't matter,

ME AND MY SADDLE-PAL

because everyone was coming back the next day to do it all over again. I thought that was a pretty clever way to solve things. Otherwise, the guy with the bike in the middle might wait for hours until he was able to maneuver it out of there.

We continued on our way to Jiuzhaigou, nervously observing the way the tires of our bus occasionally came a little too close to the cliff's edge for our comfort. By the fourth hour or so on the road, everyone was beyond nervous and had moved on to downright scared. Every so often we'd come face-to-face with a big logging truck coming the other way, but since the road was so narrow, neither vehicle could pass. There would be a stand-off, and both drivers would get out and begin talking. Whomever was coming from downhill would have to back up to find a place to pull over and let the other one pass—this was what made the trip so long.

At one point we came around a bend, and a local man—a road worker—came running out onto the road in front of us, waving his arms frantically. Our driver brought the bus to a halt. Just then, there was a big blast from the side of the mountain above the road, and a shower of huge rocks came down onto the road, scaring the hell out of us. Our driver and our interpreter got out and talked to the man, and a few minutes later the driver came back onto the bus, asking if anyone had a couple of packs of cigarettes. We'd been advised to carry a carton of cigarettes with us, and now we found out why—they were used as bribes. For a couple of packs, the road worker and his crew would clear just enough rocks out of the way so that our bus could continue on. All of these things made our drive to Jiuzhaigou *extremely* frustrating.

Jiuzhaigou was just a tiny village, with crude twig houses built along the roadsides. There was a river running through it. Believe it or not, there *was* a small hotel there, and it was in that hotel that the entire production was housed. We slept there, ate there, and had our meetings there. The place was alright if you remembered to remind yourself that you *were*, after all, in rural China.

The next morning after we arrived I went to meet with Chris Cain, Gabriella Martinelli, one of the producers, and several of the actors.

THE AMAZING PANDA ADVENTURE

We all needed to get to know one another, since we were all going to spend a long period of time together. Martinelli asked Yvonne if she would like to work on the film as the entertainment director; her duties would include arranging entertainment for the cast and crew, such as having Warner Brothers send in movies for everyone to watch, organizing barbecues, and bringing in different games to play. She even organized karaoke one night, which everyone loved. It kept her very busy during the shoot.

Chris Cain told me he was glad I was there, because he had a shot he'd planned that involved a runaway wagon carrying kids and big sacks full of vegetables. He wanted me to train the horses that would pull it, and he also wanted me to blind-drive the wagon in the shot (blind driving being where a hidden driver, crouched down so as not to be seen by the camera, drives a vehicle that appears to be out of control during the movie).

Chris had asked me to bring along a lot of gear to the shoot, but I hadn't brought any long driving reins with me.

I got busy scouting out horses. A lot of the horses in that area of China are infested with parasites, and are underweight as a result, so I knew that finding a decent-looking horse for the shoot would be challenging. During one of my scouts I found a big thirty-acre dirt field I could use to train the horses; my interpreter helped me arrange for that. Then I contacted some ranchers in the area and had some horses brought in. I started working with them and feeling them out for driving, bridling them and getting behind them, seeing how they acted. Finally I found one that seemed agreeable to being broken to drive, so I had him drag a log behind him with me standing on it, taking him through his paces until he'd pull me, and the log, behind him at a trot or a canter.

I hitched him up to a heavy Chinese wagon, and kept working with him. Every night Chris would ask me how the training was going, and then he'd laugh when I'd tell him about all of the different crazy antics each horse would pull, like rearing over backwards or running away on me. Right about then I realized why Chris was so glad to have me on

ME AND MY SADDLE-PAL

the show; not only was I directing the second unit and coordinating the stunts, but I was also training horses and blind-driving them. "That's what you're good at," Chris confirmed, when I said something about it.

We traveled up into Tibet to film a portion of the movie, and we had to go up into high altitude to reach the location where we were filming. Yvonne and I did okay up there, but there were many on the production that couldn't handle the altitude.

I got ready to shoot my second unit, and began filming the stunt with the runaway wagon. I got it set up with the big burlap sacks that were supposed to be holding all the vegetables; one of them was also supposed to contain the panda cub that the two main child characters were smuggling to freedom. I had a spot cleared in the center of the wagon where I could lay down to blind-drive the horse.

Getting ready to blind-drive the wagon for The Amazing Panda Adventure. *–M.G.*

THE AMAZING PANDA ADVENTURE

My interpreter started explaining to all the Tibetan locals where I wanted them to be, but it was not an easy task, since communication between the Chinese interpreter and the Tibetan interpreter was not at all fluid or easy. We'd get everyone lined out and rehearse, but none of the people who were supposed to be in the shots did what they were supposed to do—they kept running away instead of coming into the frame. Our director was up on a hill nearby with the first unit, and from his vantage point he could see what I was doing, and all the trouble I was having. He was laughing his ass off, even though he knew what I was going through, since he was having the same problem. All the shots seemed to take three times as long because of the language issues.

We finished in Tibet and headed back to Jiuzhaigou, and a party was organized to thank the locals from the village and our hotel for their hospitality. One of the guests was a member of the Imperial family whom our director had met; he wasn't the actual Emperor of China but he had the title in a ceremonial sense, and bodyguards to go along with it. He had a lot of power and had helped the production get into areas we needed access to in order to shoot the film. Chris came to me and told me about the party, and that the Emperor was coming to it. "I want you to sit at my table with him," he told me.

I was puzzled. "Why? I don't care about that sort of thing," I protested.

"No, I want you to be there, because these guys are going to find you fascinating," he told me with a grin.

"Oh, all right," I sighed.

"There's something I need to warn you about," Chris told me. "This guy *really* likes to drink. I mean, he can put it away like you wouldn't believe. And he drinks this *strong* white liquor that they have here—I don't know what it is, but it'll knock you on your ass. And it's going to be on our table; he's going to make toasts with it. So you'll have to drink it."

"Chris, I don't drink that crap," I told him.

He shook his head. "You'll have to, out of politeness," he said.

I started thinking. "Maybe not," I said. "I've got an idea." I told

ME AND MY SADDLE-PAL

him what I had in mind. "Yvonne will be to my right, and you'll be to my left," I said to Chris. "Your wife's going to be to your left, and then Gabriella Martinelli, then maybe some soldiers...and *then* the Emperor. Right?"

"Yeah..."

"We're going to have some empty shot glasses down below by our feet," I said, "and I'm going to have bottled water under the table we can fill them with after I pretend to fill them with this guy's liquor. That way, every time we have to toast, you, Yvonne, your wife and me will be drinking water instead of liquor."

As crazy as it sounded, it actually worked. The Emperor was a really jolly guy, and he never noticed us switching it out. I'd pour the actual stuff onto the floor under the table, and he was none the wiser.

Even though the Emperor never noticed what we were doing, one person did—our prop man. After the banquet was over he came over to me and gave me a wide, sly grin. "I saw what you guys were doing," he said. "Let's have one more toast." He reached for the bottle of real liquor and sloshed some into our shot glasses. I moaned and groaned and protested, but he insisted, so in the end we did have to drink one shot of the stuff—and it was *bad.* I mean *really, really* bad. The worst stuff I'd ever tasted, actually. But at least we only had to drink it once.

In order to get certain shots involving the panda cub, we had a number of ways of staging each sequence. We had a real panda that had been trained, but we couldn't use it for any shots that might endanger it or the actors in any way, so we also had a couple of little people that could get into a panda suit if needed. We also had a very realistic-looking stuffed panda, so when I was doing action shots I could choose between the three options to get whatever shots I needed.

There was one scene where the kids and the panda fall into a fast-moving river and are being swept down in the rapids. The water there in Jiuzhaigou was absolutely beautiful—crystal clear and deep turquoise in color, full of minerals and delicious to drink. It came out of the Mongolian mountains. I'd found a spot to film the sequence; the water was only about six inches deep but it was frothing over the rocks in a beautiful way. I came up with the idea to have the effects department build twenty-foot long sections of small tracks—like railroad tracks—that we could lay under the water and run small seats on. The children could sit on the seats and be carried through the water that way. I met with the effects team, and they built exactly what I wanted out of round pipe, and fitted them with little seats with ball bearings so they would move smoothly. When they were finished we took them out and set them up in the river, weighting them down with big huge boulders. I had a Tibetan crew of about twenty; they were not movie people but rather laborers. When they saw me moving rocks to weigh down the tracks, they immediately all came over to help me. They were incredibly hard workers and were always eager to help with even the most back-breaking tasks.

The scene was going to end with the kids and the cub being swept over a cliff and falling into a pool, so I scouted out a location for that. The two stunt doubles I found for Ryan Slater and Yi Ding, the two child stars, would be performing the fall. I found both of them in Canada. Neither of them were actual kids, just small young adults—Slater's double was a jockey, and Ding's double was a very small stuntwoman in her twenties that looked much younger than she was. Both of them were good physical doubles for our actors, but I really had to talk them into doing certain stunts—like this fall. Sometimes they even refused to do what I wanted; Slater's double had a particular problem with water stunts. I pointed out all of the safety measures we'd taken, but he was still having issues. Finally I talked him into it, and we got the shot. I was very pleased with my seats-on-tracks idea; it worked very well and gave me the exact look I wanted.

I taught the doubles how to ride the rapids safely, doing it myself first before I made them do it. We had them in wet suits and plenty of safety men positioned on the banks to ensure that nothing happened to them. It took awhile, but I eventually gained their trust.

I wanted to shoot a bit where the kids came out of the river's rapids into still water. I'd found a place where the water boiled furiously around some rocks before being forced out into a calm area. I walked

ME AND MY SADDLE-PAL

over there with my assistant and the two doubles to see what they thought of the area. I took a stick and dropped it into the fast-moving water. We all watched as it was carried on top of the rapids and ejected out into the still area. "What do you guys think?" I asked them. "That's what you'll be doing. You know the water now. Do you think you can do that okay?" They nodded. I offered to do it first for them, but they told me they trusted me and didn't need proof that it was doable.

We were getting ready to do the sequence when my assistant came to me and told me we had a problem. The area I had scouted was in a different township than where we'd been shooting, so there was a different town leader here—sort of a mayor. He wanted fifty thousand dollars in exchange for letting us shoot in that location.

"Oh, really?" I asked. "Bring him down here."

My assistant did as I said, and when the official came down I folded my hands and gave him a respectful bow, as did my assistant and my interpreter. I told the interpreter to interpret everything I said *exactly* as I said it. Then I asked the mayor, "So, you want fifty thousand dollars?"

"Yes, yes," came the reply. "Fifty thousand."

I reached into my wallet and pulled out a five dollar bill, American. "Here, give him the fifty thousand," I told the interpreter, with a completely straight face.

The interpreter did as I asked, and the mayor took the bill. He saw the five printed on it, and put his hands together in a gesture of thanks before walking off, heading back to his village, happy as a clam. My assistant looked at me with his jaw on the ground, barely able to contain his laughter. "You know, you are something *else*," he said to me. "How the hell did you think of that so fast?"

I shrugged. "I don't know, I just thought if he saw a five on an American bill, he'd go for it. But who cares why it worked, we just bought ourselves an end sequence for five bucks." We went back the next day and shot it.

One of the things that made working on this film so memorable was the jarring cultural and quality of life differences between our country and these tiny, rural Chinese villages. Yvonne had organized

THE AMAZING PANDA ADVENTURE

a bus trip to another village that was a bit bigger than the ones we'd been in; this one had a few little shops in it. Myself and about ten other people went along, and as we were walking down the street there we started getting approached by small children who lived in the village. I was wearing my western hat, and Yvonne and the other were wearing American clothes, so we were something to behold for all of those poor village kids. I found a piece of thistle rope and made a lasso, and started trick-roping for them, roping the kids and making them squeal with laughter. Pretty soon our group looked like the Pied Piper, leading all these kids down the street and getting laughs and smiles along the way.

We came upon a sign that said 'dentist.' There was a small table out in front that had various items laid out on it—vials of penicillin and hypodermic needles that were very obviously *not* sterile in any way, shape or form. The dentist came out and bowed to us, pointing at his teeth and asking if I had a toothache. "Oh, no, no," I said hurriedly. "Just looking." We couldn't believe the poor conditions there, and Yvonne actually took a picture of that dentist's table. Our director was suffering from a bad toothache, and when we got back to Jiuzhaigou I told him to go to Hong Kong to get his tooth fixed—no matter what. "Do *not* get it worked on here," I cautioned. I told him about what we'd seen.

"I wouldn't be stupid enough to do something like that," he said.

"I know, but people *do*," I said. "The locals do. It's unbelievable. The people here must have amazing immune systems." I remembered seeing similar things in Africa; dung poultices and things like that. Living conditions were almost deplorable, with no indoor plumbing, more often than not. Places that did have plumbing, like our hotel, had very poor plumbing, with the smell from sewers coming back up through the toilets. It was very eye-opening and made us even more grateful to live where we did.

Panda was a fun movie, all-in-all, to make. We saw some beautiful countryside and met some fascinating people, like my driver, whom I called "Jose," which he didn't mind at all (I couldn't pronounce his name). The car he drove me around in was a piece of junk that also

ME AND MY SADDLE-PAL

happened to be a stick-shift, which Jose didn't seem to know much about. He managed, but my ride was often very jerky and he wouldn't push the clutch in to stop. I would try to teach him to use it. "Jose, clutch," I would say, and he'd repeat it back to me—but not use it. Chris and the producers had very nice cars; I had the only clunker. "You're the second unit director," Yvonne used to tell me. "Get yourself a better car and driver, for Heaven's sake!"

"I'm having fun with this guy," I told her with a laugh. I was always trying to teach him how to work the clutch properly. Sometimes when I'd get frustrated I'd say, "Jose, use the fucking clutch!" and he learned that word, too. All I'd have to say was "Jose," and he'd finish for me, "I know, I know, fu-cking clutch!" with a big smile.

I wanted to take Chris and Gabriella out to the spot where I'd shot the water sequence, and as a gag I told them "we'll take my car!" So they all came over and hopped in the back. Off we go in the rattletrap. At every point we had to brake during the ride, the car would jerk-jerk-jerk to a stop. Jose looked at me sheepishly and said, "clutch, fucking clutch!"

"Yes, clutch," I repeated with a grin. Chris and Gabriella were looking at me. "Gilbert, what the heck do you have going on here?" they asked.

I just laughed. "This is "Jose," my driver, and he's a great guy," I told them. We eventually made it out to the spot, and Chris and Gabriella loved it.

My crew were also great people; they were such hard workers, and all for only a dollar a day of pay. I felt bad that they were getting so little pay, and I talked the Canadian crew and talked about everyone donating a dollar of our own money to give the Tibetans a little more money. We had to be careful about it because the Tibetan crew-members would get into trouble with the government if it was learned that they were making money under the table. We'd gather at the little bar in the village on Saturdays and present them with the extra money we'd collected. They knew not to say anything, but they were so grateful and worked twice as hard for us. The only thing they ever learned to say in

English was the phrase "you guys;" it was a phrase that our Canadian medic used to say repeatedly—only he'd say it with a musical lilt and it always came out "yoouu guuuys." The Tibetan crew picked up on that phrase, for some reason, and every morning they'd say it to me in unison, as a greeting.

One day Jose and I were out scouting some locations. We were on the main dirt road that ran through that part of the country when we came up behind some army trucks parked on the road, which was narrow. Jose slammed on his brakes, and we stopped about two hundred feet behind them. At the head of the procession, there was an army jeep with a loudspeaker on it. Behind the jeep were two big army transport trucks with the canvas tops gone; only the bows that held the canvas in place were there. Attached to those exposed bows were handcuffed prisoners, about twelve in each truck. Each prisoner had a strip of white-painted wood hanging from his neck, and on the wood, painted in red, was whatever crime he'd been convicted of.

Behind the transport truck was another army jeep carrying some armed guards, and one of them was calling to the people who lived up in the hills to come down and listen. I started to lift my camera, but right away, Jose reached out and pushed my arm down, shaking his head. "No, no, Mickey," he said, and motioned to me to be very quiet.

People started showing up along the road, and once the guards felt enough of a crowd had gathered, they unloaded one of the prisoners and shot him, right there on the spot.

After that, the vehicles drove to the next village and proceeded to do the same thing, until all of the prisoners had been executed. As we drove along the road, I saw rocks that were stacked about two feet high, three feet wide and six to seven feet long; these were the graves where the prisoners were buried. They were called "stinky graves" because of the odor of death wafting from them, and there were quite a few of them all over the roadsides. There's not a lot of crime in China, and after witnessing that, I could see why. That was another experience of many during the making of *Panda* that had me appreciating the good old U.S.A. that much more.

ME AND MY SADDLE-PAL

We really did have a lot of fun on that shoot, when I think back on it, and being able to spend so much time in such an exotic place made me even more grateful for being so lucky as to have ended up in the profession I'm in.

Waterworld

On our way home from China, Yvonne and I stopped off at the Big Island of Hawaii to see our boys, who were working on a post-apocalyptic sci-fi/action flick put out by Universal called *Waterworld,* directed by Kevin Reynolds and starring another Kevin—Kevin Costner.

Prior to me leaving for China, I had gotten a call from Kevin Reynolds, who had wanted me to work on the film as a second-unit director. Since I was already committed to the job in China, I couldn't take Reynolds up on his offer, but the boys were hired on for stunts, so we'd decided to visit them there.

Waterworld was a *massive* movie—in fact, the most expensive film ever made at the time of its production—and its plot centered around a time in the future where the polar ice caps have melted and the planet's continents are all covered with water. By the time Yvonne and I got there the boys had already been at work on the movie for about five months; Reynolds had a lot of stuntmen working for him, all coming and going at various times. When we arrived, the boys weren't working on that particular day, so they took us to check out one of the "atolls," a part of the set. Atolls were huge, floating structures made of scrap metal and old marine vessels that served as floating communities in the film, where all that survived of mankind lived. The thing looked like a giant piece of junk, welded together with pieces of sheet metal, ropes, and ladders, supported by pontoons to keep it afloat. After that, they took us over to see the "bone pile."

ME AND MY SADDLE-PAL

The bone pile was a collection of prototype props made at the behest of anyone connected with the film who came up an idea for something to use in it. These props would be made, then taken to Kevin Reynolds for approval. The problem was that no one told him what was being made before they made it, so more often than not, when they took something over to him, he'd say "I don't have any use for *that,*" upon seeing whatever-it-was. After getting rejected by the director, the prop or set-piece would literally get thrown on the bone pile. There must have been about a hundred thousand dollars worth of unused junk in that pile. I was flabbergasted. What a waste!

"Why is there so much *waste* in this movie?" I asked.

Troy replied, "You know, Dad, they've got ninety special effects guys on this movie. You wouldn't believe the money pouring into this thing. In fact, they had hats made up that say, 'one day of work, one million dollars. Two days of work, two million dollars' and so on. It's nuts."

One of the guys working with the second unit was there, and I talked to him. "What do you guys *do* all day?" I asked.

"Oh, you know," he shrugged. "We surf a lot. Sometimes the second unit director goes up in a plane and drops water balloons on us…"

"You've *got* to be kidding me," I replied, sure that he was.

"Nope," he said. "It's getting to be where we won't even do a shot for two or three days at a time. It's like a paid vacation."

"Must be nice," I snorted sarcastically.

Yvonne and I finished our visit and headed home, and not too long after I get another call from Kevin Reynolds.

"So, Mick, I heard you're home from China," he said.

"Yeah, we're home now," I confirmed. I told him I'd gone to China just about the time his production company had been leaving for Hawaii to shoot *Waterworld,* and that I'd stopped by the island to see my sons on our way back—and had been surprised he was still shooting there. "Guess it's a long one, huh?" I asked casually.

"Yeah, there's a lot of stuff going on," he said. He cleared his throat. "So…we're back in town now, at Paramount." He then told me he wanted me to take over the second unit for the film, the crew of which was still in Hawaii. Since I was free now, I told him I'd love to. "When can you come to Paramount so we can talk?" he asked me.

"How about tomorrow?" I asked.

"Perfect. Meet me near the commissary on the lot. We're shooting some water stuff here now and cutting Costner into some shots."

I headed over to Paramount as promised, and when I got there I was approached almost immediately by one of the film's producers. "Listen," he said urgently, "can you leave tonight?"

"*What?*" I asked in disbelief. I hadn't even seen Reynolds yet. I barely knew what the movie was about.

"There's a crew over there, just spending money," he said.

"That's not my problem," I replied firmly. "I've got to sit down with the director and find out what he wants from me. I need to look at footage, separate the good from the bad, and I want to go through your storyboards, too. I'm not leaving for the location unless I'm prepared to do the job right. Otherwise, *I'm* going to waste your money, too."

He finally agreed and let me go see Reynolds. He took me into his trailer, and in it he had *six* huge books full of storyboards—well beyond the amount normally used for one movie.

"What on earth—are you *using* all these?" I asked in disbelief.

"No, I'm really only using one of them," he told me. "The second unit is going by all of them, but they're shooting a lot of stuff I haven't approved yet."

I gave him a look. "Haven't you been discussing things with the second unit director as he shoots?"

"I've never even *talked* to the second unit director," he admitted.

I had to take a minute to absorb *that* little shocker. I'd never heard of such a thing. "That's not the way to make a movie," I blurted out. "You know that!"

"Well, I'm just so busy with Costner, and with all this first unit stuff...I just don't have time."

"Kevin, when *I* get there, I'm going to start shooting the first day, and I'm going to call you the first night to discuss everything with you.

I'm not shooting anything you don't approve. That's the way I work." He liked that, I could tell, and we started watching some of the footage they already had. I saw a problem right away with one particular scene, which I'll go into later.

We spent a long time talking, and I asked him about the storyboards. He told me to go through them and pull out anything that didn't make sense. "Just throw them on the floor," he said. I spent about two hours going through the storyboards then, watching footage of the film as I did, and by the time Reynolds came back I must have had about three hundred pages of storyboards littering the floor around my feet.

"Boy, you seem to know what you're doing," he commented with a smile.

"Well, none of this stuff *fits*," I said. It's hard to shoot a good movie solely from storyboards, because you'll inevitably end up with something you don't need if you're only working from the vision of an artist drawing something out in pictures.

Eventually I headed to Hawaii to get to work. Yvonne and I arrived on a Saturday and got settled in. That same day I met with Steve Traxler, our line producer, who would act as my right hand for the shoot. I was lucky to have Steve around me, because he'd been there from day one. He filled me in on the good and the bad of the production, and I told him my ideas about the action and pick-up shots we needed to get.

The following day was Super Bowl Sunday. I knew everyone would want to watch the game, of course, but I needed all the heads of the department to go with me out to the location the next morning. I left this assignment to Steve and promised him we'd be back in time for the game. It was really important for me to meet face-to-face with everyone so they would all know where I was coming from. Fortunately, Steve got everyone to step up to the plate and come to the meeting—something I hadn't expected. It turned out that Troy and Lance had gone around warning everyone that the "paid vacation" was going to end—and end quickly—when I got there. "You haven't seen what work *is* until our dad gets here," they cautioned. No one complained; in fact, they were excited. "We'd rather work than goof off any more," they told the boys. I held them to it. The first day there was a lot of laziness and being late to the set, but I stopped that right away with a firm lecture. Fortunately they took it to heart and I didn't have a problem with them from then on.

We got busy. One of the first things I did was go out to the bone pile again, and I noticed that there were a bunch of different boats in it. I asked my cinematographer, Gary Capo, what he'd been using for a camera boat. Nothing, was his reply—they hadn't done any of that yet.

"Well, we're about to," I replied.

I spotted a Boston Whaler that was about four and a half feet wide and fourteen feet long, and I pointed it out. I told my special effects guy that I wanted notches cut out in the front and sides for cameras so I could get good water shots.

"Don't you want us to build you a boat?" one of the producers asked me.

"Why would I want you to do that?" I asked. "We've got all these boats here, why not use one of them? This one will be perfect."

"Okay," he agreed.

After the Super Bowl was over, we really got to work.

I met with Ransom Wallrod, the man who was in charge of all the boats and anything we did on the water, to discuss my concerns about The Mariner's catamaran, which was the main watercraft featured in the movie. It didn't move through the water as fast as I thought it should go. The catamaran was made in France and it was *massive*. Each pontoon was eight feet tall, four feet wide and ninety feet in length. It had a cabin set low in between each pontoon. It had a seventy-foot sail; if a strong wind was blowing it could get up to a good speed, but that was a big *if* that I wasn't about to wait around for. I asked Ransom if he could get a high-speed motorboat to pull the cat. He said he could get ahold of a five hundred horsepower Cris Craft that could do the job.

I got the special effects department to weld a twelve-inch round rod to a plate, which would attach to the bow of the cat about two feet

ME AND MY SADDLE-PAL

under the waterline. A two hundred-foot cable with a ring attached to one end would slip over the rod, and the other end would attach to the motorboat. We did a test and it worked great. The cable was heavy enough so that it would stay under the water, and the Cris Craft was out far enough so that it never got into any of my shots.

Once that was done, I got my first shot. It was a scene involving Costner chasing one of the villains, with Costner in the catamaran and the villain in another boat. I wanted it at high speed, so we used my new cable system on the catamaran. We had it going nice and fast, and it looked great, lifting up and down out of the water as it zoomed along. It came upon its prey so fast that it actually swamped the other boat, throwing the villain right out of it—which was great. Since the actor hadn't been expecting to be thrown overboard, the shot looked really authentic, so we kept it in the movie.

While I was working on this stuff, I was keeping in contact with Kevin Reynolds, and he was thrilled with the changes. He was especially pleased with the speed I was getting out of the catamaran, and he asked how we were doing it.

"We're towing it with a five hundred horsepower speedboat," I told him, and he was surprised. He told me to use my head and shoot whatever I wanted.

"I'm still going to check in with you," I said.

"Okay. I love it."

One morning I was talking to two of our water safety stuntmen, native Hawaiians Brian Keyalana and Terry Ahuy. They told me that if I really wanted to get some great shots of the catamaran in rough water, we should keep an eye out during the day for a wind line. Wind lines are the difference of rough water that the wind creates, blowing into calm ocean water. It forms a line you can see in the distance. Each day we always had our cameras set up on standby in case we saw one. We also had two safety boats at the ready, driven by Chuck Hosack and Cowboy Yrigoyen; they were there to pick anyone up who might be thrown into the water so that we could keep going—I didn't want to worry about having to stop once we got started or I might miss the shot.

WATERWORLD

The day came, finally—we were working out on the water when Terry and Brian taxied over to me on their wave runners, hollering my name. "Hey, Mickey, there's a water line out there, coming at us!" I looked out and sure enough, there it was. We all knew what to do and took off, heading out toward the water line. We were all excited—what an experience *this* was going to be!

We got about a mile and a half out when we started getting into some wind. As the wind picked up, we turned the cat around, adjusted the sail and moved our camera boat alongside the left pontoon. Here we go! The wind caught into that seventy-foot sail and the cat took off like a rocket. We were alongside the pontoon still when it started lifting out of the water. It would come smashing down and lift again, sometimes ten to twelve feet above us. It looked like a whale lunging up out of the water, then dropping down, throwing waves of water over us. Man, it was *wild*. We got some incredible shots. I had Norman Howell, Kevin Costner's stunt double, on the cat, laying out to give it balance. During our wild ride in the camera boat, we lost one person from the boat, but Chuck and Cowboy picked him up. I had to congratulate Gary Capo, my cinematographer, for hanging in there with the camera. That wasn't an easy shot to get, with all the bouncing around we were doing. The Boston Whaler turned out to be a hell of a camera boat and we used it far more than everyone thought we would.

There's a scene in Waterworld where a plane is circling around the catamaran Kevin Costner sails. Costner's character, known only as "The Mariner," fires a spear-gun attached to the craft; the spear embeds itself in the plane. The spear has a rope attached to it, and so it tethers the plane to the craft like a dog on a leash. As the plane continues to circle, it pulls the mast of the catamaran from side to side, moving the whole thing back and forth like a sway pole. Norman Howell, Costner's double, is filmed climbing up the mast to cut the rope loose and free the craft, and he ends up doing a seventy-foot high-fall and goes into the water.

They'd shot the scene with so many different camera angles that it became impossible to piece it together as you were watching it—it didn't make any sense. Reynolds agreed that there was an issue with it, and I told him I'd re-shoot it and make it look better.

The time came to re-shoot the high fall. The problem I'd noticed with the camera angles had to be dealt with; they were not set correctly. I met with Steve Traxler and asked him about getting me a hundred and twenty-foot crane that I could mount a camera on and position it above the mast. "No problem," Steve said, and the next day I had my crane.

I had the effects team position the catamaran's pontoon parallel alongside the dock. There was a crow's nest located about ten feet down from the very top of the mast where Norman, Costner's stunt double, would be positioned. For safety's sake, Norman was attached to a cable that was hooked up to a descender unit. My plan was to attach a cable to the top of the mast, pull it over so that it was listing to the right at about a forty-five degree angle, with the left pontoon raised up about twelve feet out of the water. With our camera positioned looking straight down and seeing Norman on the mast that was leaning to its right, *bang!* The cable is released and the cat snaps back into its upright position, with Norman riding it all the way, right under the camera. Norman goes flying off, and the descender cable he's attached to lets him drop into the water. Just in case Norman didn't pitch himself off his platform far enough, the descender unit would stop him before he would land on the pontoon.

To test my plan, we took a bag that weighed the same as Norman, prepared the stunt the exact same way we would when it came time to execute it for real, and let her go. The cable was released, the pontoon dropped back into the water, and the mast snapped back into position, pitching the bag out of the crow's nest and down into the water. It worked perfectly and gave Norman the confidence he needed. I had two other cameras down below, filming at the same time, and I was pleased. It was a hell of a shot and worked just the way I'd planned it—it was the kind of shot that made you go "wow!" when you saw it.

When the studio received the footage of the fall, Kevin Reynolds called me, all excited, and told me he loved the shot. I told Traxler, my effects team and Norman how excited the studio was about the fall, and I thanked all of them for their hard work on the sequence. "All in a day's work, right, boys?" I said.

One morning I had a little bit of fun by getting all made up like one of the guys in the movie. Wardrobe dressed me up, and I got a nasty, matted beard put on, and sprayed down with grime and makeup. Once I was all done up, I went out to one of the barges and sat down, waiting for the actors and extras to get to set after breakfast. I got a bullhorn and started yelling *"all right, all you sons of bitches, get your butts out here right now! I'm tired of waiting on all of you! You're a bunch of no-talents, and I'm gonna kick all of your asses!"*

Everyone came running, and they saw who they thought was one of them on the barge, screaming orders through a bullhorn. Finally Troy and Lance looked a little closer at me and started laughing. "Oh, my God, it's Pops! He's playing one of his jokes!" Everyone else started laughing then, too, and I stayed in that crazy getup all day, directing them that way, and having a ton of fun.

All in all, Yvonne and I spent about two and a half months in Hawaii while I worked on *Waterworld*. We had a good time there; many of the other stuntmen had brought their wives and families, so Yvonne was never lacking for company.

Once we were done and home, I got a surprise call from Kevin Reynolds, asking me to fill in for *him*. He and Costner had a history of mild head-butting. They had worked together on other films such as *Robin Hood*, and Reynolds had done some shots for Costner on *Dances with Wolves*, and *Waterworld* was no exception to their pattern. I think it had to do with them both being directors—each one had his own vision for how certain shots—and the film in general—should look. Reynolds was tired of the head-butting and decided he wanted me to finish up for him. I was surprised, but I agreed to do it and headed to Catalina to direct the last remaining parts. I was shooting actors doing dialogue, and I got to direct Costner and the other stars of the film. I really enjoyed myself, and to my surprise, the studio really enjoyed what I was doing with their movie. So much so, in fact, that a couple of the bigwigs over at Universal actually came to me and told me that after seeing both my second and first unit directing, they were going to recommend that I actually direct a *whole* movie.

That shocked the hell out of me, but pleased me enormously. Directing an entire film is extremely difficult and an incredible amount of work, and to hear someone tell you they think you've got the chops to do it is a pretty amazing feeling. Unfortunately there was some internal shuffling around at Universal shortly thereafter and one of those executives left the studio, so I was never able to get the chance to do so—but it was really nice to know that they thought I'd be good at it and had wanted to give me the opportunity.

As I mentioned, *Waterworld* was the most expensive movie ever made at the time of its release. It's become infamous in the years that followed its release, but I had a good time working on it, and it certainly was one of the most epic films I've ever been a part of.

The Nutty Professor

⚜

In 1996 Universal Studios released a movie called *The Nutty Professor,* staring Eddie Murphy, who was playing no less than seven separate roles in it. I got a call from a producer on the film, Jim Brubaker, whom everyone called "Bru." I'd worked with him before on *Problem Child,* and I'd done a car chase in Phoenix for him that he'd needed put together ASAP; he'd liked the way Don McCuaig, my director of photography, and I had shot the chase—and he'd *really* liked the way we'd finished it under budget, so he'd thought of me for this film.

I went down to Universal and met with him, and with the director, Tom Shadyac. Shadyac was a young, colorful guy with a ton of energy. None of us knew it at the time, of course, but I would end up doing second unit directing on his next five movies.

There was quite a bit of action for me to work on in *Nutty.* The first sequence I shot was a corvette making a getaway through heavy traffic. I called Don McCuaig, and he and I, along with Bru and Shadyac, went scouting for a location for the scene I was doing, and for one Shadyac was shooting with the first unit. He picked a street he liked for his sequence, and I found a spot for mine one street over. He liked that because, he said, we could both shoot at the same time.

The sequence called for night work, so that meant a big lighting job for both units. I told Shadyac that that wouldn't work, because the lighting we needed to create on my street would bleed into the lighting

ME AND MY SADDLE-PAL

on his, or vice-versa. McCuaig agreed with me. I also told Tom that we'd be making lots of noise with our sequence—horns honking and tires screeching. Besides that, I knew in the back of my mind that he wanted to be on location with me when I shot my bit; he wanted to watch over me since it was my first time working with him—and it was his first big movie.

So, we nixed the same-time idea. While Tom was working with Eddie Murphy on a soundstage, Don and I were shooting our night work in Westwood. I had twenty stunt drivers working for me for two nights until we finished the sequence. Brubaker called me then and told me that Shadyac wanted to see me on stage, so I headed over.

I walked in the soundstage door and spotted Shadyac talking to Eddie Murphy. He looked over and saw me coming, and he threw his arms up in the air and hollered, "hey, hey, hey, there he is!" He left Eddie, ran over to me and gave me a big, clumsy hug. "I loved it, Mick. It was great. You guys did a super job with that scene." I told him it would look even better once we cut Eddie into it.

"By the way," I asked him, "when are you going to shoot your footage?"

"Next week," he told me. "You're gonna be there, right?"

"Oh, yeah, I'm on this movie till we wrap," I replied.

On the street where Shadyac was going to shoot, Eddie was going to drive a Dodge Viper, which, of course, is a hot muscle car. It had a lot of power; one could get on the gas and spin donuts with it all day long. I mentioned to Tom that we could make Eddie look like a hot driver by doing a stunt with the Viper where Eddie would be driving it down the street toward the nightclub. There would be two exotic, high-priced cars parked at the curb, spaced apart with just enough room to slide a car in between them. The Viper would come down the street, throw a hundred and eighty-degree turn, and slide in between the two parked cars. Tom liked the idea, so I told him I'd start working on the stunt right away.

Transportation made a deal with Dodge to loan us a Viper for the publicity it would get them from being featured in the movie. Once we had

THE NUTTY PROFESSOR

it, I took the car and some rubber safety cones, along with a water truck, and found an area at the studio's back lot. I started testing the car to feel it out and found that even with all the power it had, it wouldn't slide very well after I'd set it into the turn. Part of the problem was that the tires were fourteen inches wide and made of a soft rubber to give it traction.

I watered down the area—which we don't normally like to do because it reduces the amount of control the driver has over the car when they're doing spins and slides—and tried it again, and it actually made the Viper perform better. Now I could drive down the street, get on the power, throwing the rear end around and sliding it in between two cones. At that point I called Alan Oliney, who was Eddie's stunt double and a good wheel man besides, but he was out of town on another job, so I found another African-American stuntman who I figured could do the job and started working with him in the practice area.

He was having trouble controlling the Viper by using the emergency brake to make it go into the spin. I told him to just use the power the car put out, and then I showed him how to do it. He tried it, but wasn't really consistent with it in the beginning. We kept on working until he got comfortable with it, since they were planning on shooting the stunt the following night, after Shadyac had finished the hour and a half of shooting he had planned.

I took Eddie's double down to an alley where we'd rehearse the stunt. I went the street down and set the cones down on each side of the alley's entrance, then started rehearsing the double. All I can say was that he was having a hell of a time. Sometimes he'd slide the Viper over a cone—which, of course, represented one of the expensive parked cars. Another time he slid the car sideways between the two cones perfectly, but went in too deep, over where the curb would be in the real location. If we'd been shooting for real he would have ripped two of the car's wheels off. All the while during our rehearsal, Shadyac is able to see what's going on. Finally, he waved me over to the set.

When I got there, he shook his head. "Mick, that guy isn't getting it," he commented. "You showed it to me the other day and you did it perfectly."

ME AND MY SADDLE-PAL

I knew what he was getting at, but I shook my head. "Tom, it's against our principles for a white person to double a black person." He agreed, of course, but he was also concerned that there was nobody there that could execute the stunt.

I brought Eddie's double over to meet Shadyac and the three of us talked it over. Eventually it was decided that I would do the stunt, but on one condition—I absolutely refused to wear dark makeup, spray my hair or match Eddie's wardrobe. Instead, I wanted them to spray the inside of the windows so that the viewer wouldn't be able to see me driving. Shadyac saw my point and agreed, so we set everything up, getting the two exotic cars into their places and wetting down the street.

I said a quick prayer while I was waiting for my cue. "Lord, make my timing be good, and stay with me." The next thing I heard was *"Action!"*

I took off and when I got to the right spot, I set the Viper, turned on the curb and got on the gas. Everything worked exactly as it was supposed to. The ass-end of the car spun around and I slid it neatly in between the two cars, stopping it right at the curb. We put Eddie into the car at that point and had him step out as if he'd been driving the whole time, and what he'd just done was no big deal, walking casually into the nightclub.

There was only one problem with the whole thing. Night was starting to turn into day, and the sky was turning blue—and of course, the scene was supposed to be happening at night. Eddie wouldn't be arriving at a nightclub in at dawn. They said they'd look at the footage and have a discussion about whether or not we had to do it again.

Bru called me the next morning with some bad news: someone had turned me in to the NAACP, which meant the studio would get a slap on the wrist, and the publicity wouldn't be good, either. I wondered who it had been and guessed that it must have been Eddie's double. "We'll check it out tonight, because we have to shoot the stunt again."

"But Bru, I don't know if I have time to find an African-American stuntman and rehearse him today to the point that he'll be ready to do it tonight," I told him. He told me to do the best I could and to call him that night if things weren't working out.

I did find another stuntman and rehearsed with him, but when we got down to the location, he backed out. He was afraid he'd slam into the two parked cars. Shadyac looked at me, shrugged his shoulders and asked me what we were going to do now.

"Find Eddie's stand-in and tell him to come to the set right away," I told the assistant director.

When he got there, I went up to him. "Roger," I asked, "Why'd you turn me in to the NAACP, when you know better than anyone that I tried to get this done the right way?"

"I didn't turn you in," he responded.

I didn't believe him. "I have to do this thing again," I said, "because the other stuntman doesn't want to do it. Are you going to report it again?"

He shook his head, so I called Brubaker, waking him up, and told him I was going to have to do it again myself.

"You've gotta do what you've gotta do, Mick," he replied. "We've got to get this gag wrapped and get this problem off of Universal's shoulders."

I did the stunt again, and we wrapped for the night. The next day at the studio I called Alan Oliney, Eddie Murphy's number-one double, who I'd wanted to do the stunt in the first place, and told him the story. Alan was a veteran in our business, and we knew each other well and were good friends. He told me not to worry about it, and that he'd call the NAACP committee and straighten it out. He was as good as his word and got the studio and all of us out of trouble, which everyone was grateful for since no disrespect had been intended, of course. That was the first and last time I ever doubled for an actor of another race.

Being Around Big Stars

About six years or so my career as a stuntman, I was making a name for myself, and I *knew* that I was, because a large percentage of my work was coming straight from producers, directors, production managers and in some cases even actors. The fact that I'd doubled for so many big names, like Robert Redford, Paul Newman, Richard Widmark and Gene Wilder, helped get my name into the ears of some top people, which enabled me to get consistent work on well-known films. I've always found that as a double, the better you make an actor look, the more they're likely to remember your name and ask for you in future films.

People often ask me how I handle being around big stars, and I always tell them that first and foremost, I treat them like normal people, no matter their fame. I give them space when they need it, do my best to keep them safe if they're integrated into a sequence I'm doubling them in, and I look them in the eye when I talk to them. If they ever ask me to socialize with them, I do—but I don't fish around for an invitation, and I'm always professional when I'm working. If I notice a problem, I'll go to the director and ask for a few moments with the actor so I can take them aside and speak to them privately. No one wants to be embarrassed in front of other people—I know *I* don't.

One thing I've noticed about working with actors and actresses is that some of them treat stunt people differently than they do other

BEING AROUND BIG STARS

people involved in the production, like the director. That's because they respect us—when we double them, we help them look good through the work we do. With directors, there can be differences of opinion as to how an actor or actress should portray a scene—the director may feel they should do it one way, but the actor or actress may want to do it another. I've worked on films where it's become an everlasting battle of wills—hollering and screaming at each other, getting into each other's faces, and burning up valuable production time all the while. I've had actors and actresses come up to me and apologize for the way they've acted, telling me that they would have no problem working with me again, either as a stunt coordinator or as a second unit director, and I'm sure that other coordinators and second unit directors have experienced the same situations. I also think that it doesn't just happen in the entertainment industry, but in the real world, as well. It all depends on what size your ego is—or what size you let it become.

That rule of mine about taking people aside to speak to them instead of correcting them in front of their peers doesn't just apply to actors—it applies to everyone I work with. I remember that on one film I was working on, I was directing a car chase scene, and I wanted the stuntman driving the chase car to make a ninety-degree turn from one street onto the other by sliding the car into the turn. He must've tried it three times, and he just wasn't getting it. This particular stuntman tended to speak with a stutter, particularly when he was nervous. The more nervous he was, the worse his stutter got. The assistant was on a walkie-talkie with the driver, and I could hear that the assistant was starting to get impatient with him; his voice was starting to rise. The poor kid driving the car was stuttering back and getting very upset, and I knew I had to step in.

I walked a little bit away from everyone and waved the stuntman over to me, and he drove the car over. I got in and very patiently talked him through it and suggested a way to make it happen. "Just relax and take a deep breath," I told him. "Pretend you're just doing a rehearsal." He did as I suggested, and he got the shot. I was glad I'd been able to help him; I'd seen so many instances when guys would get overexcited

ME AND MY SADDLE-PAL

when the cameras started rolling, which can lead to heightened nerves and mistakes. In my line of work, mistakes can be dangerous, so I always do my best to try and help people stay calm and stay safe—and I do my best to be kind, too.

The thing I *really* dislike is working with ego-maniacs, but it's something that is par for the course with this business. I've found that if I can get the respect of those sort of people, it makes them so much easier to work with. Working with people who are easygoing and compatible to my personality makes my job much more enjoyable and fun, and that's the experience I've had most often. Most of the actors I've doubled over the years have treated me really well and have given me a lot of respect—something I'll always be grateful for.

Metro

I was just finishing *A Time to Kill* when I got a call from director Thomas Carter's secretary; Carter wanted me to come to his office in Santa Monica to talk to him about a film called *Metro,* starring Eddie Murphy.

"Well," I told her, "I'm still working on a film and I'm not going to be back in California for another couple of weeks. I can come in when I get back, though."

The secretary told me that Carter had heard about me through word-of-mouth in the business and was very anxious to talk to me about the project. She gave me the number to call when I got done with my current project, so I called her when I got home. "Does he still want to see me?"

"Oh, yes, very much. Let me talk to him and we can set up an appointment for you to come in and discuss things."

On the given day, I went down to Santa Monica and met with Carter, who I liked right off the bat. He told me a bit about the film, which, besides Murphy, had a good cast.

"You know, I'm a little concerned I may not be able to do what you need me to," I told him, "because I already have a commitment to another film. I knew you wanted to meet with me, but I wasn't sure when you were shooting, and that sort of thing."

Carter was disappointed. "I really wanted to bring you on for this," he told me.

ME AND MY SADDLE-PAL

"Let me give you some names of some other good second-unit directors," I offered, "because I'm afraid to get too involved with your show while I've got another one in the wings."

I gave him some names and we discussed the merits of each one, and he chose one of them. I told him it had been a pleasure to meet him, and that I was honored that he'd been so eager to meet with me and possibly hire me that he'd waited around for me to get back to California. We shook hands and I headed for the door.

Before I went out, though, I turned back and caught his eye. "You know, Thomas, I have a bit of advice for you, since you're going to shoot in San Francisco," I said. "There are some car chases in this movie, and it's a big action picture in general, so when you get to San Francisco you make sure you don't settle for the usual car-chase scenes. There have been so many of them done in San Francisco, and they're always the same. Make sure your second unit does something different besides having cars chase each other down the hills, jumping them as they go."

"That's good advice," he said, nodding, and out I went.

Two days later, Carter's office called me again. Carter had interviewed the guy we'd talked about, and even informally hired him, but he'd started thinking about things and decided that he *really* wanted me to do the job instead—so he was going to put it off a bit to be sure I could do it. I was surprised. "But I thought you'd already hired the other guy."

"Well, I sort of did—but only verbally, and I started thinking about what you said, about making the car chases different, and I want you to do it. If it means postponing it a bit, well, so be it."

I was flabbergasted, never having dreamed that a director would put an entire movie on hold just to be sure I could coordinate and direct the stunt sequences! "Wow," I told him, "I really appreciate that, Thomas, but I also feel bad for the guy I recommended to you."

"Don't feel bad," Carter told me. "He understands, believe me."

So, I got the job on *Metro*.

I called Don McCuaig, my cinematographer, and told him about

METRO

the project. Don and I went down and met with the producer and made our deals for the show. On the way back I told Don, "Mr. McCuaig, get ready for some heavy-duty action, and think about who you're going to get as your camera operators." Don and I always called each other Mr. McCuaig and Mr. Gilbert; why, I couldn't tell you.

"How many cameras do you think you'll want operated?" he asked me.

"Three operated and two to three wild cams," I replied.

Not long after that, we headed for San Francisco. Once there, as usual I took what was in the script as far as action, and I rewrote it to make it more exciting and more unique.

One evening Yvonne and I took a cable car to go out to dinner. We were heading down California Street when I suddenly turned to Yvonne and said, "I've got it!"

She stared at me. "What have you got?"

"I know what I want to do for the chase scene. It's never been done before," I said, and began moving up toward the front of the car.

"Where are you going?" she asked me.

"I'll be right back, I just need to ask the conductor a few questions."

I went up to the conductor. "Hey, do you mind if I ask you a few questions?"

"Not at all, what's going on?" he asked.

"What would happen if one of these cars broke loose?" I asked. "You know, if you had a runaway cable car?"

"Well, it wouldn't run away," he said. "We use the brakes for slowing down, you know, to let people on and off, but if there was a *real* emergency, we'd use the emergency brake." He gestured to a pedal. "If I press that pedal down, it sends a spike down into the rails. This thing would stop so fast it would make your head spin."

"Your average passengers don't know about that emergency brake, do they?" I asked him.

"Well, no..." he said, puzzled as to why I was asking.

That was all I needed to hear. When we got back I started writing the scene I had in mind. The villain of the scene, who's being chased

ME AND MY SADDLE-PAL

by Eddie Murphy, crashes head-on into another car and flips his SUV. At the same time, a cable car nearby is just taking off after stopping to pick up passengers, so the villain jumps on and the chase continues.

We had a big production meeting a few weeks later, before we'd started shooting anything for the film. *Metro* was being produced by Touchstone Pictures, a division of Disney, and one of the producers, Roger Birnbaum, attended. He'd heard about my little idea for the film, and he approached me. He was concerned about the budget—specifically, the budget I had in mind for my cable car adventure. "Mickey, what are you doing to us?" he moaned.

"Roger, this sequence is going to be amazing," I told him. "It's never been done before. We've got to do it!"

"What's it going to cost?" he asked me, skeptically.

"For the second unit, for all the stuntmen, and all the cars we're going to crash…about a million. Maybe a million-two," I said evenly. "But Roger, it's gonna be talked about as the greatest chase scene ever done in San Francisco! It's gonna sell tickets to the movie, I'm telling you! Can't you picture it?" I asked him enthusiastically. "Think about it: Eddie Murphy jumps out of this convertible and onto the back of this runaway cable car, that's crashing into all these cars…he has a big fistfight in there as the cable car's heading toward the bay…"

"All right, all right, that's enough," he said with a sigh. "I'll see about it."

I watched him go, praying he'd approve it. I *really* wanted to shoot this thing. I could picture it in my mind and I *knew* it was going to be amazing, but it *was* going to cost a hell of a lot of money, not only for my unit but for the first unit, as well.

Fortunately, they *did* approve it, and I started working out some of the different crashes we would do in the chase.

The time came when we could get to work on the sequence. I met with the special effects crew, and told them what I wanted them to do with the five-ton truck they'd gotten to create the cable car with. I wanted quarter-inch steel, four feet high that would wrap around the nose of the cable car, with a hole placed in it down low that I could mount a camera in. I also planned to mount cameras on the sides and back of the car. The mounts I had them put on the car swung in and out so that they could be hidden during various shots.

We couldn't use a real cable car track for the scene, of course, so I picked a street—Jones Street, to be exact—and we painted a realistic-looking track onto it, all the way down. It was so realistic, in fact, that a couple who lived on Jones returned from a vacation while we were working and thought the city had actually installed a cable car track on their street. I overheard the wife talking about it to her husband and I laughed, correcting her. "No, ma'am, that's just paint. We're making a movie," I explained.

The effects team started working right away and the cable car started coming together. I would check in with effects so McCuaig could give them measurements for camera positions, and I had them install tie-down safety eyelets all through the seats of the car that we could hook safety belts to. McCuaig and I would walk Jones Street with our people to map out each stunt and decide on whatever other type of camera equipment we might need.

After Thomas Carter read the sequence he flipped over it. "Man, Mickey, this is great," he told me.

I was glad, of course, that he liked my idea, but I cautioned him that it wasn't going to be cheap to stage and shoot. Besides that, we needed to think of the city—we were using busy streets for the sequence, so I knew they were only likely to let us use about two blocks of each street at a time, and we wouldn't be able to monopolize any area for very long. I told him we'd need to have the location managers for the production handle that. He agreed, so I made out a thorough budget for everything I wanted my unit to shoot on the sequence. Then when I was done, Carter could bring in his unit and cut his actors into the scene.

The special effects team did a *fantastic* job with the stunt cable car, even going so far as to put hydraulic airplane brakes on it so it would stop safely, since it was so heavy.

We got everything set up—all the locations scouted, the cars caged

ME AND MY SADDLE-PAL

for safety, and the stuntmen brought in. The cable car itself had a blind driver—a driver that crouched down in the front who had power to steer the cable car down the painted tracks, but couldn't be seen by the cameras. Both my brother-in-law Joe Finnigan and my son Troy did the blind driving for the stunt. We did some test runs, and everyone was thrilled with how realistic it looked, so we started the real thing.

Jones Street in San Francisco is pretty steep, and there were about eight or nine cross-streets we were going to continue past with the cable car, up and over each hill. We worked it out with the city to use two blocks at a time and work our way down, car crash by car crash. I loaded up the cable car with stunt people—stunt passengers, a stunt conductor, and stunt performers to double the main actors. Because of the quarter-inch steel I'd had them put on the cable car, the thing was practically indestructible. We started shooting and man, it looked *wild*.

After it was all done, we cut it all together, and the editor brought it out to Carter to show it to him. The whole crew had heard about it, of course, and they all wanted to see it too, so they showed it on a big monitor on set. The reaction we got was pretty incredible, and it was clear that this scene was going to work—and work *well*. Everyone was excited about it, and I couldn't have asked for a better result than the one I got.

Toward the end of filming Carter got a little worried about the car chase at the end, because he was thinking we needed to do something to top that cable car scene. He was planning on having different writers come in and see if they could come up with something even bigger. I talked to him and reassured him a bit.

"You know, Thomas, you don't really need to worry about topping that scene," I said. "Just have a really *good* chase scene in there, and it'll be great." I ended up coming up with something, myself, and so I wrote yet another chase scene. I wrote a scene with a truck going out of control and ending up in a ship lock. Carter liked it, so we used it, too.

I enjoyed working on *Metro*, particularly because of that scene with the runaway cable car. I was really, *really* proud of the sequence I'd created, and the work I'd done to make it a reality. Rightly so, it seemed,

METRO

because the stunt got written up in the *Hollywood Reporter* and *Variety* as one of the best car chases ever filmed, and *that* made me feel pretty damn good. The combination of a good idea, creative vision, and a talented crew can really produce some amazing results, and the Jones Street cable car chase is a perfect example of that.

The Horse Whisperer

While working on a project in 1997, I got a call from Robert Redford. He wanted to talk to me about a film he was directing and starring in, a big-screen adaptation of Nicholas Evans' novel *The Horse Whisperer*. As the title suggests, there were going to be horses involved, so already the project was right up my alley. I made arrangements to head to Livingston Montana to see Bob.

I arrived at the ranch Redford was using as a location for the movie and found him busy in a corral with a horse, shooting a scene. I waited, and when he was done I announced my presence by calling "hey?" in the same way he and Paul Newman had always done with each other on the sets of *Butch Cassidy* and *The Sting*. His head shot up and he looked around for me. "I'm up here, Bob," I told him, and he lifted his hand to me, calling for a fifteen to twenty-minute break so he could come and talk with me for awhile. He got behind the wheel of his SUV. I got in we took off for a drive around the ranch, during which he laid out what he wanted me to do.

The opening scene of *The Horse Whisperer* is a hard one to watch; it involves Scarlett Johansson and the actress playing her friend riding their horses out of their barn one snowy winter morning, intending to go for a pleasure-ride in the back country near where they live. They cross a road and start up a hill, but their horses slip and slide back down to the road. A semi truck carrying a load of logs comes around a bend and ends up hitting Scarlett Johansson's horse as it's rearing up after having thrown her off. Redford explained that he wanted me to go back to the production office in Livingston and watch what had been shot for this scene so I could give him my opinion on it.

My opinion, after watching what they'd shot, was simple: it didn't look like a Robert Redford film. It wasn't up to his standards, and some of it didn't make sense as I watched it. When he asked me what I thought, I told him, and he nodded. "That's what I thought, too," he agreed. He asked me to redo it and I agreed; the scene contained the two elements I'd become known for in the stunt industry: horses and vehicles, so I knew I could do a good job with it.

I went over the changes I wanted to make, and he suggested I check out a location where one of the film's producers had suggested we reshoot the scene. I was taken aback when we arrived there; there was a steep slope, all right, but one pretty important element was missing—the road. The producer explained that they would bring in a bulldozer and put one in for the shoot.

"Seriously?" I asked him, my eyebrows practically up to my hairline. "You gotta be kidding. It would cost a fortune to put a road in here, and even if it wouldn't, you're going to have a semi truck in here, coming down this road. But you know we probably won't get everything we need in one take. How will the semi turn around to do additional takes, if there's only one road there? It won't work. Besides that, it's not the right location for what I want to do."

"Well, what *do* you want to do, exactly?" he asked me.

"I want this huge logging truck to appear rising up over the crest of a hill and dropping down toward the girls and their horses. It's got to be very menacing-looking. And another thing, I need a turn-out around the area at the bottom, and one at the start, too so we can come back and do additional takes. If we get into an area where it's snowing, or the road freezes, he won't be able to back the big rig up the hill," I explained.

The producer wasn't happy with me, but I stuck to my guns and went back to talk to Redford. Here was another example of making

ME AND MY SADDLE-PAL

something a hell of a lot more complicated—and expensive—than it needed to be, to get the result we wanted. I put my talent for creative problem-solving to work and told Bob to work on getting the rest of the movie shot while I dealt with that opening. I asked him to let me scout out some locations on my own so I could find the perfect spot to film this thing. He was agreeable—overruling the objections of the impatient producer—and off I went. Mammoth, California was the first place I headed. I knew Dave McCoy, the owner of the ski resort at Mammoth, and I figured that he could help me out, both in finding the perfect place to shoot, and in providing equipment I might need, like snowplows and snow-making machines.

I flew into the airport at Mammoth and was met by the film's location scout. We got together with Dave and discussed possible places that might work for what I needed. Dave knew of an old road on the way to June Mountain that might fit the bill.

As it turned out, the place didn't just fit the bill—it paid it. It was perfect, with the beautiful pine forest extending out on both sides of the road, and a turn-out for the truck about a hundred and fifty yards out. I took a bunch of photos and sent them to Redford to get his approval.

About two or three weeks later I got a call from him, but it wasn't a call approving the location, as I'd been expecting. Instead, he told me to come out to Sonora, California. He never mentioned Mammoth, or the location photos. Puzzled, I did as he asked.

"Bob," I said when I got there, "what did you want me to come out here for?"

He gave me a strange look. "To shoot the opening," he said.

I was flabbergasted. "But what about Mammoth? I found the ideal location there. Didn't you get the photos I sent you?"

"No," he replied. "I never saw any photos."

It hit me that the producer must have intercepted them and never given them to Redford, in order to ensure things went the way *he* wanted them to. I was beyond irritated, but I figured I'd better work with what I had. "I'll do the best I can, Bob," I told him, but inwardly I was full of doubt. I hadn't even seen this location yet, and I knew it couldn't be as perfect as the place Dave had found in Mammoth.

Dutifully I went out to the location we were supposed to use. It was a downhill road that had been built on uneven ground and leaned a little to the left. I knew that once we got the snow machines up there, the road would become slippery and dangerous—much moreso that the road in Mammoth would've been. I told the producer my concerns, but he wouldn't hear them and insisted I shoot the scene there.

I contacted George Sack Jr, a stuntman friend, to help me out. He had stunt semi trucks that would jackknife at the flip of a switch. I also got a special effects guy I knew, Neil Trifunovich, to create an animatronic horse I'd use for the actual moment when the semi hit it. I brought in the stunt doubles for Grace and Judith, the two characters involved in the scene, and the stunt wranglers, Rex Peterson and Michael Boyle, who in turn brought the real horses we'd use.

We started the shoot, getting shots of the girls' horses slipping, falling, and losing their footing in the snow and ice on the road; the horses sliding down the mountainside back down onto the asphalt, and the truck coming up over the hill into the frame. I got a shot of Shelley Boyle, the stuntwoman doubling for Judith, being dragged from her horse with her foot caught in one stirrup, and Julie Adair, Grace's double, in the saddle as her horse reared up in front of the approaching semi. I got some shots from the truck driver's point of view, seeing these girls and their horses in the middle of the snowy, icy road. Things were coming together nicely. Redford was viewing the dailies as we worked and liked what we were doing. Pretty soon it was time to bring in Neil Trifunovich's animatronic horse and get the scene Redford was particularly anxious to see on film—the actual moment of impact. He wanted to be there when we filmed it, because it was such a pivotal moment in the story he was telling.

I had the animatronic horse in a rearing position in the middle of the road as the semi began its approach, already beginning to jackknife. Everything happens fast—within a few seconds' screen time you see the semi's massive grill hitting the horse with devastating impact. The

ME AND MY SADDLE-PAL

horse Trifunovich had created was pretty spectacular—the ears flicked back and forth, the jaw moved, and the front legs could paw the air in the same way a real horse does when it rears. He'd done a hell of a job; the horse looked incredibly realistic when the shoot was all put together and edited. I had cameras in all sorts of different positions, one inside the truck shooting out through the windshield toward the horse, one on the horse itself, and one leading the truck. I was using different angles on them all too, wide ones and tight ones, all with the idea that if shots from any of them were used, it would only be split-second portions of the footage they'd captured. Then, those portions could be edited together to create one monumental piece of accident footage that would be as realistic-looking as it was unsettling to the audience. Redford mused that perhaps I'd want the camera with the horse alone, but I explained to him that since the horse was mostly stationary, it would be far more dramatic—and effective—to do it the way I'd planned. I had confidence in the scene I'd mapped out, and I knew he wouldn't regret calling me in to do it once he saw the finished product.

I was right about that—the scene ended up looking great, and although it's a horrible thing to imagine happening to a horse, it's one of the stunt scenes I'm proudest of coordinating and directing during my career.

*

Another memorable sequence from *The Horse Whisperer* that I was involved in was a scene where Grace's horse, whom Redford's character Tom Booker is rehabilitating after the accident, gets loose from the pond Booker is swimming him in and runs off into a huge oatfield, halter still on, dragging his lead rope. Redford follows calmly at a walk, stopping about fifty yards from the horse. As the horse eyeballs him suspiciously, Redford squats down amongst the foot-high stalks, chewing on a piece and waiting. Time goes by, hour after hour, and the horse and Redford continue their staring match.

THE HORSE WHISPERER

Throughout the scene, the horse never once bends its head to eat any of the oats. We shot the scene at different times—noon, three, four, etcetera, to show the changing position of the sun and impart the passage of time. For me, it was a scene that showed the true theme of the film, which is the remarkable patience of Redford's character and the lengths he was willing to go to gain the trust of the animal he was working with. To this day I always think of that scene specifically when I think of *The Horse Whisperer*.

The Academy Awards

When you think of the Oscars, you don't typically think of stunts, but to my surprise, I got to extend my stunt-coordinating resume to a memorable moment of the 76th Annual Academy Awards. My good friend Billy Crystal was hosting that year. I got a call from the show's producer, Joe Roth, while the show was being written.

"Mickey, we want to do something a little different this year and put a stunt sequence of some kind into the show," he told me, "and we'd like your help."

He explained to me that veteran writer/director Blake Edwards (famous for directing such films as *Breakfast at Tiffany's* and the far more hilarious *Pink Panther* series), would be receiving a lifetime achievement award presented by Jim Carrey. I'd never met Edwards, but I knew Jim Carrey. Roth told me they wanted the stunt to be funny in homage to Edwards' comedic career—and he also happened to mention that Edwards was suffering from an ankle injury. Roth told me to mull it over and call him back when I'd thought of something.

My mind started working, and an idea started to form. If Edwards had an ankle injury, I could craft a stunt sequence around that, and I could make it funny. I called Roth back and laid out my idea.

"If Blake has a bad ankle, I want to play that up," I told him. "I want to put him backstage in a wheelchair—a motorized one—with his bad leg sticking out in front of him in a cast. We'll have two chicks on either side of his chair, in their fancy gowns, looking like they're gonna escort him out onstage. I'm gonna have Blake rev the wheelchair a little bit, and I'll be out of frame, holding onto a cable I'll have attached to the front of the chair. Then as we're shooting, I'll yank the whole thing out of frame real quick, and have Blake throw his head back like he's totally lost control of the damn thing. The trick is, we'll shoot this ahead of time and show it on the screen behind Jim as he's getting ready to call Blake out onstage, so it'll look like this is all happening in real time. Then, as Jim says, "Blake Edwards!" I'll shoot across the stage in the chair, doubling for Blake, and grab the Oscar from Jim as I go past."

I explained that I'd rig up up a wall at the opposite end of the stage for the wheelchair (and me) to crash through. Meanwhile Blake would be waiting behind it, and Jim Carrey would run over in a panic and help him out of there, stumbling and clutching onto his Oscar for dear life. Blake would be wearing a ripped tuxedo jacket that we'd "decorate" with drywall dust and iquid smoke so he'd look the part when Jim helped him out from the wreckage.

Roth was impressed. "Gee, Mick," he said with a chuckle, "how'd you think this thing up so fast?"

"Oh, you know me, Joe; things come to me pretty quick," I said casually. The idea had come together in my head after thinking back to an episode of *Fall Guy* in which I'd doubled for Lee Majors while his character had been in a wheelchair. I'd been incorporating the chair into a car chase scene, and that's what made me picture Blake's chair speeding across the Oscar stage. I knew those motorized chairs could get up there with their speed. I told Joe I'd start looking for a chair to use.

I found the chair and had it souped up by a special-effects crew, and when Joe came to take a look at it I did a practice run, with Roth standing in for Jim Carrey and me doubling for Blake. I whizzed past him, prentending to grab an Oscar out of his hand, and he was all smiles by the time we were done. "This is going to be hilarious," he predicted, "and just perfect. The crowd will really think you're Blake Edwards!"

"That's the idea," I chuckled.

A week before the show, I went down to do rehearsals. Even though the Oscars air live, everything in the broadcast, from skits to award presentations, has to be rehearsed, sometimes twice a day, so that no embarassing goof-ups will play out in front of that huge television audience. I rehearsed the bit to perfection with Jim Carrey, the two girls who'd be "backstage," and with Blake Edwards himself, who thought the premise of my little gag was hysterical. Making things even more perfect was the fact that I was a spot-on double for Blake, once the makeup crew sprayed my hair grey to mimic his. People who weren't in on the stunt really thought it was him in that out-of-control chair crashing through the wall. The whole thing went off like a dream the night of the show and was a complete success—made even more satisfying by the fact that the other folks involved were all nice people and a pleasure to work with.

As it turns out, the Blake Edwards wheelchair gag has earned a place in Academy Awards history—the clip of me speeding across the stage has not only been uploaded to YouTube, but also features prominently in the Lifetime Achievement Award segment of the 2014 Turner Classic Movies Academy Awards documentary special *And the Oscar Goes To.*...

Looking Back…and Forward

Writing this book has made me look back, of course, to the very beginning—not only the beginning of my career but my life, as well. It's been an amazing journey for me to think about how everything fell into place for me—working with Joe Yrigoyen and then ending up marring Yvonne, how the rodeo led me into doing horse stunts in the movies, and then how those early films earned me a reputation that led to even bigger jobs. I've worked on some great films, and some no-so-great films, too—but I've always been proud of the imagination, the creativity, and the plain hard work I've put into every stunt or sequence I've designed and/or performed, no matter what film it's part of. For me, this job is about pushing boundaries and doing things that have never been done before, and I consider myself incredibly blessed to have coordinated and performed some of the most iconic stunts ever, like the cliff jump in *Butch Cassidy*, the cable car chase in *Metro*, and the epic buffalo hunt in *The Return of A Man Called Horse*. I'm honored to think that the contributions that I made to those movies made them look a little more exciting for the people watching them, and I'm proud that I passed my love of the trade on to my boys, and my grandson Cody, who has followed in our footsteps. I'm grateful to everyone who helped me get to where I've ended up—every opportunity I've been given and every treasured friend I've made on this thrilling journey, but I'm *most* grateful to the Lord, my Saddle-pal, for keeping

ME AND MY SADDLE-PAL

me safe and looking out for me during the whole crazy ride. He's the one that's truly made it all possible for me.

While looking back has made me proud and a little nostalgic, it's also made me a little sad when I think about the enormous changes the film industry has gone through while I've been in it. Myself and the other men and women of my era took risks and used all our skills to execute some pretty amazing things—and we *really* did them. The increasing dependence on CGI and special effects means that fewer and fewer stunts are being done the old-fashioned way; now they're just put into a computer after being shot against green-screens. When I think about it, maybe *that's* one of the biggest reasons I wanted to write this book—so that you folks would know that there was a time when we did these things for real, when we put our bodies to the ultimate test, used our brains and figured things out instead of simply letting a computer do it for us. Maybe it's just me, but I think brawn and brains produce a better emotional reaction from an audience than a computer-generated sequence does. Maybe after you read this, you'll watch *Butch Cassidy* or *The Last of the Mohicans* with a new appreciation for "doin' it for real." God bless you all.

-Mickey Gilbert, 2014